Seamless Government

Russell M. Linden

Seamless Government

A Practical Guide to Re-Engineering in the Public Sector

Jossey-Bass Publishers • San Francisco

Substantial discounts on bulk quantities of Jossey-Bass books are available to corporations, professional associations, and other organizations. For details and discount information, contact the special sales department at Jossey-Bass Inc., Publishers. (415) 433–1740; Fax (415) 433–0499.

For international orders, please contact your local Paramount Publishing International Office.

Manufactured in the United States of America. Nearly all Jossey-Bass books and jackets are printed on recycled paper containing at least 10 percent postconsumer waste, and many are printed with either soy- or vegetable-based ink, which emits fewer volatile organic compounds during the printing process than petroleum-based ink.

Library of Congress Cataloging-in-Publication Data

Linden, Russell Matthew.
   Seamless government: a practical guide to re-engineering in the public sector/Russell M. Linden.—1st ed.
     p. cm.—(The Jossey-Bass public administration series)
   Includes bibiographical references and index.
   ISBN 0-7879-0015-X
   1. Public administration—United States. 2. United States—Politics and government. 3. Bureaucracy—United States.
   I. Title. II. Series.
   JK1351.L56 1994
   350'.000973—dc20   94-13232
                                             CIP

FIRST EDITION
HB Printing   10 9 8 7 6 5 4 3 2 1   Code 9496

The Jossey-Bass Public Administration Series

Dedication

This book is dedicated to our children, Rebecca and Joshua. Their lives are the truest expressions of seamlessness that I know. Most of us are trying to unlearn in order to rediscover what they already know.

Contents

Preface

My journey in writing *Seamless Government* was born out of personal values about our government and our nation. It began with a strongly held belief, an undeniable fact, and an inescapable conclusion.

The belief: our success as a nation is inextricably tied to the success of our public institutions. Our government is not an alien force somehow separated from us; in a democracy, our government is us. It reflects us, and we share a common destiny.

The fact: many Americans today regard their government with contempt; few respect it, few believe it works. According to one recent poll, only 20 percent of the public trusts the government to do what is right most of the time (Gore, 1993). The public's cynicism about government has grown enormously since the 1960s. People believe that their elected officials do not care and that their appointed officials are incompetent.

The conclusion: our public institutions are facing a crisis. They must make radical changes—literally transform themselves—if the nation is to regain not only its confidence in them but its confidence in itself. When people in a democracy no longer believe in their government, they lose confidence in their ability to govern themselves, which creates a vacuum that despots are only too willing to fill—a frightening prospect indeed.

If our public institutions face a crisis, as I strongly believe they do, how should they change? What new approaches or models can elected officials and civil servants turn to? How do they regain the public's confidence?

I have studied a variety of management innovations over the past eight years in my search for new answers. That journey has taken me over terrain familiar to many. It has included management innovations such as continuous quality improvement, empowerment, customer-driven service, self-managing teams, visionary leadership, and so on. The search also led to policy innovations such as school choice, privatizing, and community ownership of government programs such as public housing. My reaction to each has been similar—and frustrating. The innovations have much to offer, they get staff initially excited, but they seem to lack something important. Many of my clients and students have had similar reactions to these trends and models.

As I began learning about and using the principles of business process re-engineering, I finally realized why the other models left me dissatisfied: they all take current organizational structure and design as a given and look for ways to make improvements within current structures. But public institutions are built on nineteenth-century industrial structures. Those fragmented structures simply cannot produce what today's consumers expect: timeliness, variety, customization, convenience. Agencies with the most visionary leadership and the most empowered staff, working for a community-based board of directors that has genuine ownership of a program, still cannot deliver what their consumers demand. Such agencies are set up for failure in today's environment.

The more I learned about *re-engineering,* an approach designed to provide seamless customer service, the more convinced I became that it offers something truly unique. More significantly, it offers what our public institutions desperately need: a model to transform themselves for the future.

The terms *seamless organization* and *business process re-engineering* are new to many and deserve some comment here. In contrast to the fragmented bureaucracies of the past, seamless organizations provide a smooth, transparent, almost effortless experience for their customers. Staff in seamless organizations perform the full job, in direct contact with their end users.

Business process re-engineering is an awkward term, to be sure. I confess I don't care for the term *re-engineering,* because it suggests that our organizations were "engineered" in the first place. That was hardly the case in government. As Chapter Two points out, government in the United States grew increasingly bureaucratic in response to problems, abuses, mistakes, growth, and the public's intolerance for fraud and the spoils system.

Having said that, I use the word *re-engineering* because it is the term of choice for the set of powerful principles that is radically changing some public and private bureaucracies. Re-engineering requires us to challenge the fundamental assumptions on which bureaucracies are built and radically redesign these organizations around desired outcomes rather than functions or departments. In the process, it forces us to develop new ways of thinking and of seeing the world.

Benefit to the Reader

Seamless Government will benefit you in two ways. First, it will help you understand the nature of seamless organizations, why they are necessary for a government in crisis, and how they work. Second, it will show how you can use business process re-engineering principles to meet that crisis and transform your agency for seamless service.

Who Should Read This Book?

This book is for public sector practitioners, academics, and others who care about the vitality of our public institutions and want to see them change. It will benefit those who are tired of the same old management recipes and who believe that our agencies can perform far better than they do now. It is for those who believe, as I do, that public service is a distinguished calling and that it can live up to such distinction if we stop bashing the bureaucrats and instead fundamentally change the bureaucracy.

Scope and Organization

The book's organization follows the most important principle of re-engineering: organize around outcomes. The outcome of re-engineering is a seamless agency. Thus, we begin by looking at the nature of seamless service. Chapter One describes a "quiet revolution" occurring in public agencies, a revolution currently overshadowed by the crisis gripping many government agencies and the bad news that grabs the headlines. The chapter describes the consumer society that drives this revolution and the way seamless organizations respond to its demands. Chapter Two reviews the history of public and private bureaucracies. It shows how our original seamless organizations in business and government gave way to bureaucratic and fragmented institutions in the mid nineteenth century. This history is important to understand because the pressures that led to our first industrial bureaucracies are still with us, and these pressures must be understood if we are to withstand them. Chapter Three provides an in-depth look at the nature of a seamless organization—how it feels to work in one, what it is like to be served by one, how it differs in fundamental ways from fragmented bureaucracies.

The next seven chapters focus entirely on business process re-engineering, the tools for creating a seamless agency. Chapter Four details the seven re-engineering design principles, their origins, and how they transform bureaucratic agencies. Chapter Five describes an overall model for re-engineering and explores the first phase of that model: assessment. It lists the conditions necessary for beginning the process and spells out the major roles that must be filled in a re-engineering project. Chapters Six and Seven deal with the design phase of the re-engineering model. Chapter Six sets out the four re-engineering steps and illustrates them with a case study. Chapter Seven deals with several issues raised by re-engineering in the public sector: can you really begin with a "clean sheet" and redesign your agency as if from scratch, as re-engineering requires?

How do you start at the end (with customer needs) and work backwards, when agencies have multiple customers and constituents whose needs are often in direct conflict?

Chapters Eight through Ten concern implementation. Re-engineering's promise, like that of other attractive models, will quickly die if managers don't think carefully about implementation. Specifically, Chapter Eight deals with the important issue of alignment. *Alignment* is the mandatory next step after work processes and structure are changed. It is the less exciting, less visible part of re-engineering, and unfortunately the re-engineering literature has given little attention to it. Alignment means redesigning the various systems (performance appraisal, budget, information, rewards, and so on) to make them consistent with the new structure. It is critical to re-engineering for the same reason it is necessary after any organizational innovation: if the systems and processes are not realigned to support the change, the old ways will creep back in.

Chapter Nine details two government re-engineering cases. The first takes place at the Connecticut Department of Labor, which radically streamlined a fragmented process for delivering unemployment services and realigned the entire culture to support the new process. The second case involves the Defense Logistics Agency, a huge federal agency that made wholesale changes in the ways it manages and purchases products for the Department of Defense.

Chapter Ten offers tips on dealing with resistance from technical specialists, from central support staff, and from others who feel threatened by re-engineering. I look at implementation approaches that typically fail and offer some that work.

Finally, the Conclusion examines future challenges to creating a seamless government agency. Several structural barriers must be overcome—micromanaging by elected officials, warring constituencies that make it almost impossible to streamline certain processes, and our mental models that have been conditioned by the "functional silos" of antiquated bureaucracies. We look at several innovations that help overcome these seemingly intractable barriers.

A Note to the Reader

Three thoughts to guide your reading:

1. You will find a number of private sector examples in the first five chapters of this book, illustrating re-engineering principles and concepts. I included these because we have more examples of re-engineering in the business world than in government. The last six chapters of the book focus almost exclusively on government examples and cases.

2. Those already familiar with the history and development of public and private bureaucracies may find Chapter Two less relevant than other parts of the book. Those who are not aware of this history and those who believe that our regulations and oversight bodies were created by short-sighted bureaucrats trying to protect themselves need to be aware of this history.

3. Civil servants working in agencies that are feeling the pressure to change may be tempted to turn immediately to Chapters Four through Six, read about the principles, model, and steps, and skip the rest in the rush to get started. I understand this temptation, and I urge you to fight it. While re-engineering does promise radical change, it can help to achieve such change only if it is used by people who understand it. Those who read a couple of chapters, scan the model, and go right out looking for a quick fix will be disappointed. So will their staff and customers. Re-engineering for seamless service is about a new way of thinking. Take your time. Mull these principles and examples over. Talk about them with colleagues. When you begin looking at your agency in radically new ways, then you'll know it's time to begin.

Charlottesville, Virginia   RUSSELL M. LINDEN
June 1994

Acknowledgments

I owe a great deal to several people who labored through earlier drafts of *Seamless Government* and offered insightful suggestions and reflections. My sincere thanks go to Dan Stone of the U.S. Agriculture Department, Beth Harper of the University of Virginia, Bill DeLaney and Karl Mettke at the U.S. Forest Service (Karl also provided material for the Forest Service Region 9 case), Gary O'Connell from the City of Charlottesville, Tharon Greene in the City of Hampton (who helped me learn about the innovations in her city), and Evelyn Linden Baldwin, an English major who knows a poorly crafted sentence when she sees one (and had the good sense to teach her son to value a well-turned phrase as he was growing up).

Many thanks too to three academics whose critiques added greatly to this book and who pointed out problems I had not seen and solutions I would not have considered: Professors Paul Nutt of Ohio State University, Stephen Rosenthal of Boston University, and Lee Frost-Kumpf of Penn State University.

One person who read a draft of the book commented that "the strength is in the stories." I learned some time ago the value of stories in teaching (and in leading), and I am indebted to the practitioners who gave me their stories. The material for the cases came from Ann Antrobus, Jim Flanagan, Larry Fox, Jack Frank, Satyendra Huja, Carol Hunt, Hazel Johns, John Locke, Elisabeth McQueeney, Tom Malsack, Warren Master, Mike Miller, Karen Mollander, Douglas Myers, Ann Nichols, Bob O'Neill, Ursula Palmer, Bo Parker, Anne Ruscher, Gary Sheaffer, Darlene Starling, John Turner, Phyllis Watson, and Charles Werner.

I learned about the practices of concurrent engineering, just-in-time management, and lean production from several gentlemen who were more than gracious with their time and thoughts. My sincere thanks go to Minoru Hirose, Tadashi Morooka, Kiyotaka Nakayama, Kei Ogasawara, Ray Smith, Keiji Tsuchiya, and Yamahiro Watanabe.

Several groups of government managers worked with the principles and models offered in this book. I hope they benefited from those discussions—I know I did. My ideas were clarified after workshops with participants at the Navy Family Housing Management Institute, the University of Virginia Quality Management Series, members of the Forest Service Reinvention Team, students at the Federal Executive Institute, managers at the U.S. Department of Labor Employment and Training Agency, and participants in the George Washington University Contemporary Executive Development Program. My sincere thanks go to all of them. My appreciation also goes to two individuals who were most patient as I juggled teaching responsibilities and the completion of this book: Neal Callander and Russ Lentner.

There are people who provided enormous assistance without knowing it. They have a gift for encouragement, for knowing when to react and when to listen, for providing intellectual and moral support. For this, my thanks go to Tico Braun, Elliott Weiss, and most of all my wife, Jackie.

A very special note of appreciation and gratitude goes to a special individual, Bill Van Doren. Bill is a truly inspired writer, editor, designer, and thinker. He is that and more. Bill has a rare ability to sense what someone is thinking, ask probing questions, offer thoughts, improve the articulation of a concept, and get involved in the narration of a story without making it into his own. His use of words is a true art; his ability to raise the level of another's work is a real gift. He is due my great thanks.

R.M.L.

The Author

RUSSELL M. LINDEN is the principal of Russ Linden & Associates, a management consulting firm that focuses on public sector innovations. He is also an adjunct faculty member at the University of Virginia and the Federal Executive Institute. Linden's clients have included the Customs Service, Departments of the Army and Navy, Internal Revenue Service, National Association of Attorneys General, National Geographic Society, National Academy of Sciences, Treasury Department, U.S. Geological Survey, and more than three dozen state and local government agencies. He has consulted with the vice president's National Performance Review and the Federal Quality Institute about applications of process re-engineering to the public sector.

Linden has studied innovative organizations in the United States and Japan. His teaching and research interests include self-managing teams, process re-engineering, team building, implementation of innovations, and relations between career civil servants, elected officials, and their appointees. He is author of *From Vision to Reality: Strategies of Successful Innovators in Government* (1990) and contributing management editor of the *Virginia Review*, where he writes a column on management innovations in government. His articles have appeared in *PM* (the journal of the International City/County Management Association), and *The Public Manager*.

Formerly, Linden served as director of executive programs at the University of Virginia's Institute of Government and as a senior faculty member at the Federal Executive Institute. He received his

B.A degree (1967) in history and his M.S.W. degree (1973) both from the University of Michigan. He received his Ph.D. degree (1982) from the University of Virginia in educational leadership.

Part One

New Realities
for Public Agencies

Chapter One

The Quiet Revolution
in American Government

If citizens could own shares of stock in their government, this would be the ideal time to buy. The most visible indicators of government performance are bad, while the underlying fundamentals are strong and getting stronger. Indeed, I am convinced that historians will look back at the 1990s as a time when a quiet revolution occurred in U.S. public institutions.

The visible signs of governmental decline and public disaffection are everywhere, and they command the headlines: a $4 trillion federal debt growing by over $250 billion a year, continuing HUD scandals from the 1980s, a protest vote of 19 percent going to Ross Perot in the 1992 presidential elections (the largest third-party vote ever), a crumbling infrastructure with more than twenty-six thousand bridges at risk of collapse (NBC News, 1993), state legislatures passing term limits all over the country. We spend billions on schools that don't educate. We have built a record number of prisons in the past decade, and we lock up a greater percentage of our citizens than any other country (Feldman, 1993). Yet we continue to have more violent crime than any other industrialized nation, and the drug epidemic is flourishing. Amid it all, our elected officials often appear more interested in blaming each other for the problems than in working together to solve them.

Beneath these outward signs of decay, a virtual transformation is occurring in some of our public institutions, a transformation no one could have predicted even ten years ago. This sea of change is as sweeping and deep as it is quiet. It is overshadowed, for the moment, by the endless stream of stories documenting the failures

3

of our government, but the change holds enormous promise for our public institutions and for our very society.

This "quiet revolution" is characterized by the emergence of the seamless organization. By *seamless*, I mean an organization that can be described by the words *fluid, agile, integrated, transparent, connected*. Seamless organizations provide a smooth, virtually effortless experience for those who interact with it. The customers of seamless organizations are in direct contact with the service providers; there are no forms, handoffs, or runarounds. Waiting time is radically reduced. Service is delivered in a holistic, not fragmented manner. And everything about the seamless organization is "of a piece." It all fits together; it sends a set of consistent messages to both staff and end users.

Chapter Preview

We see the movement toward seamless government service manifested in at least three important ways: the fall of "Berlin Walls" within government agencies, the development of alliances between agencies and with their customers and suppliers, and an obsession with speed in customer service. In this chapter we look at these manifestations, the consumer society that is driving them, and some implications for society.

The Fall of Berlin Walls Within Agencies

Anyone who has toiled in a government agency understands why the boss worries that nobody sees the big picture. It is because nobody is *shown* the big picture. Our highly structured, bureaucratic agencies are riddled with invisible walls that keep specialized information in and other departments out. There is no motivation to see the big picture when you are rewarded only for meeting your department's immediate objectives. It isn't that people don't want to cooperate; they are punished for doing so by managers who are rewarded for building empires (bigger department = bigger budget = more power).

In 1980, Alvin Toffler wrote, "Today I believe we stand on the edge of a new age of synthesis. In all intellectual fields . . . we are likely to see a return to large-scale thinking, to general theory, to the putting of the pieces back together again" (p. 130). Our best organizations are indeed putting the pieces back together again by removing internal barriers, forming cross-functional teams, giving customers one-stop access to information and service, and viewing their world in an integrated, not segmented, fashion.

• The use of *self-managing teams* is growing in the public (as well as private) sector. Self-managing teams plan, implement, and evaluate their own work, with minimal involvement from senior management. They focus primarily on external customer needs, not the internal needs of the bureaucracy. Use of self-managing teams has reduced the ratio of supervisors to staff at the U.S. Department of Agriculture personnel office from 1:7 to 1:21. In the San Francisco district office of the IRS, use of self-managing teams has resulted in a 22 percent increase in the number of cases processed per staff hour, the equivalent of collecting $6 million more per staff year in delinquent taxes (National Performance Review, 1993).

• *Cross-functional teams* are being used in increasing numbers. Such teams, made up of staff from different functional areas, have been used on an ad hoc basis in the past for short-term projects. Today, some agencies are permanently organizing around such teams. Before the Naval Aviation Depot at Jacksonville, Florida, redesigned its process of overhauling the P-3C antisubmarine aircraft, it used the traditional approach in which single-skill employees worked on one part of every plane. Today, small multiskilled teams do all of the work on a single aircraft, which results in lower costs, higher quality, and higher worker commitment (Carr and others, 1992). The old functional walls are gone.

• *One-stop shopping* for consumers of government services and programs is radically reducing the number of people consumers must deal with. When six social workers from five different agencies are involved in managing services for a victim of child abuse, the chances of effective help don't go up—they go down, and human beings get lost in the shuffle. Today, agencies at the local, state, and federal levels are learning how to provide service through a single point of contact. The U.S. Department of Labor and over forty states are developing one-stop career development centers for citizens who in the past had to endure fragmented and uncoordinated services (Hall, 1993; U.S. Department of Labor, 1993). End result: clients learn what they are eligible for quickly, and staff spend their time assisting people, not completing forms.

• Some *schools*, those bastions of organizational divisions, are learning how to tear the walls down and put the pieces back together. We take for granted that learning consists of separate "subjects" neatly divided into forty-five-minute segments, taught by teachers who have no idea what their students' other classes contain. Today, using a "thematic learning" approach, some creative schools are putting teachers into small teams to coordinate their teaching around certain themes. If the team focuses a unit on France or visits the local city hall to learn about government, each teacher designs lessons around the theme, so the children have an integrated learning experience.

• A number of government agencies are removing internal boundaries to create *virtual teams*—teams that assemble anytime, anyplace and then disband as soon as the task is accomplished. Using a variety of software tools that have been dubbed "groupware," agencies can link hundreds of staff in far-flung offices to interact in real time, electronically. These meetings are bridging boundaries at the Team Technology Center in the Federal Aviation Administration (FAA), Fort Belvoir at Defense, and the Decision Analysis Center at the Department of Commerce. In fact, the FAA is currently seeking ways to incorporate "virtual databases" into systems available throughout the aviation field (National Performance Review, 1993).

• Even *zoos* are learning to tear down the walls, at least figuratively. The San Diego Zoo, the nation's foremost, is starting to organize its exhibits by bioclimatic zones. Rather than separate creatures by taxonomy (mammals, birds, reptiles, etc.), each in its own exhibit, the zoo is organizing them according to their natural habitat (such as an African rain forest), giving the customers a seamless experience approximating the natural environment.

Development of Alliances Between Agencies and with Customers and Suppliers

Contrary to conventional wisdom, there is nothing new about government agencies trying to work with each other and with their customers to solve problems or improve service. What is new is that agencies have developed certain structures to make these alliances standard operating procedure.

• *Partnering* is turning the adversarial world of government contracting on its head. For decades, the game of government contracting was just that, a game—and an expensive one at that. The game involved micromanagement by the government, contractors who resented the excessive scrutiny and cut every corner they could find, and an ongoing game of "gotcha" that too frequently led to delays, cost overruns, and litigation. Partnering changes that, in a big way. A partnering agreement brings the agency, contractor, and others working on the project together. They spend several days prior to the work building a united team. They view each other literally as partners in a joint venture, sharing information that was always closely held in the past, and developing something never dreamt of before—trust. The Army Corps of Engineers, which developed the partnering concept in the mid 1980s, has used it to save millions of dollars.

• *Community policing* is helping to build bridges among groups that have been adversaries in the past. In over four hundred cities and counties around the country, police officers are again walking around neighborhoods, getting to know the residents. They learn about their fears and concerns; they work together on neighborhood projects; they become part of the community. Moreover, the police have rediscovered the value of working with other agencies, businesses, and community groups. No longer up against crime all by themselves, departments now empower their officers to form ongoing relationships with merchants, gang leaders, neighborhood associations, and leverage these relationships to prevent crime. And research is showing that crime, and the fear of crime, usually go down where community policing is used (Trojanowicz and Bucqueroux, 1990).

• *Technology* is building networks and alliances among formerly disconnected groups. One example is the Legitech Network, which electronically links the science advisers of state legislators with federal labs, public interest research groups, and technical professional societies. Legitech encourages creative problem solving and information sharing among groups with important public missions. If a legislator or staffer has a question on a technical matter, he or she can put it on the network and get responses in minutes. Such expert networks are more powerful than E-mail and computer conferencing and more responsive to immediate needs, and they support the development of "anytime, anyplace" government (Peters, 1992).

An Obsession with Speed in Customer Service

In some ways, this trend is the most fascinating of all. Bureaucracies, after all, are not fast. They are not supposed to be. They were created for control. They are good at fixing accountability. At their best they provide clarity of roles. They can mass produce products and services; they can process huge amounts of information. They are capable of many things, but speed isn't one of them. Yet that "truth" is yielding to the quiet revolution in U.S. government.

• To provide faster service, the U.S. Office of Consular Affairs has streamlined its process for issuing and renewing *passports*. The normal waiting period used to be one to two months for a renewal. That has been shortened to one to two weeks. For those with emergency needs, a passport can be renewed in a matter of hours.

• The process of obtaining *permits* from a government agency can be long, tedious, and frustrating. Today, some local governments are providing permits for new businesses and buildings in a matter of hours, not days or weeks. At the Mark Twain National Forest, the time to obtain a grazing permit has been reduced from thirty days to a few hours.

• *Social service departments* are traditionally slow, bureaucratic agencies that emphasize controls and forms. Some local governments have turned that around. At agencies from California to the Washington, D.C., suburbs, applicants who once waited one to two months for Medicaid and Aid to Families with Dependent Children (AFDC) are now approved and served in a matter of days, and occasionally hours (Hall, 1993; Martin, 1993).

• Even *freeway tolls* are becoming user-friendly. An increasing number of drivers are able to "pay" their tolls without even slowing down at the toll booth. On their windshield is a plastic card read by scanners along the freeway. The drivers simply receive a statement each month showing their charges.

• A new world of speed is also coming to government's "internal customers," its employees. Making *purchases* has always been a colossal headache for civil servants, requiring multiple signatures, handoffs, and delays for the most routine of purchases. Now, some local government, state, and federal agencies are treating their staff like responsible adults, allowing them to make certain purchases by credit card. One military installation, Port Hueneme, California, enables designated staff members to use credit cards for purchases of up to $25,000 a month.

• *Nonprofit organizations* are also learning the importance of speed. The National Geographic Society determined that taking four weeks or more to respond to customer orders from its Christmas catalogue was not acceptable to consumers who can call L. L. Bean and have an item in four days. The society streamlined its customer fulfillment process and now responds within twenty-four to forty-eight hours of each request.

The New Consumer Society: Driving Force Behind the Quiet Revolution

If we knew nothing more about the preceding examples, we might reasonably suppose that they were all about technology. This is the information age, after all, and we are being overwhelmed with information because of rapid technological advances. This revolution does involve technology, but not in the sense many assume. Advanced technology can accomplish great things: it can speed up problem solving, work on several problems at once, and get paper out of the office. What it can't do is make fragmented, bureaucratic organizations more productive.

The tide of quiet revolution arises from a momentous sea of change around the globe: the enormous shift in consumer attitudes and expectations. From the dawn of the industrial age through the middle of the twentieth century, citizens in economically advanced countries have lived in a *producer-oriented society*. Requirements of mass production—a large semieducated work force willing to do routine, dull tasks; specialization of roles; interchangeable parts; interchangeable people within specialized roles; large runs of the same product; stable demand; one-size- (or color/model/style/type) fits-all products; division of labor—have driven the work routines and procedures of our large organizations for over 150 years. The industrial age shaped our roles, expectations, and relationships in fundamental ways. It tended to separate those who produce from those who consume. It rewarded nuclear families who separated from their extended families. It resulted in specialized, separate institutions to perform the tasks once left to families and communities, such as the education of children, health care, and care of the elderly and the impoverished.

Since the 1960s, the United States has been developing into a *consumer-oriented society*. The mass production economy's many benefits began giving way to its limitations—little variety, slow response, mediocre quality, and little attention to individual preferences.

The mass production system worked so well for the majority of Americans that it eventually fell victim to its own improvements. Once the problem of supply was solved and our companies were producing as much as the country wanted, consumers insisted on greater variety. As price was brought under control, consumers wanted quality. As we achieved efficiency, consumers wanted individual choice. Psychologist Abraham Maslow's hierarchy of needs comes to mind: the satisfaction of one human need leads to the next one on the hierarchy. We have satisfied the basic needs of production. We produce far more food and durable goods than our 260 million citizens can consume. The challenge now is to satisfy more developed needs and demands.

Key shifts in the transformation from a producer to a consumer society can be summarized as follows:

From	*To*
Low variety—"The American people can have any color, as long as it is black."	*Great variety*—In 1958, U.S. consumers could buy twenty-one different makes of cars from ten different producers; by the early 1990s, they could choose from over 570 car, van, and truck models (Carnevale, 1991).
Low convenience—Money was available from banks anytime we wanted it, as long as it was between nine and three o'clock.	*Emphasis on convenience*—Automatic teller machines (ATMs) provide money anytime and almost anyplace today.

From (continued)

Limited access to basic services— We could mail packages anywhere we wanted, as long as it was from the U.S. Postal Service, Monday through Friday or Saturday morning.

Few choices—We could watch anything on TV we wanted, as long as it was on ABC, CBS, or NBC.

To (continued)

Virtually continuous access— Often the service is brought to the customer: UPS and Federal Express make pickups at your office, and UPS does so twenty-four hours a day.

Seemingly endless choices— We can watch just about anything we want to on the tube, anytime, through cable and pay-per-view, and the world of five hundred channels is upon us.

Low variety, low convenience, limited access, few choices. These summarize the downside of a mass production society.

The consumer society is characterized by an increasing number of choices. The days of mass market, one-size-fits-all society are long past. Up to the 1970s, the Big Three automakers dictated auto trends, we watched three TV networks, and icons like Ed Sullivan and Walter Cronkite were able to define our culture and information for us. Today, our choices are almost unlimited—over five hundred models of cars, vans, and trucks; information on hundreds of cable TV stations; niche publications; and electronic bulletin boards appealing to every possible interest.

The explosion of information, and our ready access to it, increases the choices and power of consumers. As Hammer and Champy (1993) write, "Customers have gained the upper hand in their relationships with sellers, in part, because customers now have easy access to enormously more data" (p. 20). Osborne and Gaebler (1992) make the same point in *Reinventing Government:* "We have been transformed from a mass society . . . to a mosaic society. . . . We have come to expect products and services customized to our own styles and tastes, from television networks to restaurants to beer" (p. 168).

The increasing number of consumer options is affecting governmental agencies in major ways. The school choice movement, which allows parents to place their children in the public (and sometimes private) school of their choice, has spread across the country since Minnesota began a small pilot program in 1985. Private security guards have become one of the fastest-growing job categories in the country, which reflects many citizens' and store owners' desire for an alternative to municipal police protection. Local governments are looking for choices in the delivery of services, and the use of competition (which allows government departments to bid against private firms for the opportunity to provide a specific service) is spreading, from garbage collection to landfill operations, golf course and swimming pool management, street sweeping and repair, food and beverage concessions, printing, and custodial services. When consumers have more choices, they express their preferences loudly. Those in the public sector who have labored under the misperception that their agency has a monopoly on its services are waking up to a new day. Even those whose agencies are, technically, a monopoly (regulatory agencies, for example), are learning that the public does not sit passively by when unhappy with the agency's performance. The deregulation movement, which began in the late 1970s under President Carter and accelerated under President Reagan, is one indication of this fact.

The consumer society also reflects the emergence of a *global economy*, which depends on the technological advances and proliferation of information noted earlier. In addition, advances in transportation, the lowering of certain tariff barriers, and the emergence of regional markets crossing national borders (in Europe with the European Community, in Asia, and emerging in North America with passage of the North American Free Trade Agreement) all fuel a global economy that forces domestic companies to look thousands of miles past national borders in order to see their toughest competitors. This economy results in far more consumer choice.

The Consumer Society: How Leading Organizations Are Responding

We began this chapter by looking at three remarkable changes marking the quiet revolution in organizations: strategic alliances between agencies, the fall of Berlin Walls within agencies, and an obsession with speed. These trends are all responses to the transformation toward a consumer-oriented society. They are also initial organizational responses to the mammoth changes in technology, politics, global economics, and citizen needs and preferences.

Innovative organizations in both public and private sectors are scrambling as they learn to adapt to the new realities. The standards that successful organizations will achieve are well articulated by Anthony Carnevale (1991) in his research for the American Society for Training and Development and the U.S. Department of Labor. Carnevale notes six "benchmarks" by which all organizations will be judged in the coming decade:

- Quality
- Productivity
- Variety
- Customization
- Convenience
- Timeliness

It is precisely because these consumer demands are not consistent with the strengths of mass production and bureaucratic operations that a revolution is taking place in government agencies. If the top-down, control-oriented, segmented way of providing goods and services could meet these benchmarks, there would be no change. But hierarchical, bureaucratic organizations can't provide productivity *and* quality; they can't offer customization *and* timeliness; they aren't capable of producing high quality *and* variety. These have been the trade-offs in a mass production world. The consumer could have the benefits of efficiency, high volume, and low cost—but only at the expense of convenience, customization, variety, and timeliness.

Shamrocks, Basketball Teams, and the Seamless Organization

Some public and private organizations are shedding their old forms and styles and are learning how to succeed against the benchmarks of a consumer society. A variety of names and metaphors describe the new organizational forms:

• *Shamrocks*. Coined by Charles Handy, this term describes a three-part organization made up of core workers; subcontractors who frequently work for the organization; and the flexible labor force made up of part-time, temporary, and seasonal workers who make up the fastest-growing segment of the labor force today (Handy, 1989).

• *Jazz combos*. Max De Pree (1992) and Charles Savage (1990) use this concept to describe the kind of improvisation and flexible adaptation needed in today's turbulent environment. Innovative organizations, like jazz musicians, must share leadership, respond to change quickly, communicate laterally, and maintain good chemistry as they chart new courses. De Pree notes that a jazz performance "depends on so many things—the environment, the volunteers playing in the band, the need for everybody to perform as individuals and as a group, the absolute dependence of the leader on the members of the band, the need of the leader for the followers to play well. What a summary of an organization!" (pp. 8–9).

• *Lean production*. This term was used by the MIT team that conducted an exhaustive study of the Japanese auto industry. It refers to the system pioneered by Toyota that turns mass production assumptions on their head: use of short production runs, frequent changes of models produced on the line to provide greater variety, extremely close supplier relations sharing sensitive cost information, active involvement by teams of workers in anticipating problems and finding systematic solutions, just-in-time delivery of parts. The overriding theme: simplicity. Nothing is wasted—not people, space, materials, or time.

• *Learning organizations.* A term popularized by Peter Senge's book *The Fifth Discipline* (1990), *learning organization* describes the elements organizations need in order to continually learn and adapt: systems thinking, personal mastery (deepening the sense of personal vision so that we can see reality clearly and connect personal learning to organizational learning), mental models (deeply ingrained assumptions that influence how we view the world), shared vision that binds members of the organization together, and team learning.

• *Networks.* This term refers to the trend among some organizations to contract out 75 percent or more of their work to a variety of subcontractors, which requires constant communication and coordination. As a metaphor, networks seem to mirror the insights of twentieth-century physics, especially quantum mechanics and chaos theory. "As we penetrate into matter," says physicist Fritjof Capra (1983), "nature does not show us any isolated building blocks, but rather appears to be a complicated web of relations" (p. 87).

• *Holograms.* These are the three-dimensional pictures produced when two laser beams touch and produce patterns that can be recorded on a photographic plate. As Stanley Davis (1987) notes, when a holographic image is broken, any part of it will reconstruct the whole, because each part contains information about the whole. This forms an apt metaphor for the new organizational forms responding to the consumer society, because the ability of each unit to maintain an image of the whole is a key to success; the demands for speed, flexibility, and coordination in a fast-changing environment don't allow for top-down, hierarchical leadership styles. Every part must be acting on its own, in concert with every other part.

• *Basketball teams*. Organizational theorist Bob Keidel (1985) uses this sports metaphor to describe the kind of interaction, communication, and chemistry evident in certain organizations today. Keidel does an excellent job of depicting the similarities between the three most popular team sports in the United States—baseball, football, and basketball—and three major organizational forms: decentralized, individually oriented organizations (such as law firms, doctors' offices, university faculty, R&D centers) that focus on professional autonomy—"baseball teams"; centralized, top-down organizations (such as traditional mass production plants, McDonald's, orchestras) that focus on control—"football teams"; and small group-based, cooperative forms (such as some high-tech organizations like 3M, ad agencies, consulting outfits) that require speed, flexibility, and innovation through cooperation—"basketball teams." Cooperation-based, basketball-type organizations shine where innovation is needed. They add value through the synergy of small teams that work flexibly and quickly in response to changing consumer demands.

• *Seamless organizations*. General Electric CEO Jack Welch (1990) speaks of "boundaryless organizations." I prefer the word *seamless*, which captures the essence of what the new organizational form is all about. The walls within, and between, organizations have turned to networks. Narrow, rigidly defined jobs are replaced by generalist, multiskilled positions that change and grow over time. The precise forms and boundaries of the seamless organization are fluid, changing, permeable, sometimes invisible. At times, it isn't clear where the organization ends and another begins.

For instance, where is the "organization" when you talk with a Norfolk *city* employee, who works in a *federal* Navy family housing welcome center, about Big Brother services provided by a *nonprofit* organization that comes to your apartment? Or when the scanner at the checkout counter reads the bar codes on your items, sends that information electronically to its suppliers, who determine when to send new goods to the retailer—with no purchase orders changing hands—and receive payment without sending an invoice? Or when you deposit and withdraw money, check your current account balance, and transfer from one account to another at automatic teller machines, located thousands of miles from your bank or even from your home?

Seamless interaction marks organizations that are succeeding in the new environment. If our government agencies are to be reinvented, they will have to learn how to operate in this fashion. Some of them already do. Seamless organizations aren't primarily the result of visionary leaders, of privatizing services, of incredibly advanced hardware and software systems, or of total quality management. No, theirs is the simple, powerful story of learning to organize work in a holistic, integrated way. They are replacing specialists with generalists, using cross-functional teams instead of individuals working in isolated departments and functions, shifting from a preoccupation with internal activities to a design focused on outcomes.

Theirs is a story of taking the fragmentation out of work and redesigning it along organic, natural processes. Many agencies are learning that their employees may spend 90 percent or more of their time doing work that adds no value to the product or service they deliver. The wasted time and energy aren't caused primarily by lazy workers or old-line, top-down managers who stifle creativity. The most profound insight of the past few years for many public and private sector leaders is that their primary limitations lie instead in the ways they have organized work. Victims of their own (perceived) successes, they have taken the principles of hierarchy and mass production to such an extreme that they can't respond to the demands of a consumer society. The principles on which we have built our major government and business organizations— division of labor, specialization, standardization, clear hierarchy, individual accountability, interchangeable parts and people—produce a highly fragmented organization, keyed to separation: separation between departments, separation of line and staff, separation from its consumers, separation from its suppliers and vendors.

Seamless government agencies are putting the pieces back together and learning to organize in a holistic way. Rather than divide a government program into several different functional specialties, the seamless agency provides the consumer one-stop shopping and a simple and flexible service. Rather than force a sick patient to deal with over fifty different personnel and endure endless forms and long waits, the seamless hospital creates multiskilled "care pair" teams of nurse and technician, who provide most aspects of the patient's care and coordinate the rest. And rather than maintain strict, arm's-length relationships with suppliers and contractors, seamless government agencies are joining forces with them to form one team with a shared objective.

Seamless agencies are shedding vestiges of their mass production past and reconfiguring around a few simple, lean, streamlined models. The shift to seamless service in the public sector poses special challenges: How can agencies meet consumer demands for speed while honoring public values of due process? How can agencies lower their walls and include customers in designing and delivering services, when some of those walls were created to avoid conflicts of interest and abuses of the public trust? We will deal with these and other issues as we explore the new model of seamless agencies and the re-engineering principles used to create them. And, as the next chapter shows, these "new" models aren't really so new. Rather, they are borrowed from our earliest craftsmen and artisans and updated for a high-tech age.

Chapter Two

The Evolution of Work in Public and Private Bureaucracies

The effort to provide a seamless experience for consumers may evoke a pleasant sense of déjà vu for many. Organizations that move quickly, that provide variety, customization, and personal service are actually relearning something that once came naturally. Indeed, the seamless organization is a kind of reincarnation of the individualized craft approach to producing goods and services, an approach that dominated the U.S. economy prior to the mid nineteenth century. It's not the same today, of course, because of vast changes in the scale of operations and the speed of communications and transportation. But the emerging seamless organization shares highly significant features with the general merchants, craftspeople, artisans, and farmers who were the backbone of the country's commerce two hundred years ago; it is reintroducing a holistic approach to work and direct, personal relationships with the consumers of its work.

Chapter Preview

This chapter's purpose is to show how, and why, our public and private organizations have become fragmented and bureaucratic. I believe it is essential to understand this history so that we can avoid making the mistakes that led to the fragmentation of government in the first place.

While government and business differ in fundamental ways, they have many things in common. One commonality is a history of bureaucratic growth. As we will see, U.S. business and government organizations went through the same developmental stages, as industrial models provided the major influence on development of our governmental structures. Both industry and government began with small craftlike units led by a few generalists; they grew into large, segmented, fragmented bureaucracies characterized by division: of labor, of specialists, of management levels, of producers from consumers. For most of the past two centuries these divisions seemed to produce far more benefits than costs. Today, the costs have become unbearable, compelling us to learn how to replace division with a seamless focus on outcomes.

Seamlessness in Craft Production

As Alfred D. Chandler (1977) tells us, until the 1840s, the U.S. economy was dominated by generalists. Most people, of course, still worked on farms, and farmers understood all aspects of farming because they performed all, or almost all, of its tasks. In commerce, the general merchant dominated the scene. He performed all of the trading functions, from purchasing goods to financing and insuring the transactions. These generalists typically had a direct and personal relationship with the users of their products. Since most working Americans knew that they would see their customers over and over, they felt a sense of accountability. Trust developed, not trust born of some romantic ideal, but the kind of trust that comes from mutual interdependence and long-term relationships. Perhaps most important to us today, the generalist was highly responsive to the customer's needs and could customize goods or services to the customer's taste.

As the nineteenth century progressed, the nature of work changed radically. Personal relationships yielded to impersonal ones, a holistic understanding and performance of work evolved into the division of labor and the fragmentation of work into its smallest elements, and work became a job for many Americans. No middle managers supervised the work of other managers prior to the 1840s. No staff specialists told line managers what to do: they didn't appear until the late 1850s. Then the industrial revolution separated the roles of producer and consumer, of owner and manager, and the modern organizational hierarchy segregated people into departments and divisions, managers and workers. Americans who once identified themselves by their craft or trade increasingly described themselves by which company they worked for.

From Craft to Mass Production: Efficiency and Fragmentation in Work

In *The Wealth of Nations*, published in 1776, Adam Smith expressed his enthusiasm for a new idea, the principle of division of labor. He had observed two types of production in a pin factory: craft production and a group that divided their work into small, narrow tasks. The group that divided its labor showed vastly higher productivity.

Seventeen years later, in 1793, Eli Whitney invented the cotton gin, which quickly transformed the production of cotton in the United States. Again according to Chandler's (1977) account, cotton exports more than quintupled in the next eight years. Such quantities required financing, management, and distribution systems. A sequence of specialists—from jobber, importer, and cotton factor (who marketed the crop and financed the farmer) to broker and commission agent—participated in an efficient and impersonal chain that brought cotton to market. These changes brought to an end the personal and direct relations of the farmer and general merchant. As Chandler notes, "Rarely did a merchant know both the producer and consumer at either end of the long chain of middlemen, transporters, and financiers who moved the goods through the economy" (p. 48). Specialization had arrived on at least one major front in our economy.

Railroads as Our First Modern Hierarchies

Technology also gave rise to the railroads, which led to development of the first modern business enterprises in the United States.

The railroads faced an unprecedented task: management of a large, dispersed organization spreading rapidly across an entire continent with thousands of workers and thousands of cars. The task was as daunting as it was risky. In an age of crude information management tools, it was very difficult to know the exact location of rolling stock. Many roads ran multiple trains on the same tracks; a mistake in scheduling could prove fatal. After one such disaster occurred in 1841 in Massachusetts, the resulting outcry moved the state legislature to investigate. An early version of a blue ribbon commission looked into the matter and issued a report that would bring a knowing smile to any government employee. The commission's recommendations produced our first developed bureaucratic hierarchy.

The hierarchy included several levels of supervisors and managers. It established clear responsibility and authority for each of three railroad divisions and created functional managers to run them. It included a headquarters in which senior managers were to oversee the divisional managers. Other managerial positions were added (master of transportation, assistant masters of transportation, master mechanics, superintendent), and each level was given a set of reports to complete and pass up the chain. Precise timetables were established, and detailed instructions on how to handle breakdowns were given to conductors. In the interest of safety and efficiency, an elaborate and highly rational organization was designed. It soon became the blueprint for other railroads and for large organizations in other industries.

By the 1880s, railroad leaders completed the modern business hierarchy, developing the line-staff concept and modern accounting procedures, as well as information systems to control and evaluate the work of the many managers running the system. The organization chart of a typical railroad in the 1870s could be the chart of most large-scale bureaucracies, then or now.

The impact of the railroads was widespread, both industrially and organizationally. Their growth required new financial arrangements. The new telegraph technology spread along the railroads' rights of way, providing a communications system that complemented the railroads. The railroads' speed of delivery led to a huge increase in the volume of mail. That new volume, in turn, required the U.S. postal system to develop a hierarchical system very closely resembling that of the railroads.

The Beginning of Scientific Management

The specialization and fragmentation of work advanced by several more steps toward the turn of the twentieth century, as a group of engineers began employing scientific methods to root out inefficiencies and waste in factories and organizational systems and to increase productivity through improved accounting, cost control, and gain-sharing plans to motivate workers.

The most famous of this group was Frederick W. Taylor. Obsessed with the rationalization of work, Taylor did scientific time and motion studies of the most productive workers in various plants to identify specific work methods that all should follow, as well as to document the amount to be paid in gain-sharing plans. The goal was to break a job down into the simplest tasks that could be done quickly and learned by someone with little education: "In his [Taylor's] system the judgment of the individual workman was replaced by the laws, rules, principles, etc., of the science of the job which was developed by management. . . . The whole attitude of Taylor in this respect was described by a mechanic who worked with him. . . . Taylor would tell him that he was 'not supposed to think, there are other people paid for thinking around here'" (Marshall and Tucker, 1992, p. 5).

In order to rationalize factory work processes, Taylor proposed development of a planning department made up of highly specialized "functional foremen" who divided up the activities of the general foremen they were to replace (Chandler, 1977). This new department would oversee operations of the entire plant, scheduling daily work plans for each unit and each worker. It would recruit, hire and fire, monitor workers' output, and analyze costs. Another generalist, the plant foreman, was about to be replaced by specialists.

Although there is little evidence of factory owners adopting Taylor's system just as he proposed it, he had a tremendous impact on the nature of management and the organization of work. His ideas influenced managers in both private and public sectors, and many factories incorporated the responsibilities of Taylor's functional foreman into an expanded group of staff specialists reporting to the plant manager. His work furthered the movement toward division of labor, specialization, rigid controls, and the separation of line and staff.

Ford and Sloan: System and Structure

The development of auto manufacturing is a microcosm of the country's movement from craft to mass production. Prior to Henry Ford's innovations, most auto manufacturers used a system of craftspeople to make and assemble the car. Highly skilled workers used flexible tools to make custom-ordered cars, one at a time. Customers didn't shop at car dealerships—there were none to visit. Rather, they would visit a machine tool company and order a car to their specifications. The car was made by small groups of craftspeople, who thoroughly understood its engineering and design principles.

This craft system was decentralized. A small number of machine shops made the various parts, coordinated by an owner-entrepreneur who had a direct relationship with everyone involved. No two cars were exactly alike, because they were made to order and because machine tools could not yet cut hardened metal to precise dimensions and mass produce a design. Such tools became available in 1906, and with them automakers were able to produce interchangeable parts. This technological advance meant that auto production would soon soar and the craftspeople would lose their place in the infant industry (Womack, Jones, and Roos, 1990).

Henry Ford followed in the spirit of Frederick Taylor, continually studying the production process and looking for ways to standardize it, rationalize it, root out waste, and improve productivity. By using the new precision machine tools, reducing the number of parts needed to build the car, and making them easy to attach, Ford made revolutionary gains in productivity—and brought the final demise of the craftsperson's usefulness in auto production.

Ford had a genius for organization and a profound distrust of anyone but himself. This combination led him to divide up everything that mattered about mass production.

> Ford took it as a given that his workers wouldn't volunteer any information on operating conditions—for example, that a tool was malfunctioning—much less suggest ways to improve the process. These functions fell respectively to the foreman and the industrial engineer, who reported their findings and suggestions to higher levels of management for action. So were born the battalions of narrowly skilled indirect workers—the repairman, the quality inspector, the housekeeper, and the rework specialists, in addition to the foreman and the industrial engineer. . . . Ford was dividing labor not only in the factory, but also in the engineering shop. Industrial engineers took their places next to the manufacturing engineers who designed the critical production machinery. They were joined by product engineers, who designed and engineered the car itself [Womack, Jones, and Roos, 1990, p. 32].

In addition, Womack and coauthors show how the original "knowledge workers"—staffers who managed information but didn't understand how a car was built or even what the inside of a factory looked like—took the place of skilled craftsmen who in the past had handled all facets of production.

Ford's innovations didn't end there. He also invented the

interchangeable worker. Ford was dealing with workers so diverse it makes our current work force look homogeneous. His employees spoke over fifty languages, and many spoke no English at all. To meet these challenges, he took division of labor to the extreme. He gave assemblers just one task. A worker would perform the same repetitive movement (such as put two nuts on two bolts) thousands of times a day. Ford also built on Taylor's concept of the staff specialist, creating quality inspectors, rework specialists, repairmen, and other workers never needed when craftsmen built the entire car and inspected their own work (Womack, Jones, and Roos, 1990).

Ford provided steady employment to thousands of workers at the then unheard-of industrial wage of $5 a day, and his productivity improvements and high sales volumes brought the Model T's cost within reach of working people. At the same time, he contributed mightily to the "de-skilling" of the U.S. worker, a problem we are only now beginning to confront.

Alfred Sloan completed the modern mass production system with his creation of the divisional structure at General Motors. Sloan took specialization another step when he established separate divisions for each car model (Oldsmobile, Buick, Pontiac, Chevrolet, and Cadillac), plus additional units for separate components (generators by Delco, steering gears by Saginaw, and so on). Divisions were organized by function (such as accounting, manufacturing, engineering), and each function was run by specialists. Sloan also created new staff specialists of financial management and marketing, giving each division its own dedicated experts. The division of labor had become complete.

The automakers' relations with labor unions only added to the system's fragmentation. Eventually, unions accepted the basic tenets of the mass production model and fought for job seniority and job rights. They wanted more—more security, more rights based on seniority, more job rules, and, of course, more money and benefits—within the system. One could hardly blame them for such demands.

Unfortunately, union priorities and management's treatment of unions only led to a more rigid work force that focused on equity, not organizational success and improvement.

In the mass production model, few people understood what it took to build a car from start to finish, but everyone knew what his or her individual job and unit did. The divisional structure, using the principles of mass production, became the model for virtually all manufacturing industries and most services. Work, and the workplace, had been rationalized and fragmented in ways that lowered prices, increased volume, and provided work for millions. Few Americans in the 1920s would have believed that organizational systems producing such manifest benefits would be overcome by their own built-in limitations.

From Craft to Mass Production in Government: Post Office, Education, Health Care, Police Work

Our government agencies and their structures mirrored the movement from craft to mass production in U.S. business. Just as commerce two hundred years ago was dominated by generalist merchants, farmers, and craftspeople, the government was also run by a small number of generalists. A typical federal department in 1800 was administered by the secretary, aided by clerks and a small field establishment (White, 1963). There were no bureaus, no middle managers, few specialists. This simplicity was primarily a function of size; the country's population simply didn't require a large, central governmental bureaucracy. It was also due to ideology. As Matthew Crenson (1975) notes in his study of early U.S. bureaucracy, "Hostility toward 'bureaucracy' has been a durable feature of American political life for generations" (p. ix).

But as the country and its government grew, our government agencies were influenced by new management thinking. They developed a specialized, hierarchical form that reflected the bureaucracies emerging in the private sector. Growth and new technologies were partly responsible. In addition, fraud and corruption created demands for improved controls, and those demands led to checks and balances, more hierarchy, more layers of management. The organizational forms that emerged resembled those of the railroads and, later, the automakers. The move to rationalize and the need to control wrongdoing spawned bureaucracies heavy with senior administrators and staff specialists, bureaucracies that fragmented the work once done holistically by professionals. And in each case, the professional was further separated from the end user of services.

The country didn't want a large, controlling federal government; it distrusted the notion of career civil servants, yet it needed certain business done. Our first presidents found an answer to this dilemma by placing government departments in the hands of people chosen on the basis of character. There is a certain irony here, given that our Constitution had established a government of laws, not of people. But it was not until Andrew Jackson became president in 1829 that the notion of formal rules and regulations, impersonal standards, and performance measures was established. For an entire generation prior to Jackson, public officials were selected for their personal virtue and reputation for honesty.

The government that Jackson inherited was a highly personal, informal one: "Command . . . was personal. Authority and responsibility for the affairs of an agency were concentrated in a single human being. The functioning of a department depended less upon its formal organizational apparatus than upon the personality and preferences of its chief. Indeed, formal organizational apparatus hardly existed. To a considerable extent, the agency was the creature of its chief—his character, his commands, and his personal taste" (Crenson, 1975, p. 51).

But Jackson didn't leave government as he found it. In spite of his own preferences, he began the growth of bureaucracy and specialization in U.S. government. His change of heart was caused by abuses of public office. Just as hierarchical, bureaucratic systems were begun by the railroads in response to a problem (safety), the federal government created administrative layers to deal with a different problem: the use of public office for private gain. Since Jackson had been roundly criticized for expanding the spoils system in government, he had to be especially sensitive to allegations that his appointees were guilty of corruption. The abuses were first discovered in the Post Office Department, and it was there that our first nonmilitary government hierarchies grew.

Postal Service

Until the 1850s, the entire postal system was administered by three assistant postmaster generals and a few clerks: no middle managers, staff specialists, or transportation hubs. Each of the almost seventeen thousand local post offices in 1849 was run locally (Chandler, 1977). In essence, the system had been run during its first three decades by one man. Abraham Bradley, one of the first public officials to come to Washington when the government was established there in 1800, was the department's real power. The department became a "thing of his own making," as he supervised the letting and performance of contracts, all financial matters, and the behavior of local postmasters (Crenson, 1975, p. 112). When he was forced out during Jackson's first term, his successors confronted a major dilemma. It seems that old Bradley had written very little down! There were a few official records, but most important information was noted on old scraps of paper or remained in his head. He must have been one of the first U.S. bureaucrats to use the strategy of building a power base by making himself indispensable.

Abraham Bradley's personal approach to administration didn't outlast him in the post office, because of the problems discovered there during Jackson's presidency. The major problems concerned the letting and oversight of contracts to deliver the mail. Since the Post Office Department had no transportation capability, it paid contractors to get the mail through. When a House committee investigated these contracts, it found plenty to report. A mail delivery route awarded to one contractor for $4,500 a year increased to $38,500 just twenty-four months later. Contractors provided unnecessary services to jack up prices; some charged for services that they never delivered (Crenson, 1975).

Congress's investigation of postal abuses led to a thorough housecleaning and a new postmaster general, Amos Kendall. Taking charge in 1835, Kendall brought in a trusted colleague to control finances. He then did what many bureaucrats do today when they want to make a splash and get people's attention: he reorganized. He split the country into two regions and assigned an assistant postmaster to each. More significantly, he separated the supervision of financial accounts from all other management responsibilities and took responsibility for overseeing the accounts himself. He thus established the principle of separation of powers in the federal administration. Checks and balances were being extended from the Constitutional framework to departments and agencies within the executive branch.

Congress furthered the trend a year later when it added a treasury department auditor to the post office staff. This auditor (and forty staff) oversaw department accounts, keeping a special eye out for abuses of contracts. Then, it created an additional system to control expenditures and abuse, which added to governmental fragmentation. It directed that all postal revenues be sent to the U.S. treasury, only to be returned later in the form of annual appropriations. Congress was far more concerned about curbing misconduct than about administrative productivity. As has often been noted, the framers of the Constitution worried about abuse of power, not about efficiency, and Congress followed in the same path. Finally, Kendall compounded the fragmentation when he replaced his two-region organization with a tripartite model: offices for appointments, contracts, and inspections, each run by an assistant postmaster. In a very short time, Amos Kendall and the Congress brought division of labor, specialization, and a degree of hierarchical bureaucracy to one of the country's largest government agencies.

In the ensuing decades, the Post Office Department developed an organizational structure very similar to that of the railroads. In 1855, to meet the increasing pace and volume of mail, Congress funded fifty distribution centers staffed by middle managers. They were given detailed position descriptions on how to coordinate the flow of mail. Specialized mail cars came into use. Difficult as it may be to imagine today, the newly organized postal system was considered highly efficient. By this time it was the government's largest operating agency, and as such it had no lack of political patronage. Still, it developed a highly professional cadre of managers who oversaw its growth (which continued until, in 1992, Postmaster General Marvin T. Runyon responded to a $2 billion deficit with the largest government reorganization in several decades, eliminating thirty thousand management and support positions and prompting the early retirement of forty-seven thousand workers). Hierarchy and bureaucracy were spreading in the federal government.

Education

Through the first half of the nineteenth century, those Americans who went to public schools were taught all their subjects by the same teacher. This individual passed on both the knowledge and the morals of the community and was expected to model the high standards taught in the classroom. Usually single, often male (females came to dominate later in the century), the generalist teacher had the important responsibility of helping to pass on the community's culture and beliefs.

As Marshall and Tucker (1992) have shown, a new model began to spread by the early 1850s. The one-room schoolhouse gave way to buildings in which students were divided by age. Some classes were led by teachers who specialized in different subjects.

And students began to be separated into different ability groups.

By the turn of the twentieth century, the nature and purposes of public schools changed. The numbers of children going to school mushroomed, and for the first time many children went on to high school. Compulsory education meant mass education, and mass education required a new organizational approach. Reformers of the nineteenth and early twentieth century, indignant over the corruption and abuse of public office by politicians and their cronies, had been remaking local governments through the introduction of council-manager plans, giving the policy-making function to the elected officials while maintaining the ongoing administrative functions for a professional manager. The reformers were enthusiastic about the promise of scientific management and sought to apply its principles to education.

They began by replacing the ward system of school board appointments with a corporate style, giving a smaller number of (business)people a policy-making role. The boards would then select the superintendent, a professional to run the schools. The superintendents selected were attracted to the new scientific management methods and apparently borrowed from Taylor's concept of the large planning department in building their own central administrative staffs. Result: an explosion of administrators. According to the U.S. Office of Education, in 1899 there was an average of four central staffers in the 484 cities surveyed. Between 1890 and 1920, staff numbers grew exponentially: from 9 to 144 in Baltimore, 7 to 159 in Boston, 10 to 159 in Cleveland, and 235 to 1,310 in New York (Marshall and Tucker, 1992). The trend has continued to this day, unfortunately. In the New York public schools, the ratio of administrators to students is sixty times higher than in the New York City parochial school system (Peters, 1992).

More significant than the change in school governance was the application of scientific management methods to the schools' curricula and staff management. In order to fill the needs of the country's booming industries and to meet the perceived needs of the influx of immigrant children for whom English was a second language, schools were transformed into deliverers of an educational "product," one that fit the requirements of Henry Ford's mass production plants. Thus, conformity, precision, and regularity, the skills and attitudes needed in industrial employees, were emphasized. Factory labor required workers who showed up every day on time, took orders willingly, and did their repetitive tasks without complaint, and schools learned how to turn out such a product. Franklin Bobbitt, professor of educational administration at the University of Chicago and an influential proponent of Taylorism for the schools, said that efficiency depended on "centralization of authority and definite direction by the supervisors of all processes performed. . . . The worker [that is, the teacher] must be kept supplied with the detailed instructions as to the work to be done, the standards to be reached, the methods to be employed, and the appliances to be used. . . . [T]here can never be any misunderstanding as to what is expected of a teacher in the way of results or in the matter of method" (Marshall and Tucker, 1992, p. 17).

Schools divided knowledge into "subjects"—science, social science, math, reading—and each of those subdivided again and again. Following in the spirit of Adam Smith, many school leaders concluded that the nation's schools would be most efficient by dividing up the curriculum and giving teachers specialized roles. Just as there was "one best way" to organize work in the factory, there must be one best way to teach and to learn.

The schools, operating with scientific management efficiency, performed a wondrous achievement. They turned out millions of children, including many immigrants, who were literate in English, knew basic math, were punctual, understood the rules of work, and were willing to do the jobs required in the factories. That is no small accomplishment. The price we paid wouldn't show up until the second half of the century, when our economic competitors' productivity and quality started to exceed our own, in part because of the advanced skills of their workers. While other countries were investing in the education and development of their youth, we were mass producing an obedient but largely de-skilled work force. The "scientific" approach that reduced learning to its smallest, most fragmented elements and micromanaged teachers by dictating their every move, would prove disastrous for the country.

Health Care

Most Americans born before 1950 can remember being treated by a family doctor. Memories of the good old general practitioner are not a nostalgic fiction: for much of this century doctors had a generalist role, providing most, if not all, of the outpatient's medical care. And hospital staffs were far less specialized than they are now. The catalyst, again, was technology. Prior to the development of penicillin and other miracle drugs, most doctors were generalists because little specialization was possible.

The family doctor of the 1940s and 1950s would scarcely recognize the medical field today, as physicians increasingly engage in specialties and subspecialties. Prior to World War II, 77 percent of physicians were general practitioners. That number declined to 56 percent in 1955 and 31 percent in 1966 (Starr, 1982). According to an Associated Press article published in the *Daily Progress* of Charlottesville, Virginia (June 6, 1993), by 1992, the percentage of graduating medical students opting for generalist roles dropped to 15 percent. Today's hospitals are bastions of segmentation, for the patient (who encounters forty-eight different personnel during an average hospital visit) and for the professional. The 629-bed St. Vincent Hospital in Indianapolis, for instance, had 598 separate job classifications before it was reorganized, and over half of those slots had but a single occupant (Lathrop, 1991).

And the problem involves more than specialization. The entire field of health care providers is caught up in a range of activities that add little to the patient's health. A three-year study by Booz Allen & Hamilton described the situation in hospitals in stark terms:

record keeping, scheduling, transporting, supervising, meetings, cleaning up, meal service, and idle time consume 84 percent of hospital personnel activity. "Put another way, for every dollar spent on direct care, we spend $3 to $4 waiting for it to happen, arranging to do it, and writing it down," noted J. Philip Lathrop, Booz Allen's vice president of health care practice (Weber, 1991, p. 24).

The Booz Allen study looked at one 650-bed acute care facility that provides a full range of health care services. It has a favorable financial position relative to comparable facilities in its state. The study found that, of each dollar this facility spends on employee wages,

- fourteen cents goes to scheduling and coordinating care,
- twenty-nine cents goes to documenting what is going on,
- twenty cents pays for idle time,
- eight cents goes to the hotel services hospitals provide,
- six cents pays for transportation services, and
- seven cents goes for management and supervision.

That leaves a paltry sixteen cents for actual health care. Lathrop (1991) places most of the blame on the health care industry itself: "No one told us to fragment our large hospitals into 150 responsibility centers or to manage our business—patient care—in a way that requires seven to nine layers of management between the CEO and the bedside caregiver. . . . No one dictated to us that to provide a chest film for an inpatient we should perform forty discrete tasks, involve fifteen different employees, or take three hours to do it all" (p. 18).

It hasn't always been this way, of course. Our health care system has evolved through many of the same stages that characterize private industry's development. In the first half of the nineteenth century, most Americans dealt with illness themselves. It was a personal and family problem, and they went to doctors rarely. As urbanization became a fact of life and more Americans separated work from home life, it became more difficult to care for the ill at home, and specialization crept into health care. Physicians became an accepted part of daily life. Two hundred hospitals existed by the 1870s, but they were dedicated more to charity and mental health problems than to the general public's health.

Spurred by the growing American love affair with science and technology, the number of hospitals exploded to over six thousand by 1920. Technological advances as well as financial incentives led more and more doctors into specialized practices. Hospitals could afford the newly developed equipment needed for many of the tests and procedures becoming popular. In addition, doctors (never a well-paid profession during the nineteenth century) found that they could treat more patients in their offices than at home; those too sick to go to the office were hospitalized. The result: home visits became obsolete as hospitals were transformed from communal, informal places to highly bureaucratic organizations. An orientation to wellness changed into treatment for disease. And hospitals went from the "periphery to the center of medical education and medical practice." What once were "refuges mainly for the homeless poor and insane" had become "doctors' workshops for all types and classes of patients" (Starr, 1982, p. 146).

Fragmentation, compartmentalization, and specialization characterize the organization of health care today. In health care, as in education and private industry, we have fragmented the work such that the once proud craftsperson/professional no longer performs the full scope of work and is increasingly separated from the patient.

Police Work

Those who can remember being cared for by the family doctor may also recall knowing the cop on the neighborhood beat. It wasn't long ago that most police departments in the United States were organized to support the patrolman or woman who walked the streets of a neighborhood, knew many of the residents, and often got their cooperation in preventing crime and apprehending suspects. Technology and applications of "modern" management systems have changed that, generally for the worse. But now many departments are becoming aware of this problem and returning to a holistic role for the police officer.

The evolution from the all-purpose cop on the beat to the highly trained, technology-driven police officer of the 1990s parallels the development of our health care system, with one major difference. Like physicians, police officers played a generalist role through the nineteenth and early twentieth centuries. They knew the residents; they knew the community; they understood community issues and concerns. Specialization came with increasing professionalization of police work beginning in the 1930s and with the advent of sophisticated technology and exploding urban problems of the 1960s. The one major difference between the bureaucratization of police work and that of health care lies in the element of corruption.

Police were victims of the political spoils system that did so much damage to U.S. government through the mid to late nineteenth century. Municipal police departments began to form as early as the 1830s, often as a response to urban unrest and riots. Police chiefs were usually appointed by elected officials, who used their appointment power to reward political supporters. Many departments became corrupt tools of politicians, going after their political enemies and turning their heads when politicians' friends broke the law. Late nineteenth-century reforms helped reduce some of the corruption, especially that associated with hiring, but abuses continued, largely because corrupt elected officials continued appointing the department leaders. Major reforms followed in the 1930s, when a commission established by President Hoover made recommendations leading to the professionalization of the police.

Higher education requirements, systematic training, professional standards for hiring and promotion, establishment of crime prevention units, and professionally appointed leadership turned politicized departments into professional ones (Trojanowicz and Bucqueroux, 1990).

Ironically, the very professionalization that led to major police improvements during the 1930s, 1940s, and 1950s led to serious problems in the 1960s and 1970s. For as departments became more professional, they began using scientific management tools that separated the patrolman from the community. Police division of labor, overreliance on technology, and specialization created a feeling of isolation in many communities, and that isolation was magnified by the urban explosions of the 1960s.

By the 1960s, the police were under siege. Excesses of radical protest movements spilled into the streets, and cops were often on the receiving end of the violence. The protest movements died down, but urban violence continued and escalated. Most departments pulled patrol officers off their walking beats and went to a random patrol/rapid response method. They put the cops into cars, equipped them with the latest technology, took them out of the neighborhoods they once patrolled, and instead gave them large areas to cruise. It seemed to make sense. As crime spread, as criminals became more sophisticated and their use of guns increased, police roles became narrower and more specialized. Investigations, narcotics, and youth divisions developed subspecializations to cope with escalating gang problems, drugs, and violence. Further, the spread of 911 emergency systems rapidly increased the numbers of calls going to the departments.

The situation was complicated by the courts. A tide of decisions protecting the rights of the accused forced police to spend huge amounts of time documenting what they were doing. Like the hospital personnel who devote far more time to paperwork, management, and reporting than to actual health care, police across the country faced a rising tide of paper in the 1970s and 1980s. It's doubtful that the social problems plaguing us would be any better if police had less paper to handle. However, like their colleagues in the schools and hospitals, police officers have found themselves separated from the work they signed on to perform and increasingly distanced from their chiefs by the ranks of middle managers who push paper and manage information. They work in highly special- ized roles, they feel extremely limited in their range of options, and they have lost contact with people in the neighborhoods who once were their potential partners.

The End, and Cost, of Mass Production

Thus, in several important parts of the private and public sectors we see the same patterns repeated. Individual generalists who work in personal relationships with their consumers are replaced by large, impersonal hierarchies in which work is reduced to its smallest ele- ments and workers are separated from the consumers and from each other. Given the technologies developed during the nineteenth and early twentieth centuries and the country's need to feed and manage its growing numbers, it's doubtful that any other pattern could have developed. A producer-oriented era called for central- ized, segmented organizations.

Separation in business (division of labor, specialized positions, separate "line" and "staff," and so on) was mirrored in government. Public agencies adopted similar management models. Moreover, many governmental reforms used the principle of separation to meet public demands for accountability and honesty. For instance, the Pendleton Act of 1883 tried to separate politics from administra- tion in federal hiring; the council manager form of local government that emerged in the early twentieth century separated policy-mak- ing from policy administration; and the rise of oversight boards and commissions created an additional layer of review, which separated management functions among two or more bodies.

The costs of separation have been enormous. While division

of labor and specialization have allowed government agencies to manage complex problems, they also led to enormous fragmentation, overlap, and duplication. Worse, these relics of the mass production era have tied the hands of bright and committed civil servants and reduced the quality and effectiveness of government programs.

The costs show up in the proliferation of programs: the federal government has over 150 employment and training programs, administered by fourteen different departments (Gore, 1993). It shows up in the numbers of people whose job it's to check on, audit, or control others—700,000 employees, fully one-third of the federal nonpostal work force, according to one U.S. Office of Management and Budget estimate. And it shows up throughout state and local government as well. A study by the National Commission on the State and Local Public Service describes state and local government as "fragmented and balkanized." The budgetary process in many states is a nightmare, splitting one budget into several hundred bills. Authority at the local government level is fragmented among dozens of commissions and boards, which divides executive and legislative authority and makes it difficult to form coalitions around common interests. The legislative process sifts bills through endless committees, which break what should be broad comprehensive bills into hundreds of pieces. Personnel systems become absurd, which results in narrow job classification systems containing anywhere from 551 job titles (South Dakota) to as many as 7,300 (New York). As the commission concludes, the fifteen million state and local employees need to be turned loose from "command and control" and rule-bound systems that tie their hands and be given clear missions with authority and responsibility to achieve them (Ehrenhalt, 1993).

The costs show up in the turf wars that managers fight, encouraged by personnel systems that reward people by the size of their staffs and budgets. The costs show up in poor service to customers who have to put up with delays, shoddy quality, runarounds, and lack of accountability. And perhaps most insidiously, the costs are reflected in unspoken *assumptions*—that government *has* to be slow, will *always* buy from the lowest bidder, can *only* be organized in a fragmented manner. It's such assumptions, as well as outmoded structures and systems, that force otherwise smart and conscientious civil servants to do stupid things.

The rise of the consumer society, along with the development of new technologies, has transformed some organizations, giving them the capability to provide seamless service to their customers. In the next chapter, we look at the nature of seamless organizations, what it's like to be served by them, and what it's like to work in them.

Chapter Three

A New Approach to Work: Re-Engineering and the Seamless Organization

Chapter Preview

It is one thing to define the new organizational form as "seamless" and quite another to grasp what a seamless organization is all about. This chapter's purpose is to help readers understand what a seamless organization is, how it differs from fragmented bureaucracies, how it feels as a consumer to be served in a seamless fashion, and what it's like to work that way.

To get a sense of what it's like to interact with an organization that doesn't create bureaucratic delays and engage in turf wars, consider the following scenario.

A Stay at the Hospital

You have just learned that you have to go to the hospital for a series of tests. The doctor thinks it's probably nothing serious, but just to make certain, she has you check into a local hospital. You don't object—it's your body, after all—but you wonder whether the doc would have recommended all the tests if this weren't such a litigious time.

At any rate, you leave for the hospital at eight the next morning, insisting that your spouse not come along.

"Last time I had to go in, it really helped that you came with me. But something's changed at the hospital; they've reorganized—it's really different."

45

"What's different about it? You mean, now you have three hours of paperwork instead of two?"

"Well, I understand your skepticism, but it really is different. I went down there last week for a preadmission meeting, and I didn't even talk with anyone in that horrendous admitting department. I met with a support person from the unit where I'll be staying. She seemed to understand all of the tests and services I would need; in fact, she did some lab work and took an X ray while I was there. She took care of all the paperwork, and even introduced me to some of the staff who work on that unit. They all knew about me.

"She scheduled my admission, so by the time I left everything was ready for me. My paperwork's done, so are the initial tests, they gave me my room number . . . in fact, I go right to my room when I get there today. The whole thing is really streamlined."

And that impression continued to be borne out when you arrived at your room. Two of the staff you had met at your preadmission interview were waiting for you. They introduced you to the doctor who did the full assessment of your condition, they stayed with you during the tests, and they made certain you understood what she was saying when she gave you the results. This pair, and another pair who worked with you during the evening shift, seemed to be there whenever you needed anything. As you learned later, they are called "care pairs" in the hospital's new organization, and their responsibility is to take care of all your medical needs, either providing the service themselves or coordinating it when they can't provide it (such as pharmacy). They were with you when you went to physical therapy, and when you had questions they couldn't answer about medication and therapy, they used the computer terminal in your room to get you the information.

Once, when the three of you had a quiet moment, you asked the pair how they really like the new approach. "It seems you're always in motion. I mean, you do everything. Doesn't it get stressful?"

"Are you kidding?" one replied. "We love this new approach. We got into health care because we wanted to help patients get well, but we used to spend so much time with paper rather than with patients, a lot of us were looking to leave. With this new system, we really get to know the patients. We figure we spend twice as much time with patients now, and we like being able to coordinate their overall needs. See, even under the old system, we saw the patients more than anyone else, but we had no ability to manage their care; we'd see things falling through the cracks, things we could easily prevent, but we had no power to do anything about it. Now, we see them throughout every aspect of their stay here, we make sure it's the right medication, that paperwork doesn't take over the system, that the doctors understand what you need, and that you understand what they're saying."

"The physicians like the new system as much as we do," said the second. "They were worried, before it started, that they'd lose control, but in fact they feel like they have more control. With this system, there's less paperwork for them as well as for us. And test results get turned around much faster. It really is a win-win. The docs get to spend time doing what they like to do, and we're with patients most of the time, which is what we're here for. And we'll be following up with you after you leave."

Which is exactly what they did. The doctor who did the diagnosis at the hospital met with you and your family physician, along with the care pair, to summarize what was learned and what you need to do to get well. The care pair went with you to the pharmacy unit, where you got your medication. When you were ready to leave, they went over all your charges, indicating which your insurance company should cover and which would be left to you. They also left you their cards and asked you to call within a week to let them know how the therapy was going.

"And if you don't call us, we'll call you!" one of them said, as you thanked them and left.

The Thread of Seamlessness

The preceding story is not fictional, although it may appear too good to be true. This seamless care is what patients at the Lakeland

(Florida) Regional Medical Center encounter every day. The 897-bed hospital, which provides a full range of health care services, began to change in 1989 after an analysis revealed that only 16 percent of the staff's time was spent delivering medical, technical, and clinical care. The staff has been breaking down old functional walls that created delays, fragmented work, and reduced the quality of care. Today, four units have been transformed and now operate on a model of patient-focused care.

In the new model, care pairs and care trios (registered nurses and technicians) provide most services to the patient. To handle their extraordinary range of tasks, they go through an intensive six-week training program during which they learn procedures formerly farmed out to specialized departments: EKGs, respiratory and physical therapy, laboratory testing, diagnostic radiology. Once they pass a rigorous test in each area, they begin working as a team. Backed up by computer terminals in each patient room, they are linked to the hospital's mainframe and can oversee a complicated scheduling procedure that involves admissions, discharge, and bed control. This saves them time, and more: it keeps information and control where it belongs, in the hands of the people who spend the most time with the patient.

The results have been overwhelmingly positive:

- Average turnaround time for routine tests dropped from 157 to 48 minutes.
- Care pairs and trios have doubled the amount of time they spend caring for patients.
- Medication errors on the four patient-focused units are the lowest in the hospital.
- Physician, staff, and patient satisfaction levels have soared.
- Patients interact with thirteen hospital staff, on the average, compared with fifty-three in traditional units.
- Direct bedside costs are down—9.2 percent lower than in traditional units.

It hasn't been cheap. The hospital spent $5 million to develop and support the new approach. But those costs are being made up in lower ongoing costs. Nurse turnover on the patient-focused units is the lowest in the hospital, which further reduces costs. And the idea is spreading. Lakeland plans to put all units onto the new model by the end of the decade, and a number of other hospitals around the country are trying to adopt similar models (Lathrop, 1991; Weber, 1991).

For the end user, interacting with a seamless organization like Lakeland is an incredibly positive experience. Everything feels congruent; it's of a piece. Service providers care for the whole patient; there are few handoffs, no impersonal treatment. Services are available on an "anytime, anyplace" basis; there are no sharp divisions among staff (care pairs and trios stay with the patient when the doctor is there, so that nothing falls through the cracks). Much like our earliest craft producers, staff in a seamless organization produce the whole job and are in direct contact with the end users.

Making the transformation to seamlessness is far from easy, however. Everything, from jobs to technology to role definition and performance measurement, must change. Table 3.1 details the shift from fragmented, mass production to seamless organizations. We'll look at each shift next.

Jobs

The hierarchical, mass production model requires narrow, segmented jobs. While the 598 distinct job classifications in one Indianapolis hospital may seem appropriate in the health arena, where information and technology are exploding so quickly that subspecialists are needed to keep up with their field, the downsides make it impossible for the hospital to function effectively. As one consultant noted, this system leads to "the presence of specialists and technicians whom we wouldn't dream of asking to do anything but their own, narrow, and often self-defined duties, even it if means they are idle much of the time" (Lathrop, 1991, p. 17). The same

Table 3.1. The Shift from Mass Production to Seamless Organizations.

To Provide Seamless Service, Agencies Shift . . .

From	To
	Jobs
Narrow, segmented, little control over how work is done or decisions made	Broad; multi-skilled teams; generalist individuals exercise great control over work procedure and decisions
	Measurement
Based on inputs and activities, size of one's staff and budget	Based on outcomes, consumer satisfaction
	Technology
Used to control, centralize activities	Used to enable decentralized activities
	Internal Organization
Fragmented departments and functions, driven by the organization's internal needs	Integrated process teams formed to deliver according to consumer's needs
	Time Sensitivity
Low; works best when able to maintain its own rhythm; slow to respond to external demands and opportunities	High; focus on end user and outcomes places a premium on quick response; services delivered faster
	Clarity, Distinction of Roles
High; internal division of labor; clear distinctions between organization, its customers, and its suppliers	Low; organized by cross-functional teams within; suppliers and consumers share tasks formerly done by the organization
	Nature of Products or Services
Standardized, oriented to what the organization produces most easily; low variety, high volume, little customization	Customized, oriented to what the consumer wants, high variety, high volume

problems crop up in functionally oriented police departments and other government agencies that are highly specialized.

In a seamless organization, people have broad responsibilities and great authority over work procedures. They are trained to take on new tasks, and their training and education continue throughout their career (see Chapter Eight). St. Vincent Hospital in Indianapolis has begun its own care trio model (a cross-trained RN and two well-trained technicians). In the units in which the care trios operate, they have pared down those 598 specialties into just *five* job classifications (Weber, 1991).

Another example of the broad roles given by seamless organizations is found in community policing agencies. Consider the guidelines given to officers in the Phoenix Police Department:

- Is it the right thing for the community?
- Is it the right thing for the Phoenix Police Department?
- Is it ethical and legal?
- Is it something you are willing to be accountable for?
- Is it consistent with the Department's values and policies?

When the answer to all these questions is yes, the guidelines state "Just do it" and don't bother asking for permission. That is the sort of "policy manual" that encourages employees to think; and when they think, they can come up with flexible, personalized, creative solutions and services for their end users.

The issue here is not delegation, not even empowerment. In seamless organizations, the work has been defined differently. Employees don't need to be given more authority; managers aren't trained to encourage their employees to take greater risks. Rather, the work, and the jobs, have been radically changed, and it's obvious that the worker is trained and responsible for a wide range of tasks and outcomes. When that responsibility is made clear, when there is no longer a series of handoffs and sign-offs required before each decision, the employee or work team understands the obvious: it's their job, and they are trained to do it well and do whatever it takes to achieve the desired outcome.

Measurement

We've all heard the story from a friend or relative: "Why'd the cop stop you? Everyone drives that fast on that highway."

"I don't know; must be because it's the end of the month and he hadn't filled his quota of tickets yet."

The only problem with that explanation is that it's frequently true. Number of tickets, number of arrests, number of cases "cleared"—those are indicators that can be counted. In many bureaucracies, government and corporate, the size of one's budget and number of direct reports are also used to measure responsibility (and thus salary). This approach leads to nothing but empire building, creates more barriers and competition between departments, and takes employees' minds off the reason they are there: to meet the mission and satisfy the end user's needs.

Seamless organizations learn to focus their measurement systems on the most important measures: *outcomes*. Organizations, both public and private, have historically measured inputs and outputs, rarely outcomes. Inputs, such as the number of staff hired, tax revenues collected, technology purchased, are easy to count. The problem, of course, is that they are irrelevant to what citizens care about, which is results. Outputs, a measure of what the agency does, are also easy to count. With inputs of staff, money, and equipment, the agency produced certain outputs: x bridges repaired, y flu shots given to low-income children, z arrests of criminal suspects. Outputs *seem* to be about results, but they aren't. They measure organizational activity, not results.

Systems that measure results focus less on number of highway miles, more on the reduction of accidents on bridges. They go beyond the number of flu shots given and report the number of children who got sick. They speak to safety on our streets, not numbers of arrests. Such measurement systems are difficult to develop in government, because many government services are difficult to quantify. How does one quantify the outcomes and quality of research at the National Institutes of Health, for instance? Standards such as peer recognition and number of awards won aren't outcome measures, although they are frequently used.

The government making the most progress in outcome-based performance measurement is that of Oregon. Beginning with a Futures Commission in 1986, the state's leaders and thousands of citizens have joined forces to create long-term goals that have been broken down into more than 270 "benchmarks," or specific outcomes for which various state agencies are accountable. Administered by the Oregon Progress Board, these benchmarks apply to three general areas: people, quality of life, and the economy. The goals are quantifiable, they focus on outcomes, and agencies are accountable for results—budgets reflect agency accomplishments of their benchmark goals (a sure way to get managers' attention!). Examples of benchmark goals: the teen pregnancy rate will fall from 19.5 to 8 per 1,000 by the year 2000; fifth graders with age-appropriate math skills will rise from 77 percent to 91 percent by 2000.

Under Governor Barbara Roberts, the benchmarks are becoming a reality for the state's civil servants. Agencies must develop specific performance measures tied to the benchmarks (the legislature is actively involved in the process). And a senior state official is formally responsible and accountable for each of the state's 17 "lead" (or urgent) benchmarks. Since many public problems (crime, health, education, and the like) cut across government departments, it's especially important to focus accountability in one place. Oregon is learning how to do that.

Technology

In bureaucracies, technology often becomes a control mechanism. Indeed, the massive mainframes we once relied on exclusively were very clearly used for control. Mainframes emphasize centralization, with all information going through one source. Even in a PC-based organization, the information systems department is often seen as a group of arrogant control artists who believe that only they can decide what hardware and software the employees really need.

In an era of PC networks, we have the luxury of both centralization and decentralization. The care pairs at Lakeland can check the terminals in their patients' rooms to monitor and coordinate all services being provided, and so can everyone else serving those patients. Managers in numerous agencies now make their own purchases using credit cards. They have no more forms to complete; a credit card and the bank's tape provide all the paper flow needed. Information technology in seamless organizations doesn't control; it enables. The term *expert systems* doesn't really capture what the new on-line databases do for the generalists who will dominate seamless organizations. A better term is *system for experts*, experts in their clients/consumers and their needs.

Four key technologies are enabling multiskilled work teams and generalists to handle very broad tasks: graphical user interfaces, networking software, relational databases, and imaging software.

• *Graphical user interfaces* have become a popular user-friendly piece of software. Those familiar with Windows or Apple Macintosh understand how much time is saved when they can access computer files by selecting them as "objects" on the screen rather than by typing in commands and through the use of context-sensitive pull-down menus.

• *Networking software* is a key to breaking down old bureaucratic models, in which information flowed up and down the hierarchy with mind-numbing slowness. It's now estimated that 60 percent of all business PCs in the United States are able to trade files and documents and work together on E-mail, because they are hooked into a common network. Networking gives everyone equal access to relevant data in real time.

• *Relational database management systems* enable retailers to scan the item sold at the cash register and transmit the information instantaneously to its suppliers, who know exactly what has been sold, in what colors, sizes, and so on, and when to resupply the retailer. Relational databases also offer new ways of storing information in several small files rather than relying on one huge mainframe. Agencies can put information about their customers in one small computer and accounts payable data in another. Then, they can link the two as needed. This approach saves money, gives managers a decentralized approach to maintaining their own records, and avoids hassles with a centralized data processing department.

• *Imaging software* converts hard copy to digitized images, which allows documents to move through an organization electronically. It encourages the use of parallel rather than sequential processes (see Chapter Four) by making information available for use throughout the organization. Through imaging software, a document—an insurance claim, for example—can be read, used, and incorporated in other documents by an adjuster and that person's supervisor (and others) at the same time, without the need for redundant data entry and without having to pass from one desk to another in assembly-line fashion (Schwartz, 1993).

Internal Organization

Since Alfred Sloan put the crowning touch on the mass production model with his introduction of a divisional structure and specialized staff departments, almost all medium and large public and private organizations have organized in hierarchical fashion around functions. Staff are identified and organized by function: product development, public information, budget, personnel, administration. It's such a prominent part of the organizational landscape that most of us can scarcely imagine any other way to organize.

In seamless organizations, these "Berlin Walls" are falling. People work in "process teams" that include most of the key functions that go into the process of producing a given deliverable. When a bank organizes around the loan process, the deliverable is making appropriate loans. Loan process teams include a mortgage loan officer, title searcher, and credit checker who work together (not in sequence) to handle all aspects of each application. If the team is a community policing trio, they are trained to handle the various complaints and needs that people in their neighborhoods once brought to different departments. And the care pairs and care trios in hospitals that use them now handle 90 percent or more of the patients' needs. The organization of the future will likely be organized around its key processes. As one business executive said, "Every business has maybe six basic processes. We'll organize around them. The people who run them will be the leaders of the business" (Stewart, 1992, p. 92).

Time Sensitivity

Speed, as we have noted, is one of the most important factors in meeting consumer demands in the 1990s. Hierarchical organizations weren't designed for speed—they were designed for stability, clarity, efficiency, volume. Those who go to a private physician for their own care or the care of their children have probably experienced these features of mass production. You arrive for your 2 p.m. appointment, check in, have a seat, and wait. Like all mass production workplaces, a clinic is oriented to meet the needs of the producers (especially the doctors), not the consumers. Unlike at Burger King, we do it *their* way at the doc's office.

Seamless organizations are very time sensitive, which is one reason that they are developing—to respond quickly to a chaotic environment. At Lakeland Regional, as noted, turnaround time for routine tests dropped almost 70 percent in the care pair units. Building projects using the partnering approach (see Chapter One) come in on time more frequently than others. One reason for the greater time sensitivity: fewer people are involved passing information, signing off and checking off forms and approvals.

Clarity and Distinction of Roles

For decades, management consultants (including this one) have stressed the importance of role clarity. This is indeed a strength of bureaucracies. The jobs are narrow, the lines between departments usually clear, the turf important (and, therefore, well marked out and protected); most people in hierarchical, bureaucratic organizations understand what their job is and what their unit does.

The opposite is true in seamless organizations. When a process is the responsibility of a care pair, a police trio, or four to seven managers from two organizations in a partnering relationship, roles are fluid and changing. In fact, the very notion of a seamless organization is that there are very few dividing lines. That's the point—get rid of the segmenting, the specialization, the walls that separate and divide up natural work flows, and replace them with small, multiskilled teams that take ownership for the whole process, start to finish.

Roles also change when organizations are flattened ("delayered," in current jargon). Information flows more quickly when there are fewer channels, and since middle managers have traditionally been information brokers (recall the development of hierarchies in the railroads), they are becoming obsolete in a high-tech age. Groupware, E-mail, PC networks, and other technological wonders provide information far faster and more directly than any managers can.

One reflection of the trend toward delayering is the emergence of self-managing teams. Teams that plan, implement, and evaluate their own work (and often evaluate each other's contributions) with minimal management involvement are frequently part of seamless organizations. Such teams typically share a variety of tasks, teach one another, stay in direct contact with the end users of their products and services, and worry far less about who is "supposed" to do what than about whether the consumer was pleased with the product.

My own favorite example of blurred roles in self-managing teams comes from music. In New York City, the Orpheus Chamber Orchestra has been playing beautiful classical music since 1974, *without* a conductor. It's not that they've been carrying on a long job search; the group was formed to be a conductorless orchestra. The Orpheus musicians, who have played in the world's finest concert halls, select an executive committee to plan each year's repertoire, and the job of providing an interpretation for each piece is rotated among different musicians.

Thus, there is no one leader; there is leadership to be sure, but nobody stands in front of the group when it performs. Much like a jazz ensemble (or basketball or soccer team), Orpheus members share leadership through their lateral communications. One member noted that she always had to cut her bangs when she played in a traditional orchestra, because she had to be able to look up and see the conductor. After joining Orpheus, she could let the bangs grow, because now it was *peripheral* vision she needed to interact with the flow of the musicians (CBS *Sunday Morning,* 1987).

The blurring of roles is also reflected in some very interesting changes going on "outside" seamless organizations, with their suppliers and consumers. Consider the following:

• Contractors and subcontractors are taking on new roles and relationships as they become more integral to the organizations they serve. Professional Parking Services (PPS), which provides valet parking service for many large U.S. hotels, wants the driver to believe that its valets are employees of the hotel, not contractors with no vested interest in the hotel. One technique to create a seamless impression: PPS sends its employees to the training programs Marriott Hotels runs for its own employees. As PPS delivers, its client hotels turn over more work (such as the doorman job) to them. Some Marriott customers report that they cannot tell the difference between a Marriott employee and one hired by PPS (Peters, 1992).

• In many respects, the move toward more consumer involvement in producing goods and services has been coming for some time: we produce our own movies—through camcorders. We can measure our own cholesterol levels, blood pressure, and blood sugar or test for pregnancy. We get our own money at ATMs, pump our own gas, and pay with a credit card without ever talking with an employee. Fast-food restaurants and cafeterias involve the customer in the "meal production process" not only through salad bars but also when they have customers fill their own drink cups outside of the food-ordering line (this is also an example of "maintaining a continuous flow of the main sequence"; see Chapter Four).

• The state of Oregon has given state-created software to vendors who want to maintain real-time communications concerning state requests for proposals; the software allows the vendors to send in proposals electronically and saves the state time and postage costs.

• Technology enables new networks to take the place of old-line bureaucratic relations. One fairly astonishing example began in Pittsburgh in late 1991: electronic surgeries! Well, almost. At the University of Pittsburgh Medical Center, a multimedia network permits neurophysiologists to assist in operations from remote workstations. As Alexander (1991) reports, the electronic network links physiologists at seven hospitals making up the medical center. Physiologists sitting far from the actual surgery can monitor a patient's brain-wave activity, see what the surgeon is seeing through the microscope during surgery, and communicate with the surgeon and others in the operating room without coming anywhere near it. This high-tech network gives the surgeon real-time advice on complicated procedures from colleagues sitting at their desks.

Nature of Products or Services

Standardization—of products and of people—is a key to mass production. The mass education system the United States developed in the early twentieth century was modeled after manufacturing principles of Frederick Taylor and Henry Ford. Just as it was assumed that only long runs of standardized products yielded efficient and productive plants, educational leaders wanted the same in the schools. As in Taylor's remark that "there are other people paid for thinking around here," teachers were expected to teach the prescribed curriculum. They were interchangeable cogs in a mass production school system.

Such systems yield a highly predictable, consistent product or service. What they don't produce is what today's consumer society demands: variety, customization, choices. Fast-food restaurants provide the predictable, consistent, standardized offerings that Americans have grown to love (especially if you are traveling far from home and your kids are hungry; those golden McDonald's arches actually start to look good!). The limits of such establishments are running straight into the desires of a choice-happy public.

When I called a favorite fast-food deli recently to ask if I could give them my order and pick it up later (hoping to avoid the usual noon-hour crush), I was politely told that they didn't offer that service. When I suggested that it would certainly help people like me to be able to call ahead, would no doubt increase their business, and could reduce the number of people waiting in line, the manager groaned, "Oh, my God, then we'd have to hire more people and add another cash register." Where she could only worry about a problem of capacity, I saw an opportunity for variety (as well as a way for her to smooth out some of their demand during peak hours).

Seamless organizations provide the choices, variety, and customization we want today, without losing the many benefits of mass production. A community policing officer spending time with neighborhood groups and merchants is looking for ways to customize a solution to local problems. Because the officer knows the neighbors and residents, he or she can go beyond "Band-Aid" measures, help residents identify the causes of their problems, and involve them in solutions—forming tenant councils that take control of their public housing project, organizing adult literacy programs that enable parents to help their kids with school work, working with neighborhood associations that want to "adopt" nearby parks and take them back from drug dealers, and so on. An officer working in the traditional random patrol model simply lacks the time to learn about particular neighborhood needs and can only offer "mass production" solutions to our problems: tell your neighbors when you go on vacation, leave a light on in the bathroom when you're out for the evening, keep your kids in after dark, teach them to just say no to drugs. Such well-intentioned advice might have gone down well in the 1950s; it doesn't work today.

Function Versus Process and Outcome

The two most important words in our comparison of mass production, bureaucratic organizations and seamless ones are *outcome* and *process*, and they are closely related. What these examples have in common, more than anything else, is a radically different process for achieving the desired consumer outcome.

Since most people work in hierarchical, bureaucratic organizations, they are used to thinking in terms of departments and functions. "Personnel" (or "human resources"), for instance, is a department. Within that department, there are many functions: training, benefits, compensation and classification ("comp and class"), recruitment, and the like. Most personnel shops divide their employees into these specialized functions. When your job description is functionally oriented rather than process and outcome oriented, you have a very narrow understanding of your role and how you can add value to your agency. You know what specific activities you perform, but do you understand what *outcomes* you and your colleagues are responsible for?

Figure 3.1 shows how a typical city's human resources department chart might appear. What does this chart tell us? It shows a variety of activities that are performed by different people; we know who gives advice on EEO matters, who handles staff grievances, who trains employees. But do we know who is responsible to see that the organization as a whole behaves in accordance with equal opportunity principles? Do we know who sees to it that the city's managers improve their staff relations skills, reducing the number of grievances against them? Is it clear who is to think about the needs of the city five years from now, the kinds of skills needed to meet those needs, the career progression options employees should consider, and what needs to happen to prepare managers for future possibilities?

In most cities, the answers would be no. The personnelists would be very clear about what they do each day, but as to these "bigger picture" questions, they would probably shrug and point to the city manager's office.

Contrast this functional approach with that used by the U.S. Forest Service Sheffield Ranger District. The Sheffield District was organized like most bureaucracies—by function. At Sheffield, that approach included such areas as timber management, wildlife management, recreation and fire management, law enforcement, facilities management. District-level employees handled specialized jobs within one of these functions. They knew a great deal about a relatively small technical area.

Most employees were fairly comfortable in this setup because

Figure 3.1. "Typical" City Human Resources Department.

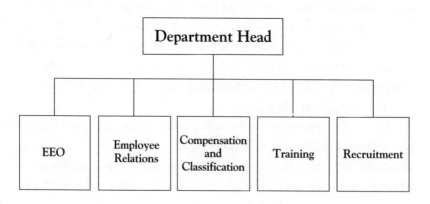

it was familiar. However, they were most uncomfortable with the problems it created: major turf wars, lack of flexibility in budgeting, little information sharing across functions, difficulty in dealing with complex issues that crossed functional areas. Most important, there was little integration and communication among functional specialists. The walls and turf prevented them from bringing an efficient, interdisciplinary approach to their work.

In 1988–89, Sheffield threw out the functional walls for a process-oriented approach. Employees are now organized into information management teams, design teams, and operations teams. All functional and technical people are represented on each team. Thus, when a forest area needs a new program, the cross-functional design team assesses the needs and resource requirements and writes the plan. When that program is ready for implementation, the design team works with the cross-functional operations team to make the design a reality. And the information management team assists staff through each phase of development and operations. Figure 3.2 illustrates the shift Sheffield made from a function- to process-oriented approach.

The result is a huge increase in communications and integrated management. Specialists are becoming generalists, learning from each other and dealing with the forest in a holistic manner, much as care pairs or trios are able to deal with a patient as a whole person. There are problems caused by the process approach, to be sure—handoffs from design to operations must be carefully managed, and staff worry about losing their program's quality and technical integrity—but they are handling these and have no interest in going back to the functional walls (Jack Frank and Karen Mollander, personal communication, 1993). Like care pairs in a hospital and community police officers in a neighborhood, Sheffield's professionals are dealing with a system (in their case, a forest), not isolated parts. To deal effectively with systems, the organization must be designed by natural processes, not artificial functions.

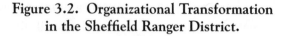

Figure 3.2. Organizational Transformation
in the Sheffield Ranger District.

The Old System: By Function

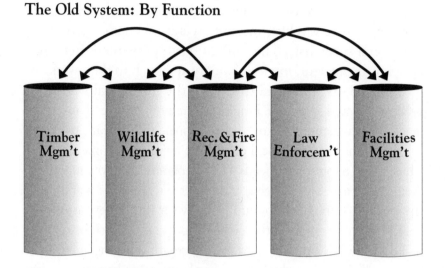

| Timber Mgm't | Wildlife Mgm't | Rec.&Fire Mgm't | Law Enforcem't | Facilities Mgm't |

The New System: By Process

Inputs:
Information, requests, problems, conflicts

Information Mgm't

Design

Operations

Customer Outcome:
Public access to national forests, sustainable forests

Process teams: Represent nearly all functions.

Core Processes and Support Processes

Since many people are not accustomed to thinking in terms of organizational processes, a definition is in order. To adapt the definition in the *Re-engineering Handbook* (AT&T, 1991) for our purposes, a *process* is a set of related activities designed to produce a particular outcome. There are two kinds of processes in organizations: core and support processes. Core processes meet the important needs of the organization's external consumers. Support processes meet important needs of internal customers—the employees and, increasingly, the suppliers. The following lists, which describe the processes, are not complete but are intended to make the concept of processes more concrete.

*Core Processes Common to Many Government
and Service Organizations*

- *Customer fulfillment,* from customer request for service or product, to delivery of service or product, to receipt of payment, to evaluation and customer feedback, to action on feedback as necessary

- *Program delivery,* from program concept to program planning, to publicity, to registration, to delivery and payment, to evaluation and planning for future program improvements

- *Information delivery,* from request for information (about services, taxes, program availability and eligibility, anticipated waiting time, and so on) to information delivery, to tracking and analysis of information requests, to feedback to program departments

- *License and permit acquisition,* from request for permits and licenses, to application, delivery, and payment

- *Complaints management,* from receipt of complaint, to investigation, to decision and communication of decision, to resolution, to analysis of complaints and action on any root causes found

- *Contracts management*, from identification, to writing specs, to publication of request for proposal, to contractor selection, to coordination through entire project (including ongoing evaluation), to final review and payment
- *Emergency services*, from call for assistance, to dispatch, to provision of emergency service (fire, police, ambulance, and so on), to resolution of need, to analysis of patterns of calls and action on that analysis if necessary
- *Policy-making*, from need for policy or policy change, to understanding end user's needs and priorities, to research of options, to determination of pluses and minuses of each option, to presentation of options with recommendations, to decision

Support Processes Common to Many Government and Service Organizations

- *Visioning/planning*, from identifying future opportunities and threats, to analysis of internal strengths and shortcomings, to stakeholder input on strategy development, to strategy formulation and communication to all stakeholders
- *Purchasing*, from identification of need, to requisition, to order, to delivery, to payment
- *Filling positions*, from position vacancy, to identification of position requirements and downstream concerns, to advertising, to interviewing and selection, to orientation, to employee feedback about the process
- *Employee development*, from determination of employee goals and needs and (simultaneously) determination of future agency priorities and skill needs, to individual or team development plan, to ongoing development activities, to feedback and plan revision
- *Budgeting*, from annual goals and revenue projections, to

communication of goals and resource availability with all employees, to budget requests, to public input, to budget decisions (and communications of those decisions to employees), to budget adoption, to revision of departmental or team budgets

- *Information management,* from analysis of present and future information requirements, to development of information plan, to purchase and installation of hardware and software, to training, monitoring, and updating plan and resources
- *Team building,* from identification of need for teamwork, to explanation of benefits of greater teamwork, to team self-assessment, to team plan for improved performance, implementation, evaluation, and follow-up

Several things should be noted about these examples. First, there is no separate "evaluation" process. In an organization designed by processes, no separate evaluation office is needed. Evaluation is an integral part of many ongoing processes and should be done by the process team itself.

Second, many support processes can and should be managed by line managers themselves. The planning department (if one exists; many are being disbanded) should support each program manager's planning efforts; the program manager is the process "owner" for his or her planning process. Likewise for filling positions, orienting new employees, training and team building, or purchasing. In all these instances, a seamless organization gives a program manager or a team ownership of the internal, support processes. Staff specialists (human resources, purchasing agents, budget analysts, and the like) are distributed to the line departments, where they provide consultation and technical backup to the program managers and participate on cross-functional teams.

Third, when processes are made visible to employees and they start to see where they fit in, a "leveling" effect arises. Processes cut *across* organizations; a senior manager may serve on a process team with an entry-level support staffer; a trial attorney may work on a process team with a purchasing manager. And, as the Sheffield Ranger District showed, staff from totally different functions work together. The process owner is the team leader, and others should have equal input. (For more on the process owner role, see Chapter Five.) When the process's desired outcome is clear (for example, "The purpose of the customer fulfillment process, and our reason for meeting as the customer fulfillment team, is to ensure that we get the customer what she orders, at the quality and price agreed to, as quickly as possible with absolutely no hassles for the customer"), when everyone understands the process owner's role, then formal authority is much less relevant. The most relevant personal attribute people bring to the table is the quality of their ideas and expertise, not their official power. And the only relevant question is, How do we design processes that lead to our stated outcomes, consistent with values of equity, openness, and accountability, as quickly and seamlessly as possible?

Some government managers have told me that they have difficulty identifying their agency's core processes. After all, we've organized government bureaucracies around functions and departments; that's how the budget is divided, that's how staff efforts are measured and rewarded, that's what elected officials understand. How do civil servants identify their agency's core processes?

Some agency staff have found the following questions useful when they try to determine their core processes:

- What work do we do that distinguishes us from other agencies?
- What outcomes do we produce that our customers most value?
- What work can't be outsourced, because we have a monopoly on it or because we do it so well?
- What work do we do that is vital to our agency and critical to our mission?

- What work begins with an important customer need or request, cuts across functional boundaries, and ends with a product or service delivered to the customer?

When senior staff at the Department of Defense asked some of these questions, they came up with these core processes (U.S. Department of Defense, 1994):

1. Conduct strategic operational planning and operations
2. Raise forces
3. Maintain force readiness
4. Provide forces
5. Sustain operations
6. Return/restore forces

A senior staff team at the U.S. Customs Service spent six months during 1993 and 1994 to chart a new course for the agency. With the passage of North American Free Trade Agreement (leading to much lower tariffs), very close scrutiny by Congress, and the trend toward lower tariffs around the world, the agency needed to re-define its mission and strategy. Under the leadership of Deputy Commissioner Michael Lane, the team decided it needed to deter-mine its core processes. After several weeks, they developed a first draft of core processes that included the following:

1. Passenger compliance
2. Cargo compliance
3. Informed compliance
4. Strategic trade
5. Anti-smuggling
6. Investigations and intelligence

To understand the agency's business from a process point of view, the team then mapped each process end to end, beginning with the suppliers and ending with the outcomes produced. Table 3.2 presents the full map for the Passenger Compliance process.

Table 3.2. Full Map for the Passenger Compliance Process at the U.S. Customs Service.

Suppliers	Inputs	Work Activities	Outputs	Customers	Outcomes
Carriers port authorities	Passengers, conveyances	Inspections, analysis	Arrests, other violations	Passengers, taxpayers	Voluntary compliance with laws at border

Source: U.S. Customs Service. *People, Processes and Partnerships: A Report on the Customs Service of the Twenty-First Century.* Washington, D.C.: 1994.

The Path to Seamlessness

This chapter has described the nature of seamless organizations. The move from bureaucracy to seamlessness requires a new way of thinking and a different set of organizing principles. These organizing principles, which have come to be called *business process reengineering* (BPR), provide powerful tools for transforming organizations. They focus staff on customer outcomes rather than internal activities. They organize work flows around processes rather than functions. They make clear the costs of long, tedious processes. And they provide major gains in productivity, because staff are organized in a holistic way that gives them the complete job and puts them in direct contact with the end users.

In today's organizational climate, the demands for radical change explain why so many people are interested in learning about reengineering. And BPR is proving an attractive solution. A recent Conference Board survey showed that 72 percent of the organizations using BPR began seeing results within the first six months, and in all but one case the annual financial benefit of BPR was the same as or greater than the *one-time* cost of re-engineering.

Chapter Four reviews BPR's basic design principles; Chapter Five introduces a re-engineering model and discusses its first phase.

Part Two

Re-Engineering Public Organizations: Principles, Strategies, and Guidelines

Chapter Four

Principles of Re-Engineering

Chapter Preview

The term *business process re-engineering* is new, but its design principles have been developing for some time. In this chapter, we examine those principles—where they come from, how they are being applied, and how they can transform public bureaucracies into seamless organizations.

As we explore these principles, it is helpful to recall the definition of re-engineering offered in the Preface: *challenging fundamental assumptions on which the organization is built by radically redesigning its processes, systems, and structure around desired outcomes.* Re-engineering design principles are certainly important, but none is as important as the first part of the definition: *challenging fundamental assumptions.* Each design principle reverses long-accepted organizational truths, verities developed during an age that assumed we needed people to check people who checked other people in order to ensure accountability and control. The world has changed, and so must our assumptions.

Origins of the Design Principles

The process re-engineering design principles we can articulate come from three sources. First, and best, they come from *successful experiences.* Dozens of corporations and governmental agencies have made major advances by re-engineering their processes, and their experiences provide us with the most useful data from which to draw general principles.

Second, re-engineering draws from its first cousins in the manufacturing world, *concurrent engineering* and the process of *lean production* developed by Taiichi Ohno for Toyota. Davidow and Malone (1992) have described concurrent engineering as an approach geared to involve everyone in the design and production process at the start, so that all "downstream" needs are met: "everyone affected by design—engineering, manufacturing, service, marketing, and sales personnel, as well as suppliers and customers—should participate as early as possible in the design cycle. Through this communication, trade-offs can be made and consensus reached, which will reduce product cost, improve manufacturability and serviceability, and ensure that the product's features match the market's desires" (p. 91). In other words, the process involves the various functions in a parallel, not linear fashion.

Taiichi Ohno helped create the Toyota Production System (now often called *lean production* as it spreads through many Western industries) to meet the particular needs of Toyota in post–World War II Japan. As Ohno said, the system was "born of the need to make many types of automobiles, in small quantities with the same manufacturing processes" (Stalk and Hout, 1990, p. 52). Toyota's situation—its market in postwar Japan was severely limited, there was no need to produce millions of cars like the U.S. auto giants, and it had very few resources to invest in plants and equipment—required a different approach to auto production than that used in the United States, and Ohno created it. He met consumer needs for variety, responsiveness, and low cost within Toyota's limited resources and within the constraints of a union agreement Toyota signed in 1949. The agreement included a commitment to provide lifetime employment to workers and pay based on seniority, in exchange for union agreements to abide by flexible work assignments and active involvement in seeking work procedure improvements.

Ohno's strategy was to build on the fundamental Japanese value of simplicity. He had the traditional Japanese impatience for any type of wasteful practice, and he responded to the huge waste he saw in the Ford plants he visited by creating a simple system that uses every inch of space, every human resource—especially the workers' minds—and every bit of time. His system is being adopted by many other manufacturing companies.

A third source is the increasingly important focus on *time-based competition*, which includes elements of concurrent engineering and lean production. Time-based competition developed in the United States from the successes the Japanese were enjoying from just-in-time production methods. It is a systems approach that scrutinizes every step in the value chain, from supplier relationships through design and manufacturing or service development to distribution and consumption, with the goal of eliminating wasted time and effort in the chain. It uses the principles of just-in-time manufacturing, short production runs, instant communications and close coordination with a small number of suppliers, and flexible manufacturing to shorten production and delivery cycles and provide the timeliness and variety consumers demand. It expands on concurrent engineering and lean production by extending these principles throughout the whole value chain.

The major design principles of these three sources of process re-engineering can be summarized as follows:

Principles of Concurrent Engineering

- Bring downstream information upstream.
- Integrate upstream processes.
- Simplify design cycles: fewer handoffs, fewer steps.
- Substitute parallel for sequential processes: overlap phases of program or product development.
- Create and empower cross-functional teams to be responsible for the entire product and process development cycle, start to finish.
- Maintain constant communications within the team and between teams.
- Institute "multilearning"—ongoing learning; trial and error;

benchmarking at individual, team, and organizational levels. (Sources for these items: Takeuchi and Nonaka, 1986; Webster, 1992; Ray Smith, personal communication, 1993.)

Principles of Lean Production and Time-Based Competition

- Use just-in-time methods throughout the assembly process, so that parts are "pulled" through the line when needed rather than "pushed" through by predetermined production goals.
- Ensure continuous flow processing by locating related processes close to each other, using a simple plant layout, and processing parts one at a time rather than in large lots.
- The goal is to reduce time from conception to consumption—eliminate idle time at every step of the value chain.
- Organize around the main sequence (those activities that directly add value to the end user).
- Foster close, synchronized, long-term relationships with a small number of suppliers, who are viewed as partners in the enterprise; assign whole components (such as the entire seat) to them, not parts of the product.
- In manufacturing, use small production runs, quick product changeovers, small inventories, parts located in close proximity, and a simple plant layout (elements of the "flexible factory").
- Organize around self-contained, multifunctional, self-scheduling teams of workers empowered to perform the key activities, make the key decisions, stop the line, and find defects.
- Treat information as the key variable: it must be exchanged, in real time, face-to-face and electronically, with workers, suppliers, retailers, and customers.
- Use "stretch objectives," challenges so great they require totally new ways of thinking and organizing, in order to break down walls between departments and functions. (Sources for

these items: Womack, Jones, and Roos, 1991; Stalk and Hout, 1990; Monden, 1983; Kiyotaka Nakayama, personal communication, 1993; Blackburn, 1991; Davidow and Malone, 1992.)

The just-in-time, or stockless, production system (sometimes called *kanban*) sweeping so many Western manufacturing plants is a major element of a time-obsessed organization. Just-in-time production is a key element of lean production, and like lean production, it was inspired in part by a U.S. organization.

As Ohno (1988) recalls:

Kanban [is] an idea I got from American supermarkets. . . . In 1956 I toured U.S. production plants at General Motors, Ford and other machinery companies. But my strongest impression was the extent of the supermarkets' prevalence in America. . . .

A supermarket is where a customer can get (1) what is needed, (2) at the time needed, (3) in the amount needed. . . . From the supermarket we got the idea of viewing the earlier process in a production line as a kind of store. The later process (customer) goes to the earlier process (supermarket) to acquire the required parts (commodities) at the time and in the quantity needed. The earlier process immediately produces the quantity just taken (restocking the shelves). We hoped that this would help us approach our just-in-time goal and, in 1953, we actually applied the system in our machine shop at the main plant [pp. 25–27].

As Davidow and Malone (1992) point out, *kanban* is brilliant in its simplicity. By focusing on providing "the necessary units in the necessary quantities at the necessary time" (p. 120) and working only with suppliers who deliver high-quality products in the precise quantities and at the time needed, a great deal of the mass production overhead costs are eliminated. Through precision about what is needed, where and when, advanced companies are eliminating the need for incoming inspection, large inventories, billing, ordering, shipping, and receiving procedures. Lean production on the floor leads to lean office procedures. And lean, simple procedures compress time.

Companies around the world have little choice: they are focusing on timely response to consumer desires because consumers do have choices in this global economy and show a great willingness to exercise their choices. As companies compress cycle times, bring products and services to market faster, and even learn how to provide "virtual" products and services (available whenever and wherever the customer wants them), they are discovering an irony about time: *it does not cost more to deliver products and services quickly—it costs less. Compressing time in the design and production process improves an organization's overall performance.*

From successful re-engineering experiences, from concurrent engineering, lean production, and time-based competition, we can list the following values and design principles for government re-engineering projects:

Key Re-Engineering Design Principles

1. Organize around outcomes (customers, products, processes), not functions.
2. Substitute parallel for sequential processes.
3. Bring downstream information upstream.
4. Capture information once, at the source.
5. Provide a single point of contact for customers and suppliers whenever possible.
6. Ensure a continuous flow of the "main sequence" (those activities that directly add value to the customer).

   A. Identify value-adding and non-value-adding steps.

   B. Eliminate or separate every non-value-adding step, so

that the main sequence flows smoothly and quickly.

   C. Use a triage approach to sort out complex and risky cases from the routine ones.

7. Don't pave cowpaths; first re-engineer, *then* automate.

We will examine these design principles one at a time.

Organize Around Outcomes, Not Functions

When Louis Henri Sullivan articulated the basic architectural rule of thumb "Form ever follows function," he expressed the essence of the principle of organizing around the outcome. This principle is obvious to any consultant—or marketing person, reference librarian, city planner, or others in the professional helping professions. When a client asks me whether I suggest total quality management, self-managing teams, intensive customer service training to the front-line employees, or any other organizational approach, my answer is generally the same: it depends on what outcome you are trying to achieve. That is, TQM and other approaches are *means* to an end. Before deciding on the means, the client has to clarify the desired end. It's an obvious, if somewhat overlooked truism in the helping professions, that you start at the end. Once the desired result is clear, you can organize around it.

Like so much about organizational life in the 1990s, this principle involves more unlearning than learning for people toiling in rigidly structured bureaucracies. Organizing around outcomes is a natural approach for most people, *until* they have been trained to separate, segment, and divide projects and problems for the presumed sake of efficiency.

Take a common task: planning a family vacation. When you sit down with your family to think about the next vacation you will take together, what do you do? Do you begin by assigning each member a function or task: "Bob, you're in charge of packing and unpacking; Mary, you and your baby brother gather all the toys you want to take; honey, you're the trip finance department, so make sure we have all the money or credit we need; I'll plan logistics"? If that sounds familiar, either your family has long ago decided where it's going and only has to divvy up the chores, or you may be having some very unhappy vacations.

The way most families, and individuals, think about vacations begins with the outcome, not the functions: Where do we want to go? What type of vacation do we want to take? What sort of experience do I want? Those are the conscious or unconscious questions we ask ourselves, and that is the natural way to think about using vacation time. The same sort of thinking goes into buying a house, looking for a new job, choosing a college, buying a new suit. We start with the end in mind, unless past training or certain constraints severely limit our choices.

Unfortunately, our organizations haven't functioned this way since we moved to a mass production economy. Division of labor, specialization, interchangeable parts, and fragmented work made sense when technology was basic and consumers were glad to have whatever producers gave them. In a high-tech economy driven by consumer preferences for speed, variety, quality, and convenience, the old fragmented system doesn't make it. It takes too long. It's too rigid. It's demeaning to an increasingly well-educated work force that expects interesting, challenging work. And ironically, it no longer produces what was once its greatest asset—the lowest-cost method to produce large quantities. Today, leading organizations are learning that to meet these expectations, they must organize around the desired outcome.

In their path-breaking book *Competing Against Time*, Stalk and Hout (1990) ask, "What distinguishes a time-based organization from a traditional one? Basically, it has asked two simple questions. What deliverables do my customers want? and what organization and work process inside my company will most directly provide these deliverables?" (p. 169). Asking "What deliverables do my customers want?" is another way to state the first principle: organize around outcomes, not functions.

Stanley Davis (1987), in his fascinating book *Future Perfect*, describes the phenomenon of organizing around outcomes through the use of the future perfect tense. The future perfect tense—"by Friday I will have completed work on this project"—puts you into the future, looking backward. As Davis says, this perspective means that "the present is the past of the future" (p. 26). The emerging economy requires such instantaneous response to consumer desires that successful managers must think, plan, and lead with a future perfect perspective: "The manager visualizes the completed strategy before visualizing the component actions that will bring about the completion" (p. 26). In today's real-time environment, the only way leaders can succeed is "lead from a place in time that assumes you are already there" (p. 25).

The U.S. military has long understood the principle of organizing around outcomes. The primary outcome, or "deliverable," that the military's customer (the country) expects is national defense. When our political leaders give the military a clear and specific *military* mission, as in the Persian Gulf War, it typically performs very well. That is because the entire organization is aligned toward the very clear outcome of national defense and fighting preparedness. The various training and educational activities it provides, the chain of command concept and discipline that it forces, the culture that supports absolute unit cohesion and loyalty, the distinctive code of justice—these and many other elements of military life are all aligned to the outcome we expect: strong national defense. Our military doesn't perform as well when given missions that are unclear (such as the defense of Beirut during President Reagan's first term), not clearly associated with vital issues of national defense (its role in the war against drugs), or both (Vietnam). In such cases, we are asking it to provide an outcome for which it's not organized.

Examples of organizations designed by function rather than by outcome follow:

- Schools and universities, fragmented into academic departments and "subject matter," are organized for the professional's convenience, not for the student's learning. Organizing for the students to learn, an outcome that makes sense for education, cannot be done effectively when those responsible for achieving the outcome are divided by specialty and discipline.
- Police departments that continue to operate under the random patrol and rapid response mode, which separates officers by function—traffic, patrol, investigations, narcotics—rather than by outcome.
- Most hospitals, welfare agencies, city halls; in fact almost all organizations of any size that belong to an industry begun before the 1960s. As organizational theorist Henry Mintzberg (1989) points out, most of our organizations, whether new or old, are designed as their earliest predecessors were. New hospitals function as early ones did, so too with publishing houses, hotels, fire departments, and so forth. Industries that have grown up in recent decades such as electronics, computers, and other high-tech industries, don't have the same bureaucratic, fragmented structures.

Three Approaches to Organizing Around the Outcome

As Lewis Branscomb, former director of the National Bureau of Standards, has noted, there are two ways one can specify standards for a new bridge. One is to give bidders *design* specifications: annotated drawings of the bridge, detailed design of the parts, how they are to fit together, materials to be used, and so forth. The second way is to give bidders *performance* specifications: the peak load the bridge must carry, distance it must cross, how long it must last, and so on.

Branscomb concludes that performance (read "outcome") specifications are always superior to design specifications (Marshall and

Tucker, 1992). Employees can follow design specs to the letter and still produce a bridge (or government program) that doesn't do what it's supposed to do. And when that happens, who is responsible? The finger pointing begins before the job is even completed. Performance specs, on the other hand, give staff an incentive to find creative ways to meet end user requirements. They make the organization accountable for the desired outcome, rather than micromanaging it by focusing on the means to achieving that outcome.

There are three ways to organize around outcomes: by customer, by product, and by process.

Organize Around the Customer. The first step to take when organizing around outcomes is to determine whether an identifiable customer is requesting a specific service. If so, that customer's needs can form the basis of the deliverable, or outcome. The Human Resources Department's self-managing team in Hampton, Virginia, for instance, is organized around its customers. The department used to be organized around areas of specialization—training, compensation and classification, and the like. They work as generalists now, organized around specific customer departments. Rather than specializing in employee relations, each team member now "specializes" in serving a half dozen or more customer departments, providing all of their human resources needs.

The state of Connecticut has re-engineered its unemployment offices, organizing them around the customers and their needs. The former system required applicants for unemployment insurance to wait in long lines. Once registered, they were directed to a second line where they waited to apply for job-matching services. Then, they were sent to yet another line where they could seek job training. The sequential approach was tiresome and time-consuming to the citizen and turned well-intentioned civil servants into unapproachable paper pushers focused on control, not service.

The new process has demolished the long lines. Now, applicants call for a scheduled, sit-down interview. With the help of new computer systems, each employee is able to provide applicants with the office's full range of services. The employees have been trained to work as generalists, not specialists, so that they can handle all the applicant's needs (for more details, see Chapter Nine).

This change involves new roles, new technology, a change in attitude concerning the purpose of the job, and a lot of cross-training. To ensure success, hundreds of state employees were interviewed before the new system was designed, and many of their ideas were used in the new process.

Organizing around the customer is also a theme of the federal Job Training Partnership Act, which pays vendors according to the number of people they place in actual jobs (outcomes), not the number that complete training (outputs).

Organize Around the Product. When the customer is not easily identifiable (their numbers are too large, their needs change too frequently) or when the deliverable is a tangible good and not an intangible service, then organizing around the product is the approach to take. The San Diego Zoo is an excellent example of organizing around the product—the physical presentation offered, with the associated educational and support services. Organizing in the conventional way, around taxonomy, was convenient for the staff; it enabled them to work with those who shared their professional expertise. If the organization's primary purpose was to meet the needs of the staff, such a design would make sense. It makes no sense if the outcome is defined in terms of the consumer's experience of the product. Plant and animal life don't occur in nature in a segmented, specialized fashion. Studying our environment is an exercise in integration, not separation, and the zoo is now moving in that direction, organizing around bioclimatic zones.

An educational approach sometimes called "thematic learning" provides another example of organizing around the product. Some schools now integrate the students' learning experiences by focusing several classes on a common theme. At schools like the Governor's School for Government and International Studies in Richmond, Virginia, teachers work in teams to coordinate the curriculum for groups of a hundred students. The teachers each have responsibility for one subject area but share responsibility for the students' overall learning; they are focused on outcomes. Rather than fragment the day into discrete and disconnected forty-five-minute periods, the teachers use a flexible schedule and core themes (such as a unit on South America) to facilitate integrated learning. Every day for a month or more, each member of the four-person teaching team uses that theme as a focus for the students' work.

Ninth-grade students also do a year-long research project requiring skills in all academic areas. Teachers work as a team to help students with their research and coordinate the project—the math teacher helps with statistics, the literature teacher with writing skills, and so on. The teamwork (with students as well as with each other) forces teachers to become generalists, breaking down traditional academic walls as they take responsibility for the "product" (and outcome), student learning (Steven E. Ballowe, personal communication, 1991).

Another example of organizing around the product involved one auto company in which it used to take two to three weeks to estimate the costs of new parts needed in its factories. The delay was caused by a classic assembly line process; six different functions added their information to the work package as it made its way to the end user: from product engineering (preparing blueprints and specifications), to manufacturing engineering (developing routings which show how to assemble the pieces), to industrial engineering (estimating the number of hours of labor for each type of work required to make the part), to purchasing (for quotes), to finance (for overhead), and finally to sales. The process, organized strictly around functions, violated many of the re-engineering principles: it relied on sequential steps; downstream information wasn't brought upstream, so that inappropriate numbers showed up late in the process and required extensive rework; information was captured several times.

After a team mapped out the process to distinguish the value-adding steps from the delays, they interviewed the end users of the cost estimates to better understand their expectations. The team reorganized around the end product, the cost estimate. Their main recommendation reduced the number of steps from six to two. Now, product engineering prepares blueprints and specs as before. It sends them to a group of four employees representing manufacturing engineering, purchasing, finance, and sales. This group meets twice weekly and works together in one room, with one member acting as chair. There are no handoffs—if a difficult case cannot be decided during a meeting, it's researched during the week and settled at the next meeting. The result: average cycle time went from two to three weeks to half a week, and the quality of the estimates improved (Stalk and Hout, 1990; and see Figure 4.1).

Organize Around the Process. When there is no consistently identifiable customer needing a specific service, no tangible good or product, organizing around the outcome means organizing around the process itself.

The Union Pacific Railroad (UPRR) used to be an example of a rigid, hierarchical bureaucracy; it certainly had plenty of time to perfect this form, having helped to create it in the first half of the nineteenth century. Before Mike Walsh was named CEO in 1986, the Union Pacific was as stodgy as anything government ever produced. One example: the manager of one UPRR business function with a $22 million budget "didn't have the authority to spend more than two thousand dollars without the written approval of Omaha [headquarters]. And it took eight weeks for that!" (Peters, 1992, p. 88)

Walsh created a revolution in structure and systems at the Union Pacific—it's truly a new organization today. For instance, before Walsh restructured, there were ten levels of management

Figure 4.1. Organizing Around the Product: Cost Estimating Process.

Before Re-Engineering

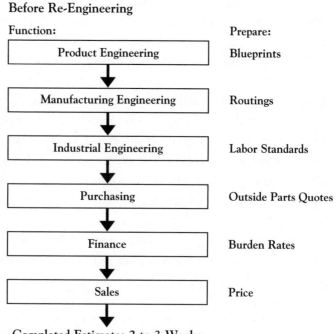

Function:	Prepare:
Product Engineering	Blueprints
Manufacturing Engineering	Routings
Industrial Engineering	Labor Standards
Purchasing	Outside Parts Quotes
Finance	Burden Rates
Sales	Price

Completed Estimate: 2 to 3 Weeks

After Re-Engineering

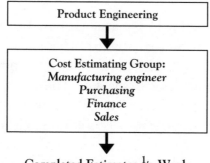

Product Engineering

Cost Estimating Group:
Manufacturing engineer
Purchasing
Finance
Sales

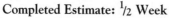

Completed Estimate: ¹/₂ Week

Source: Adapted and reprinted with permission of the Free Press, Macmillan Publishing Company, from *Competing Against Time: How Time-Based Competition Is Reshaping Global Markets*, by George Stalk, Jr., and Thomas M. Hout. Copyright © 1990 by the Free Press.

on the operations side of the organization chart. When a track inspector found bad track located in a customer's yard, he had to send his message up eight of those levels. When it reached the general manager, that person sent the message to the assistant vice president for sales on the sales and marketing side, who then sent it down four levels where it finally reached the customer.

The organization and its reporting process have been streamlined in a big way. Walsh eliminated five organizational levels in his first ninety days, letting go of hundreds of managers whose main job was to collect and pass on information. Now, when the track inspector finds bad track in the customer's yard, he or she simply tells the customer. No sign-offs, no handoffs, no approvals, no levels of review. The track inspector only contacts management for help if the customer fails to act (see Figure 4.2).

The state of Oregon organized around the process when it reengineered its requests for proposals (RFPs). In the past, when Oregon wanted to solicit bids from private contractors, it did what most agencies do: it used a long, paper-intensive process to determine the work requirements, compile the job specifications, write them up, put them in envelopes, and mail them to hundreds of contractors. Fifteen state employees were needed just to address and stuff envelopes and update vendor lists. The annual cost of postage alone exceeded $100,000.

State officials examined basic assumptions. Two assumptions underlying the old process were that RFPs had to be sent on hard copy and that it was up to the state to pay for vendors to learn about business opportunities with the state. The new process turned those assumptions on their heads. Now, RFPs are sent on-line, and interested vendors use state-provided software to learn about bid opportunities. The state no longer spends $100,000 for postage—vendors now pay the "postage" through their monthly long-distance bills, and there is no hard copy to stuff and send (eliminating the need for those positions). Further, vendors can log on to learn who won each proposal and at what cost, which has gradually brought down the vendors' bids (Martin, 1993).

Figure 4.2. Union Pacific Railroad Decision Flowcharts, Before and After Re-Engineering.

Reporting Bad Track to Customer:

Before Re-Engineering

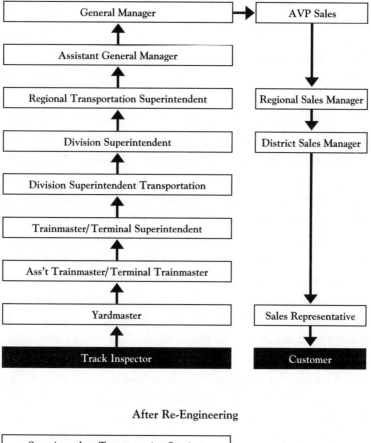

After Re-Engineering

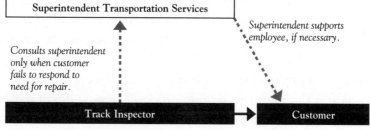

Source: © 1993 Video Publishing House, Inc. Used with permission.

Whether an agency organizes around customers, products, or processes, the objective is the same: orient staff and their work to outcomes, not activities or outputs. Focusing on outputs—number of job training sessions given to unemployed people, fire department response time to emergencies, percentage of pregnant women who receive prenatal care—is a measure with very little meaning. What citizens want to know, what managers must expect to find out, has to do with outcomes, not outputs: How many unemployed people are finding and keeping jobs? Is the overall number of fires decreasing? Is the percentage of babies born healthy going up?

When government agencies organize around outcomes and give staff the tools, authority, and responsibility for achieving certain outcomes, it provides an ingredient critical to any organization—focus.

Many civil servants would love to put more focus into their work by organizing around outcomes but find that the policies they are trying to implement lack a clear outcome. The lack of clarity comes from the legislative process; in order to get a bill passed into law, elected officials usually have to compromise. They add amendments, put money in for tangential purposes, and engage in the give-and-take that our system requires. Thus, it's sometimes impossible for the career staff to implement the "intent of Congress" (or of city council or the state legislature), because there was no one intent. The legislation contained multiple intents, reflecting the multiple constituencies and interests that had to be satisfied. Can staff organize around outcomes in these cases?

The answer is that they can't, until they articulate an outcome that appears consistent with the legislation or policy directive and gain support for that outcome. And that isn't as difficult as it may seem. When elected officials grope with controversial public policy issues and can't achieve a clear consensus (such as whether to make going through the review process for new development extremely fast and user-friendly for builders, or slow and filled with public hearings to accommodate environmentalists), they are sometimes privately happy for the staff to help them out. Staff can fill the policy vacuum by designing approaches that are consistent with public sector values (openness, accountability, equity). Some staff prefer not to fill such vacuums; others see them as opportunities to act creatively and move forward. And when staff are willing to move forward, articulate (perhaps limited) outcomes, and craft programs that succeed at achieving those outcomes, the elected body is often quite happy to share the credit.

Organize Around Outcomes: The Shift in Assumptions

Old assumptions: Those who perform the same function should work together. We can't control the results of our work, so we can't be accountable for those results, only for the activities we directly perform.

New assumptions: Those who work on the same processes should work together. We can't control the results of our work when we aren't organized for results; if we organize around outcomes, we will find that we can control the results far more than we imagined.

Substitute Parallel for Sequential Processes

Anyone who has ever successfully cooked a multi-dish meal for a group understands this principle. You can't get all the dishes ready at the desired time if you cook them individually. The experienced chef knows when the food needs to be served and plans backward, working on several different dishes at once.

Unfortunately, most bureaucracies don't support the principle of using parallel processes. They still work sequentially. One day on vacation, I went to buy a newspaper. The sales clerk told me I had to pay at the front counter. When I arrived there and offered my $0.35, none of the three clerks was able to take my money. They were all engaged in helping someone in front of me. The first clerk was waiting to take the person's traveler's check; the second was waiting to ring up the sale (once the check was verified by the first); the third clerk was waiting patiently for the first two to finish, so that she could put the item into a bag. The sequential assembly line, perfected by Henry Ford in 1914, was alive and (too) well eighty years later.

One obvious example of parallel processing in the organizational world involves high technology. In an age of E-mail, there is no reason for a leader to rely on trickle-down communication, giving information to the senior managers, who pass it to the middle managers, who send it on down to first-level supervisors, and then (if anybody still cares about it) to the worker bees. Push one key on the boss's computer, and everybody with access to a computer has the same information, simultaneously.

Stan Davis (1987) has a wonderful example for this sort of communication. He cites the old mechanical TV knob as the metaphor for sequential, one-level-at-a-time communication. To go from channel 2 to channel 7, you must go through every intervening channel on the knob, just as communications have traditionally gone one level at a time. Today, remote control replaces the knob in most Americans' living rooms. To go from channel 2 to 7 using the remote requires one quick movement; you can go instantaneously from one channel to any other one, because each channel has direct access to every other channel. So, too, with organizations that emphasize rapid, complete communications. Everyone is wired to everyone else, so there is no need for middle managers to play "information cop" and decide what gets passed on or held up. The MCI Corporation is one of the leading examples of simultaneous communications. Its leadership encourages every employee to use the company's E-mail system to send ideas and suggestions directly to the president; many do, sometimes from their home computers. He reads them and responds to those that interest him, directly to the employee.

In re-engineering, substituting parallel for sequential processes has several clear advantages. The more steps in a process, the greater the likelihood of errors, delays, and information falling through the cracks. When each unit works on one aspect of a product or process and then sends it on to the next unit, there is little ownership and a lot of finger pointing when errors occur. A parallel process speeds up the outcome and allows errors to be caught much sooner.

Examples of substituting parallel for sequential processes:

- Concurrent engineering of new products is being undertaken, in which the phases of design, development, prototyping, and manufacturing overlap (see the earlier discussion).
- Electronic linkages between producer, supplier, distributor, and retailer can compress time by passing information instantaneously. This system, called electronic data interchange (EDI), helps companies like Wal-Mart turn over inventory 50 percent faster than their rivals. By scanning the bar code of each item sold and transmitting that information from its computers directly to its suppliers' and manufacturers' computers, Wal-Mart lets suppliers such as Procter & Gamble know what a local outlet needs before the store does, so that they can deliver the items "just in time" to keep the shelves (but not the warehouse) stocked (Hammer and Champy, 1993; Davidow and Malone, 1992).
- Becoming ever more common are "all hands meetings" via teleconference (the only way a decentralized organization can communicate face-to-face with all of its employees, simultaneously).
- Many agencies now put their program staff in direct contact with their customers. Rather than filter customer feedback through layers of management, those who plan and provide the program or service get real-time customer reactions.
- The mortgage approval process in some lending institutions (a sequential process that typically takes four to eight weeks) is

being re-engineered at certain banks now. Teams of up to seventeen employees are linked together electronically so that they can make decisions on dozens of applications in a matter of hours (Verity and McWilliams, 1991).

• No doubt you have come across the employee who takes your order while you stand in a fast-food line, writes it down, and hands it to you to give to the cashier.

• Some insurance companies are re-engineering the way they process applications for mortgages. The old system was an assembly line. The application went through as many as sixty different people, five to six different departments, and thirty different steps as credit checks, quoting, rating, underwriting, and so forth, were done in sequential fashion. Companies like Aetna Life & Casualty have re-engineered the process. Now, a generalist (sometimes called a case manager) has full responsibility for the application, from the time it's received to the point when a policy is issued or declined. Case managers have been cross-trained and can handle 90 percent or more of the applications with the help of expert systems run on PC-based workstations. When case managers do need help, specialists are available.

Before it redesigned its processes in 1992, Aetna had three thousand employees staffing twenty-two business centers at which insurance applications were processed. Applicants waited three weeks to learn whether their application was approved.

Those three thousand positions in twenty-two centers have been reduced to seven hundred in four work centers. A single Aetna representative, sitting at a PC tied to a network, performs all the steps an application needs. Result: The applicant receives a policy within *five days*. Aetna predicts that the new system for issuing policies will save the company about $40 million a year and improve productivity by about 25 percent (Gleckman, 1993; see Figure 4.3).

• Parallel processing is exciting many in the computer field.

Figure 4.3. The Re-Engineered Application Process
at Aetna Life and Casualty.

What used to take three weeks . . .

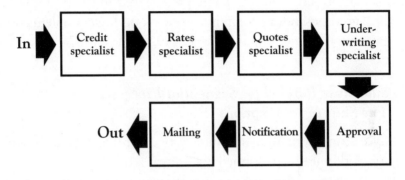

now takes no more than five days.

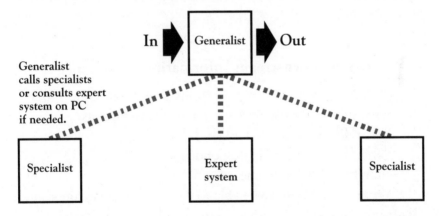

Computer scientists are designing systems that allow massive computers to work on several aspects of complex problems at once. To do so requires a shift as major as the change from bureaucratic, segmented, step-by-step work procedures to lean production and concurrent engineering. Some predict that in the future we will link up thousands of computers to work on huge problems simultaneously (Davidow and Malone, 1992; Davis, 1987).

Substitute Parallel for Sequential Processes: The Shift in Assumptions

Old assumption: To maintain quality control and fix accountability, work must be performed one step at a time.

New assumption: A consumer society won't wait for sequentially produced programs and services. Bright people, supported by appropriate technology and a seamless work process, can perform many things in parallel.

Bring Downstream Information Upstream

When I saw a doctor about pain in my knee some time ago, he diagnosed it as a torn cartilage, probably due to jogging.

"What do you suggest?" I asked.

"What do you want?" he responded.

I didn't know what he meant.

"What do you want to be able to do with the knee: run again? Play tennis again? Horse around with your kids on the floor? What I recommend depends on what you want to be able to do. We can do some minor things if you want a slight gain in usage. To jog or play tennis will require surgery and an extensive rehab program. What I do depends on what you want to do."

The doctor, quite appropriately, was trying to get downstream information (how I wanted my knee to function) upstream, at the start of our work together. He was also using our first principle, organizing around outcomes.

The concurrent engineering approach in design and manufacturing is making us aware how much time and quality is lost, and how much finger pointing is generated, when information is dispersed through a process or system. When each function (engineering, marketing, manufacturing, accounting, and so on) works on the product separately and doesn't know downstream needs and requirements, the lack of integration creates serious problems. Concurrent engineering solves the problem by putting specialists from all functions onto a team that designs and creates the product from start to finish. Since every function is on the team, the information needs of every step are known from the start.

Our third principle—bring downstream information upstream— leads to something near and dear to most people in organizations: no surprises. It also leads directly to our first principle, focus on outcomes. It's far easier to focus on outcomes if all downstream information is brought upstream. When you go to a restaurant and your server remembers to tell you that they are out of one of the specials, downstream information has been brought upstream, which makes the outcome you had in mind when you chose that restaurant more likely. It also saves you time and reduces your disappointment. (The special becomes much more important after you go ahead and order it, and *then* learn that it's unavailable!)

The "no surprises" rule is of great importance to most managers, of course. When a quality improvement team works for months on a task without knowing the parameters of its work, this principle is violated. I once worked with a middle management task force for six months, helping it come up with ideas for improving an agency's performance appraisal system. The task force reported its ideas, some of which were very creative for the agency—include self-assessment on the appraisal, use bottom-up assessment of managers, focus on goals rather than traits. Unfortunately, the deputy who reviewed the report never commented on its substance. He was upset that the task force hadn't sought input from all levels in the agency before issuing its report. That downstream information— how the deputy wanted us to gather data—was never given to us, nor had we taken the time to ask. Needless to say, when members of the task force were asked to go back and start their project again from the beginning, they rolled their eyes and opted out.

One of the most interesting examples of this principle is seen in the new approach called partnering, mentioned in Chapter One. Partnering is often employed when a government agency has a contract with a private firm for a building project. Frequently in the past, such projects came in late, over budget, and below the quality requirements of the customer. The main reason: the entire process was conducted in adversarial fashion, with both parties trying to reduce the damage inflicted by the other.

Partnering makes the two (or several) parties into one team with a common objective: satisfy the customer's (agency's) need. By the end of a partnering session, the full group has brought downstream information (what each needs during the project stages) upstream. Before the project begins, agency and contractor leaders have located potential pitfalls; they have agreed on methods for resolving disputes; they understand what each needs from the other at various milestones; and they have a common vision for how the project will proceed and a common information base from which to start.

In addition to the U.S. Army Corps of Engineers (see Chapter One), the Arizona Department of Transportation (ADOT) also swears by partnering. During fiscal year 1991 (prior to instituting partnering), 27 percent of the construction projects done for ADOT were not completed on time, and there was $23 million in claims filed during that year. Two years later, after the introduction of partnering, no claims were filed, fewer projects were completed late, and ADOT saved over $400,000 through "value engineering," an approach that engages the contractor and department staff in suggesting ideas for efficiencies and improvements (Cole, 1993). A key ingredient in these successes: bringing downstream information—concerning mutual expectations—upstream.

Other examples of bringing downstream information upstream:

- Sometimes staff will tell a customer the information needed to obtain a permit or license, before the customer even walks in the door (see the discussion of the Charlottesville Social Services Benefits Division in Chapter Eight).
- Employees may visit the external customers who use the program, product, or service that the agency produces, so that the employees understand how it's used, what the customers like and don't like about it, what changes would be helpful, what features are nice but not needed. (One intelligence agency, after a visit with the customers of its various reports, found that it put great effort into certain reports that nobody read!)
- Prototyping, when designing an innovative product or program, can be an effective strategy. Unlike traditional planning, in which extensive time is spent designing the innovation before it's produced and brought to market, prototyping creates a "quick and dirty" version of the product, which allows others who work in the production process, as well as potential end users, to react. These reactions constitute "downstream information" that is fed back to the designers, who can make changes before extensive time and resources are expended on the initial concept. In the field of software development, application prototyping (the use of test programs) is common; a software model is developed and given to likely end users to determine their needs. U.S.–Japanese joint ventures in auto manufacturing use prototyping to get information from those who must manufacture and market the new model. Prototyping's many benefits include improved collaboration among staff, suppliers, and customers and better use of time, since planning and production are done in parallel, which shortens the feedback loop (Marsters and Williams, 1993).

Bring Downstream Information Upstream:
The Shift in Assumptions

Old assumption: Information is time-specific, is produced in sequence, and can only be accessed at the relevant point in the sequence (or "We'll find out when we get there").

New assumption: Information can be accessed any time, any place; it's most valuable up front.

Capture Information Once, at the Source

Every time I go to the dry cleaners, we go through the same ritual. The service people are polite, remember my name, and quickly find my clean clothes. Then I leave them some clothes to clean, and as they fill out the slip they ask for my phone number. Why do they continually ask for the same information? My number hasn't changed in a dozen years. I ask the same question when I check into Holiday Inns, a chain I have frequently used. In a high-tech age, why does the desk clerk have to capture the same information about me every time?

Why haven't they figured out what Domino's Pizza knows— that it's a waste of the customers' and employees' time to capture the same information over and over? Domino's has all the information it needs on its repeat customers. Once they see the caller's phone number on their caller ID system, they need only get the order and they're ready to go. Domino's doesn't need your address again. They captured the information once, at its source.

Every time information is passed through another person, it runs the risk of being distorted, as in the childhood game of Telephone, which demonstrates how a message, whispered from one child to the next, rarely comes out at the end resembling the words the first child spoke.

The fourth principle—capturing information once, at its source—is a long-sought goal of many chief executives, who despair that they typically receive information late, with few options and little time to decide (Peters, 1979).

Capturing information once is important not only for executives. For an unemployment applicant to fill out three different forms at three different lines for three different agency personnel not only is demeaning and a waste of the citizen's time, it also adds needless layers of bureaucracy and costs to the agency and provides many opportunities for mistakes and lost information. It makes professional staff into clerks who spend far more time checking for accuracy than providing a service. For the applicant and employees, it's important to capture information just once, at its source.

In a mass production, fragmented organization, it's virtually impossible to capture information once. The various departments are too specialized, each uses its own computer system, each collects data from the same customer or vendor separately, and their technology doesn't allow them to share it. Moreover, the lack of trust created by separate missions and reward systems gives them no reason to share information.

Capturing information once becomes possible in an age of on-line databases, bar codes, and PC networks. It becomes a necessity in a consumer-dominated age. Many consumers simply will not waste their time filling out multiple forms, and increasingly, consumers demand that professionals deal with them in a holistic, not fragmented, fashion.

Technology now enables the railroads to capture information once, at its source. Keeping track of thousands of rail cars forced the railroads to create our early organizational hierarchies. Today cars are marked with machine-readable symbols, which are read by sensors and fed into computer systems that do the tracking. Such change is required when progressive executives take over old-line hierarchies, as happened at Union Pacific Railroad.

Capturing information once, at its source, is also seen on the nation's highways. Toll booths on many highways are being replaced by electronic toll systems. The motorist doesn't slow down, and nobody stands at the booth to collect money. Instead, scanners read credit card–size windshield tags and send a bill to the home or office. Begun in the late 1980s, the electronic system is spreading rapidly for three reasons: convenience to the motorist, cost savings to the highway authority, and less road congestion. The electronic system can process three times more cars per hour than a person taking cash, and it costs less than 10 percent of the manual system.

Other examples of capturing information once, at the source:

• The Charlottesville, Virginia, Fire Department issues incidence reports to citizens who have suffered a fire loss. Preparing these reports used to be absurdly tedious, in part because the necessary information was captured and entered at least five times, and often by two or three officers entering the information multiple times after the call. The process has been re-engineered: now *one* officer enters the information, *once*.

• Bill Marriott, Jr., insisted for years that he see the complaint cards sent in by Marriott Hotel guests. Marriott knew that only this direct connection with his customers would keep him truly in touch with their needs and preferences.

Capture Information Once, at the Source: The Shift in Assumptions

Old assumption: Information must be captured frequently, to assure control and accuracy.

New assumption: Information must be captured once, to streamline the process and ensure accuracy.

Provide a Single Point of Contact for Customers and Suppliers Whenever Possible

You know the feeling all too well. You call a government agency (or virtually any large bureaucracy) and ask for information about a particular product or service. After being put on hold, you are switched to a department, where you again explain your needs. You're then told that you have reached the wrong department: "We

don't provide that service here; you need to call department X."
Two or three calls later (each time dutifully repeating your story),
you may get the help you need—if the right person is in today.

Consumers are so used to getting the runaround in dealing with
government and large commercial establishments that we take it
as a given. Bureaucracies aren't user-friendly because they're designed to meet their own needs, not those of customers. Thus we
aren't surprised when we have to deal with three, four, five, or more
employees in order to purchase a product or service. In a producer-
oriented world, consumers take what is offered.

In a consumer-oriented world, we have choices, and the choice
most of us make is to deal with as few people as possible in making
a purchase or dealing with a government agency. Customer service
experts report that the more people we encounter in obtaining a
service, the more dissatisfied we are (Albrecht and Zemke, 1990).
In the traditional pyramidal bureaucracy and in the absence of current information technology, there was little choice but to subject
consumers to several service personnel.

As convenience and speed become more important to consumers, the principle of providing a single point of contact becomes
essential in service delivery. A single point of contact requires several important organizational shifts: from specialist to generalist
positions (backed up by specialists and on-line systems); from
departments that hoard information to process teams that share it
freely; from adversarial relations with hundreds of suppliers to close,
long-term relationships with a small number of suppliers; from clear
and rigid lines separating departments and functions to fluid situations in which employees may work in other departments, at a supplier's location, at home, or at the site of the customer; and from a
control orientation to a service orientation for the front-line
employee who deals directly with the consumer.

Large government bureaucracies are learning to provide a
single point of contact. As noted earlier, applicants for unemployment assistance in Connecticut used to deal with at least

three different employees in order to be declared eligible and receive unemployment compensation and related services. After a major re-engineering project, that has all changed. Now applicants are given a scheduled interview with one service provider. The waiting, the time filling out repetitive forms, and the bureaucratic runaround are relics of the past.

Other examples of single point-of-contact service:

• The Family Housing Office serving the Norfolk (Virginia) Naval Shipyard opened a Welcome Center in 1991. The purpose is to meet all needs of an incoming military member and his or her family. The Welcome Center provides the services normally offered at Navy family housing offices, but goes much further. It provides a landlord-tenant mediation service for military families having disputes with their landlord. It gives information on food stamps, religious services, and a variety of community programs. The staff will help military families review a lease for a unit being considered, and offers counseling for those with special needs. It also provides space for a Norfolk city employee, who registers new families to vote, gives vehicle registration and public school information.

• Merced County, California, re-engineered its applications for social services. Applicants who once waited four weeks just to get an interview now wait three days or fewer. An individual caseworker, aided by an expert system, handles all the programs applicants may apply for, radically reducing processing time. Accuracy in determining eligibility is up, staff turnover is down, and productivity increased 148 percent in 10 months (Mechling, 1994).

• One of the most ambitious efforts to create one-stop shopping is being developed at the U.S. Department of Labor (DoL). In an attempt to streamline and coordinate the various services available to people who have lost their jobs, the DoL is developing a comprehensive Worker Adjustment strategy for the entire country. The federal government alone funds more than 150 employment and training programs, leaving many people confused and unaware of their options. By the DoL's own account, the system is fragmented, complicated, a vast maze that serves a bare fraction of those eligible.

The DoL plans to pull the pieces together by offering grants to states that implement a one-stop approach for those needing unemployment services. The department envisions a national network of Career Centers that enable workers, students, and employers to access information and services about jobs, the labor market, career education, training opportunities, financing options, apprenticeship programs, and certification requirements for certain jobs. Rather than the old top-down, bureaucratic approach in which Washington told the states what to do (but provided little if any money to do it), the DoL wants to use grants and seed money as incentives to states that will streamline their current operations and join this network of one-stop Career Centers. The DoL is leaving room for creative approaches as long as states provide a single point of service; offer rapid response, information, and services on job and training needs; deliver career planning and job search assistance; and help employers by providing applicant recruitment and screening.

Provide a Single Point of Contact: The Shift in Assumptions

Old assumption: Organizations should be organized by distinct functions, for the convenience of the departments.

New assumption: Organizations should be organized by processes. Customers and vendors should deal with one person representing the entire process, for the convenience of the customer.

Ensure a Continuous Flow of the Main Sequence

Quick turnaround and prompt service are becoming more important to government bureaucracies as well as to business. Stalk and Hout (1990) identify two keys to quick turnaround and prompt service. To compress time, it's necessary to (1) organize around the main sequence and (2) maintain a continuous flow of work.

The principle of *organizing around the main sequence* means focusing on those activities that directly add value to the end user. All other activities should be eliminated, reduced, and/or done "off-line" (separate from the main sequence). There are different ways to define the term *value adding*; perhaps the most common one has to do with those activities that a customer or end user would pay for (Harrington, 1991).

Examples of Value-Adding Activities:
What the Customer Is Willing to Pay For

- Activities that bring a service or product closer (backyard refuse pickup, home delivery of purchased goods)
- Activities that bring a product or service to the consumer faster (fax, overnight delivery, 911 emergency systems)
- Activities that add features we care about (mushrooms on the pizza, cruise control on the car, enrichment programs for talented students)
- Activities that combine or refine ingredients to produce something more useful to us (clearing and landscaping a vacant field to make a city park, assembling component parts to make a car or stereo)
- Activities that make a product or service more user-friendly (PC with built-in modem and fax)
- Activities that enable front-line employees to better meet our needs (training for specialized staff to become generalists and provide one-stop shopping)
- Activities that provide the customer with accurate, real-time information (medical procedures that diagnose a disease, information on highway traffic conditions)

Many organizational activities are totally irrelevant to consumers; these add no value and should be reduced, eliminated, or removed from the main sequence.

Examples of Non-Value-Adding Activities:
What the Customer Is Not Willing to Pay For

- Inspection
- Supervision
- Accounting, budgeting, and virtually all overhead activities
- Sign-offs, handoffs from one unit to another
- Credit checks
- Rework
- Reconciliation
- Documentation

Some non-value-adding steps will always be needed, of course. Our principle states that such activities must be separated from the main value-adding sequence, so that the process moves along smoothly.

Maintaining a continuous flow of work is exactly what it sounds like. Several of our principles (capture information once at its source, provide a single point of contact, substitute parallel for sequential steps) are aimed at maintaining a continuous flow. This one is easy to understand from a consumer's point of view. For instance, few of us value waiting in lines. At Four Seasons Hotels, their best customers are checked in before they arrive (through their information system), so that the customer does nothing upon arrival but pick up the room key (Stalk and Hout, 1990). That approach is maintaining a continuous flow.

Another example is found in universities around the country that have re-engineered the classic of all bureaucratic processes: student registration. Gone are the hours spent in the gym going from one line to the next, filling out forms, learning that desired classes are filled, completing drop/add forms, and waiting in more lines for second and third choices. All of those non-value-adding steps are gone. Many students today find out their grades, check class offerings, and register without leaving their rooms. It's all done electronically. The Integrated Student Information System (ISIS) is used at many colleges and universities to make registration user-friendly for both students and staff. Students receive a work sheet to guide them in using their push-button phones, and they register their decisions in a matter of minutes. A voice response system tells students which numbers to push to access information and make class selections. It tells them when a class is full or restricted. Students learn immediately when they're accepted into a course and can complete the entire registration process without hassles or forms. The entire focus is on the only steps that add any value: accessing information and making decisions. And it's all done seamlessly.

Maintaining a continuous work flow not only eliminates consumer waiting time; it also makes better use of employees' time and therefore the organization's resources. Some total quality management gurus like Dr. J. M. Juran estimate that employees in service organizations spend 30 percent or more of their time doing rework. Of all the activities performed, rework is surely the least value-adding activity of all. It adds costs, reduces employee commitment, and takes the focus away from the customer.

How do organizations organize around value-adding activities and maintain a continuous flow of work?

Identify Value-Adding and Non-Value-Adding Steps

First, the value-adding steps must be identified. One of the most useful and powerful activities for a senior manager is to review all of the steps in a process with those who perform the steps. The results are usually shocking, as they reveal the huge amount of waste and rework that is a normal part of the process. Often, the shock that comes from understanding the current process provides the needed motivation for change. A simple flowchart is sometimes sufficient.

After the current steps have been outlined, those involved ask the same question about each step: *would a customer or end user pay for this?* I had an experience with one city government that demonstrated the power of mapping the process and asking that simple question. During a workshop on quality service, we were discussing current organization processes. I asked for an example of a current process that seemed overly long, and someone volunteered "internal utility billing." Several people rolled their eyes, so I knew we had a winner. The process has to do with identifying the utilities each department has used during the month and billing the department accurately. Some departments occupy several buildings, so it takes some care to get the billings right.

However, when we mapped out the current process, it astonished all of us. Three different departments with three different computer systems were involved in a nineteen-step process that was incredibly tedious, with very few value-adding steps. As I began to identify some steps that added no value or that could be combined with others, an old timer in the city leaned back, smiled, and said "Hell, when I started here in the early sixties, we didn't have *any* of those steps. The finance department simply notified us at the end of each month what our usage was and how much it cost from our budget." The process was soon streamlined from nineteen steps to three. It wouldn't have happened if we hadn't mapped out the existing process.

Eliminate, Reduce, or Separate Non-Value-Adding Steps from the Main Sequence

When non-value-adding steps can't be eliminated, they should be removed from the main sequence and run in parallel. Freightliner, a heavy-duty truck producer, doubled its market share when it learned how to cut weeks off its delivery time. It removed such non-value-adding support activities as pricing and credit checking from the main sequence and performed them "off-line" (Stalk and Hout, 1990). Figure 4.4 shows the streamlined system.

The collection division in the IRS Hartford, Connecticut,

Figure 4.4.　Separating Non-Value-Adding Steps from the Main Sequence: Freightliner's Streamlined System.

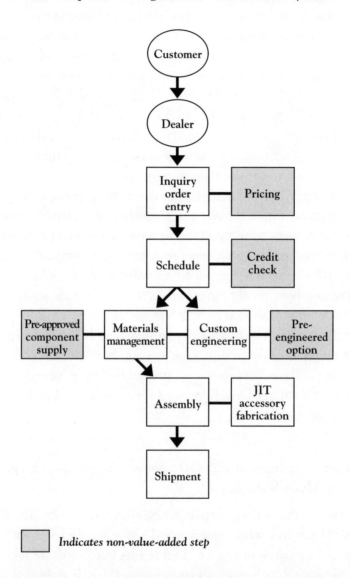

Indicates non-value-added step

Source: Adapted and reprinted with permission of the Free Press, Macmillan Publishing Company, from *Competing Against Time: How Time-Based Competition Is Reshaping Global Markets*, by George Stalk, Jr., and Thomas M. Hout. Copyright © 1990 by the Free Press.

office has made impressive gains since 1992 by ensuring a continuous flow of the main sequence. Through the use of Entity, an automated case management software program developed by employees in the Hartford offices, the division has fundamentally changed the group managers' and revenue officers' roles and relationships with each other. By putting all taxpayer information on computer, Entity enables revenue officers to quickly identify the information they need and ends a very paper-intensive process. It's helping the office create a paperless system for the front-line revenue officers (ROs), who now can provide one-stop service for taxpayers. The ROs quickly see the status and priority needs of each taxpayer case, which is vital since they handle fifty to a hundred collection cases at any one time.

Before using Entity, ROs could only resolve single issues for taxpayers, such as the fact that a taxpayer hadn't paid taxes the previous year. Now, they play a much broader role. They do an assessment of taxpayers' situations, educate them on different approaches for coming into compliance with IRS requirements, counsel them on related financial issues, as well as collect delinquent taxes and secure delinquent returns.

As the ROs became more comfortable using the automated system, the division began to explore the possibilities for streamlining key processes. One major change: they eliminated the tedious case reviews that group managers had always done on the ROs and transformed the group managers' roles from controllers to coaches and facilitators. Group managers had been reviewing four cases per RO per month; these reviews covered five critical elements and 102 subelements for each case. The chief of the collection division, Elisabeth McQueeney, encouraged by her innovative district director, Jim Quinn, convinced her staff that these reviews added no value and only served to slow down the process. In 1992, after extensive discussions with the ROs, group managers, union leaders, and others in the IRS hierarchy, her division dropped the monthly reviews. By focusing on the ROs' main activity—resolving delinquent cases—and removing the time-consuming reviews, cycle time for case resolution has dropped from 40 to 21.6 weeks. Delinquent tax dollars collected rose by 14 percent during the same period.

The staff accomplished an even more dramatic reduction in the "currently noncollectibles" process. It used to take an average of 14.7 days from the time an RO determined a case was uncollectible to the time that information was entered into the computer. The delay wasted staff time and invited errors. The staff flowcharted the existing process, questioned each step, and found steps that added no value—for example, they eliminated multiple handling of the same document.

As the staff studied the existing process, they determined which steps were time-consuming, which could be combined, which eliminated. Working together, they found a quicker, leaner method for determining noncollectibles and put the new process into effect. Result: what used to take 14.7 days now takes 1.4 days (Elisabeth McQueeney, personal communication, 1993).

Use a Triage Approach

A variation of the preceding step is to provide more than one alternative for a process. Most organizational processes are relatively rigid. We have maintained the "one-size-fits-all" mentality of mass production firms by requiring the same process for each need: every citizen wanting a building permit goes through the same steps, regardless of the complexity of the situation; every consumer wanting to apply for a loan goes through the same process; job applicants, promotion decisions, customer complaints tend to have a single routine, regardless of circumstances.

Some of the best examples of this rigid approach are in procurement. In most organizations, making a purchase is a major headache. A $10 purchase often requires the same procedures, paperwork, sign-offs, and even quotes as a $1,000 purchase. Staff at the Navy's Port Hueneme facility studied their purchasing process and found that they spent $250 in staff time for each purchase, no matter how small. The reason the process is so tedious, especially in government agencies, is usually a record of past abuses. Someone was caught making purchases exclusively from a company owned by a relative (or political official), the purchases cost more than they would have elsewhere, and the result was a flurry of regulations requiring multiple bids and documentation.

Progressive organizations deal with different needs differently. They apply the concept of triage, so that complex and high-risk instances follow one process, while routine actions are given a different, streamlined process. The idea is adapted from the way hospitals deal with a sudden crush of badly injured patients, some of whom can be saved, some of whom can't, some needing more immediate attention than others. Airport ticket counters use a sort of triage approach when they form separate lines for those needing tickets and for those with tickets who just need to check their luggage. It's precisely because the concept is hardly new that its absence from so many organizations is striking.

The State Department's Bureau of Consular Affairs made creative use of triage when it streamlined its process for issuing passports. The change was required to meet a huge increase in the number of passport renewals expected in 1993, an increase the bureau had to meet with fewer people and financial resources.

Under its old system, a citizen could go to the local post office or a federal building or, in large cities, a regional passport office, to fill out the application. Every application—for first-time applicants, renewals, and emergency requests—ended up in one of the regional offices. Once completed, the work was sent back to the applicant. Renewals typically took six weeks or longer.

The bureau staff saw that too much pressure was being placed on the regional offices and used a triage system to remedy the situation. Today, a citizen wanting to renew a passport can save time by sending a one-page application and current passport directly to a bank in Pittsburgh, which has contracted with the government for the initial data entry. It puts that data on a tape; bar-codes the applications; and sends tapes, applications, and passports overnight to a central passport office in Portsmouth, New Hampshire. There, government employees do the final verification and process the renewals. A computer prints the new passport, which goes back to the applicant.

Typical turnaround time for renewals is now one to two weeks. In addition, pressure has been taken off the thirteen regional offices, which allows them to process the increasing number of first-time applications more quickly. And those who have an emergency can go directly to a federal building and get a passport renewed in a matter of hours. This triage approach—sending renewals to one location, first-time applications to the regional offices, and handling emergencies locally—created greater capacity to handle the 25 percent increase in passport-related work (Gary Sheaffer, personal communication, 1993).

Ensure a Continuous Flow of the Main Sequence: The Shift in Assumptions

Old assumptions: To maintain quality control, slow down the process. All applications must go through the same process (one size fits all).

New assumptions: Speed and user-friendliness are key customer needs that can be met without sacrificing quality (one size fits only a few).

Don't Pave Cowpaths: First Re-engineer, *Then* Automate

This principle (Hammer, 1990) comes last as a reminder that automation is essentially a last, not a first, step. To make major, even radical improvements in work processes, you can't begin with technology. Bringing in new generations of the most advanced technology can be very helpful. It's not usually helpful, however, until the end of the redesign process. First the *work* must be re-engineered, then it can be automated. As Harvard Business School professor Gary W. Loveman put it, "Gains come not because the technology is whiz-bang, but because it supports breakthrough ideas in business process" (Gleckman, 1993, p. 57).

The term *paving cowpaths* comes from Boston and the way its streets developed. Apparently, they really did pave old cowpaths when setting up the first streets in Beantown. Today, the advocates of process re-engineering use *paving cowpaths* to describe our misuses of advanced technology. Like the early streets of Boston, we have laid vast amounts of computerization over outmoded work methods. A cartoon shows a man proudly displaying his modern computer system and saying, "Now that we've automated, we do the wrong thing faster" (Carr and others, 1992, p. 89). The long-heralded office revolution that computers were supposed to bring never occurred. The main reason: we tried to automate inefficient, fragmented work procedures.

There are interesting historical parallels for our misuses of modern technology. As James Martin put it, "The first motorcars were called 'horseless carriages' and were the same shape as a carriage without a horse. Much later it became recognized that a car should have a different shape. Similarly, the first radio was called 'wireless telegraphy' without the realization that broadcasting would bear no resemblance to telegraphy. Today we talk about the 'paperless office' and 'paperless corporation,' but we . . . duplicate the previously existing organization of work" (Carr and others, 1992, pp. 88–89). If work is currently designed in an awkward manner, automating awkwardness is no answer. If anything, it makes matters worse, because investment of resources in the current approach only delays the time that management will be willing to take a new look at it. "The costs are sunk," they will say, "so we'll have to live with it."

An oft-cited example of automating without first changing

basic work practices occurred at General Motors. During the 1980s, the auto giant invested $30 to $40 billion to automate its processes. It failed and often produced mass chaos instead. For instance, at one new plant GM opened in 1985, the company used 260 robots for welding, assembling, and painting cars; fifty automated vehicles that serviced the assembly line; and other high-tech equipment using laser beams to inspect and control the whole process.

The results, as documented by auto industry analyst Mariann Keller (1989, pp. 206–208), "read like a 1950s B movie that might have been titled *Robots from Hell . . .*"

- Robots designed to spray-paint cars were painting each other instead.
- A robot designed to install windshields was found systematically smashing them.
- Factory lines were halted for hours while technicians scrambled to debug the software.
- Robots went haywire and smashed into cars, demolishing both the vehicle and the robot.
- Computer systems sent erroneous instructions, leading to body parts being installed on the wrong cars.

An MIT study of the auto industry documents the results of misusing technology. The least automated Japanese plant, as of 1989, was also the most efficient auto plant in the world. The most automated car plant in the study, a European factory, required 70 percent more effort to perform a set of standard assembly tasks than the most efficient plant (Womack, Jones, and Roos, 1990).

It's true that almost all re-engineering projects make use of the latest technology: local area networks, client/server computing, graphical user interfaces, electronic imaging (EDI), and the like. But technology can only enable, once work is redesigned. American industries spent an incredible $1 trillion in information technology during the 1980s and got nothing more than stagnant productivity out of it (barely a 1 percent rise during the decade, compared to almost 5 percent in Japan). Moreover, the service sector, which received more than $800 billion worth of new technology, showed the worst productivity results of all. Now the enormous investment is finally paying off, not because of the technology, but because of "the sweeping changes in management and organizational structure that are redefining how work gets done. . . . 're-engineering,' a process that questions traditional assumptions and procedures—and then starts over" (Gleckman, 1993, p. 57).

Several of the re-engineering examples noted earlier demonstrate the proper order in which to use technology. The single point of contact approaches used by some city and state social service agencies, Oregon's new RFP process, Connecticut's unemployment agencies, and hospitals like Lakeland Regional didn't lead with technology. Technology was brought in only after assumptions were changed and processes were re-engineered to focus on the outcome.

First Re-Engineer, Then Automate: The Shift in Assumptions

Old assumption: Advanced technology increases productivity.

New assumption: Streamlined work processes increase productivity. Technology amplifies strengths (or weaknesses) in the process.

This chapter has described seven basic re-engineering design principles and one overriding theme: challenge fundamental assumptions. Because the word *re-engineering* sounds technical, people sometimes assume that its principles must be difficult to learn and even harder to apply. Yet, as the examples in this chapter show, the design principles are little more than common sense. It's not common sense that most bureaucracies have taught their employees how to take natural work processes and separate them into multiple steps among various people and departments. Thus, re-engineering requires unlearning as well as learning.

While these design principles may be natural and basically simple, practitioners are wise to reflect on them and discuss their possible applications with colleagues before embarking on radical change. They also need to think through how to apply them in a way that makes sense to staff and customers. The next chapter introduces a model for putting those design principles into action and describes the steps involved in the model's initial phase.

Chapter Five

Setting the Stage for Re-Engineering

Chapter Preview

This chapter offers a model for applying design principles in the re-engineering of a public agency and describes the model's first phase: assessment. We will explore the four conditions necessary for successful re-engineering and certain key roles that must be filled.

A Note to Innovators

In 1986 I began research for a book on public sector innovators who had succeeded in producing major management and organizational changes (Linden, 1990). Some were middle managers, some senior executives, one an elected official. I found that they shared one personality characteristic: they were extremely driven individuals who pursued their vision with tremendous focus and energy—as well as seven strategies. One of those strategies I called "Starting with Concrete Steps." I found that these innovators did a good deal of strategic *thinking* before they took action but very little formal planning. They thought through their goal, decided where their support lay, then began with some concrete steps. Such steps included getting customer feedback, reorganizing, beginning a rotation system, putting potential allies in key positions. They were very action-oriented managers who were not at risk of "paralysis by analysis." They acted, got some feedback, changed course, and acted again. One astute public management theorist, Bob Behn (1988), calls this "management by groping along."

Unlike those innovators, however, managers who successfully re-engineer organizational processes do not jump right in with concrete actions. That's because re-engineering creates profound changes in virtually every aspect of organizational life, changes that must be anticipated and planned for. What begins as a redesign of one specific process spreads to other processes. Soon, employees realize that other changes are needed to support the re-engineered processes: performance appraisal (from individual to team based), budgeting (from function to activity based), the management information approach (from controlling to enabling), and so on. That is, the organization must be realigned to support the new focus. Those interested in re-engineering must therefore spend considerable time up front thinking about what they want, why they want to embark on re-engineering, whether they are willing to actively support it over the long haul, whose support they will need, which processes they will begin with, and how they will articulate the purposes of change. They must understand the necessary conditions for re-engineering and the roles that need to be filled to make the project successful. These conditions and roles are shown graphically in Figure 5.1.

Necessary Conditions for Re-Engineering

As shown in Figure 5.1, determining whether the conditions for re-engineering can be met belongs to the assessment phase and is carried out by senior leadership. The first of the four conditions is beyond the control of the leadership in most cases; the other three require action by senior agency officials.

Real Pain, Present or Anticipated

It has been said that most change is pain driven. Few organizations make major changes just because they haven't changed in a while. Rather, it usually takes a major threat or real loss to prompt people to let go of what they know and enter the unknown. Just as some people disregard their doctor's advice about their unhealthy living habits until their life is threatened by a heart attack or other

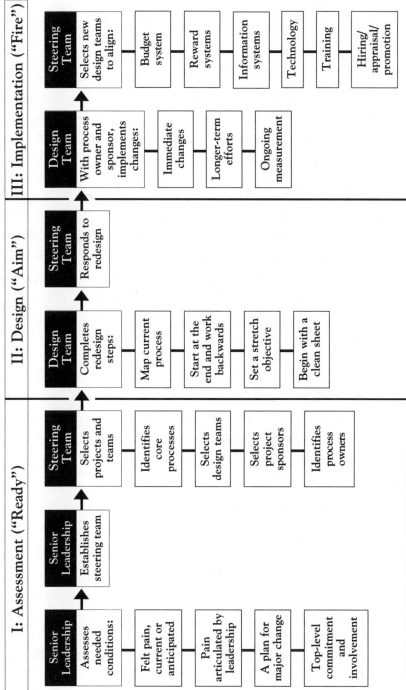

Figure 5.1. A Model for Process Re-Engineering.

serious condition, organizations typically need some threat to over-come inertia.

Ford, Xerox, and Motorola are three well-known examples of successful private firms that underwent transformations in their cul-tures and ways of doing business because they were facing serious pain: lost market share and profits. Examples of pain-induced change have also emerged in government: the IRS, the Federal Emergency Management Agency, and the Naval facilities at Jack-sonville, Florida, and Norfolk, Virginia. Organizations that embark on fundamental change without the spur of any immediate pain—General Electric's radical downsizing (close to 200,000 employees let go since 1981) and restructuring in the early 1980s, Procter & Gamble's 1993 plan to cut its work force by 12 percent and the number of manufacturing plants by 20 percent—are quite rare. Indeed, a study of forty companies by Gibb Dyer, management pro-fessor at Brigham Young University, showed that in every case the company had to experience very rough times before it could change (Dumaine, 1993b).

Because re-engineering is threatening, disruptive, and poten-tially costly at first, it is important for the organization to be expe-riencing real pain. Without such pain or tension between the current and desired state, the staff won't feel the need for radical change and probably won't support it.

Articulation of the Pain or Threat and the Cost of Not Dealing with It

The leaders' job is to make the pain, or threat of it, clear. When the threat is financial, that situation is usually fairly easy to describe. Unless the leadership is totally mistrusted by the employees, losing market share (or a declining budget for a government agency) is a clear statement that business as usual won't work. Other threats come from falling behind in meeting customer preferences, as Wang Labs and IBM did during the 1980s; losing the most talented people, as happened to the U.S. Department of Housing and Urban

Development; losing the support of key constituencies (often because of a loss of credibility), which happened to the Environmental Protection Agency in the early 1980s; or losing a reason for its primary mission, which is affecting most Department of Defense agencies as the communist threat diminishes and the department tries to justify its budget requests.

One caveat: the threat or pain must be real, and it must be perceived by the employees; it cannot be made up (Davenport, 1993). An agency head may be a visionary and anticipate a threat over the horizon—indeed, the best leaders excel at looking past tomorrow to anticipate future challenges—but the threat or pain must be genuine and well articulated if the employees are to believe it and act on it. The former head of a government management development agency tried to get his faculty to be open to major changes by telling them that their customers were no longer pleased with the agency's programs. The director had a point; some of their customers had grown disenchanted. However, the faculty didn't feel that disenchantment because they didn't see it. The director was new and had not yet established his credibility with the faculty. Moreover, the faculty had gotten very little indication of customer discontent—classes were filled, and overall evaluations continued to be high. Had the director taken various faculty members with him to meet their customers (those in agencies who decided how many slots to buy at the management center) so that they could hear customer concerns directly, the director would have had more success in showing the faculty the threat that did exist.

I observed a city manager do an excellent job of perceiving a threat and articulating it to employees. During a workshop on quality services, the participants learned about the use of flowcharting. To illustrate, I asked the group to describe one process that was onerous to external and/or internal (employee) customers. That's when someone came up with the utility billing process described in Chapter Four. By the time the group finished flowcharting the nineteen steps in what should have been a simple and quick process, everyone looked at the chart, astonished. The pain (terrible use of staff resources, wasted time, poor use of automation) was clear.

The manager said, "What do you think our customers would say if they were sitting here watching us describe this process? What do you think would happen if we were a private company, operating like this? Would we even have any customers if we functioned this way?" The way he framed his questions, his own concern with the unwieldy process, the fact that it was clearly unacceptable to everyone, resulted in a clear understanding of the pain, the challenge, and the consequences of not dealing with it.

A Clear Plan for Dealing with the Pain or Threat

This is where re-engineering comes in. Without some approach, model, or theory with which to deal with the threat, employees will flounder. If employees can understand what challenges the organization, how that challenge will hurt them if no change is made, and *what the change will mean to them and their roles*, they will usually respond well to a clear plan for dealing with the challenge. There is a lot of talk among those who lead seminars on "Managing Change" that people resist change. I see a lot of people who resist *being changed*, but most of the time I find people in organizations respond well to change when the problem, its impact, and a potential solution are candidly laid out for them by someone with credibility. Those managers who throw up their hands in despair, muttering about employees who resist change no matter what, should look at themselves and ask whether they have credibility with the staff, before blaming the staff for not heeding the message.

I observed the city manager of a city near Washington, D.C., make a compelling argument for the need to change and the paths to take when he told his senior staff why change was so important and why he wanted to use a combination of quality management and re-engineering to manage the change:

"We have been the victims of our own success, or maybe it's our perceived success, here for quite a while. . . . By 'perceived success' I mean that our customers, the citizens, usually say very good things about us. They even tell us we're running the city well. So we've gotten kind of complacent, we tell ourselves we're running things well, and in general we're right.

"But you know as well as I that we drop the ball a lot, in ways the citizens don't see. What should take a few days takes a few weeks. What should cost a few thousand dollars costs much more than that. Why? Because we don't coordinate well internally. To use the TQM jargon, we don't treat each other as internal customers. We can't afford to maintain these walls between the departments. We won't be able to keep covering up the glitches, and, as our citizens start expecting much faster execution on our part, which we all know is coming, we won't have the luxury of arguing over turf anymore. Exactly how this will play out for each of us isn't clear yet, but I'm committed to getting as much input and involvement from you as possible so that we can design our own solutions to these questions.

"I want you to participate in a seminar that explains two approaches open to us—TQM and process re-engineering—to decide if they give us the tools and models we need to get rid of our walls and become a faster, leaner organization."

At that point, he fielded some questions. Then he and his department heads spent the better part of a day learning about the principles of quality management and process re-engineering. At a follow-up session, the entire group decided to pursue both approaches. They understood the need and threat, they saw consequences of not acting, and they liked the models put before them.

Active Involvement of the Senior Leadership

Of course, you say, *every* innovation requires top-level support. Whether it's TQM, customer service, a move to self-managing teams, or an aggressive plan to compete by reducing cycle times and focusing on speed, virtually every consultant and management book emphasizes the need for support from the top.

Process re-engineering is different in that it requires more than support from the top—it requires active, continuous *involvement* at the top. The organization's leadership needs to understand what re-engineering is all about and must be involved at each step. The reason is simple: unlike TQM and most other innovations, process re-engineering doesn't take the current organization structure as a given. Quite the opposite, process re-engineering demands that we begin with a "clean sheet" (discussed later). Ultimately, a re-engineered organization will have few specialists; it will be organized around processes rather than departments and functions; it will take the power away from the remaining staff specialists; it will force most employees to adopt new roles. The disruption and perceived threat is great. Moreover, some people may feel very threatened because their turf, as they define it, will vanish. Rather than a series of "stovepipe" departments that control segments of work, re-engineering will force staff to let go of their terrain and find ways to coordinate on an entire process (Stewart, 1993). Thus, it can only succeed with actively involved leaders who model the needed changes in their own behavior and push those leading the redesign effort to persist until the changes are complete. As Hall, Rosenthal, and Wade (1993) note, "Without strong leadership from top management, the psychological and political disruptions that accompany such radical change can sabotage the project" (p. 119).

When the leadership shows the present or anticipated pain or threat of the status quo, when it articulates how the pain or threat will hurt the organization if not dealt with, when employees are given a clear plan for dealing with the threat, and when the leadership is actively involved throughout, then re-engineering has excellent chances to succeed.

Re-Engineering Roles

Once the senior leaders have determined that the four conditions for re-engineering are in place, it's time to select the key players and get started. To envision new processes and fight the battles to implement them, the right people need to be involved. Senior people with clout and respect must lead the process throughout; those in the organization who fear they have much to lose will practice the art of wait 'em out and wear 'em down, and only people with real power can counter such resistance. In addition, those who will work in the redesigned processes must be involved in changing them; they know where the problems are, and they must make the new processes work.

In government, it's especially important to get the right people involved, because work outcomes tend to be less quantifiable than in industry. It's one thing to show that a re-engineered process can develop a new car in thirty-nine months rather than sixty, as the Chrysler Corporation has done. It's quite another for a police chief to re-engineer the department toward a community policing orientation, with all of its initial costs and training and disruption, when there are only a few long-term studies documenting its impact on crime. When the work being redesigned is difficult to quantify, the decision to support a proposed innovation is often made on the basis of the innovator's reputation and judgment (Linden, 1990). Thus, the re-engineering leader needs more than power; she or he must have a solid track record and reputation as a successful change agent.

The emphasis on getting senior people involved doesn't mean that the process is totally top-down, only that it requires active top-level involvement—not passive support, but active involvement—at every step. The actual creative work is likely to be done by some of the staff who currently work in the process being re-engineered. As Thomas Stewart (1993) has written, "When the consultants move on and the process map comes down from the wall, the painfully won gains will leak away unless the employees who have to live with the new work design had a hand in creating it" (p. 48).

Following are the four components of the ideal re-engineering group: the steering team, design team, project sponsor, and process owner.

Steering Team

Made up of senior agency staff, this team's job is to coordinate the various re-engineering projects. It identifies core processes and decides which processes should be re-engineered earlier, which later, and which not at all. It ensures that the learning from one project is shared with others. It hears recommendations from the re-engineering design teams and decides whether to approve them. It also looks at infrastructure changes needed to achieve consistency throughout the process. For instance, if some units begin providing one-stop shopping through the use of self-managing teams, a number of issues will be raised that a senior team should decide: What are the new roles of the teams' managers? How do we evaluate and reward team members, and who makes those decisions? What are the performance standards for the teams, and are they individually or team based? These alignment issues, discussed in Chapter Eight, are critical to long-term re-engineering success and require the assistance of a senior steering team.

This team may also assist if there are strong disagreements about agency restructuring. For instance, during the summer of 1993, when it became known that Vice President Gore's National Performance Review would recommend certain agency mergers, such as the Immigration and Naturalization Service with the Customs Service, and the Drug Enforcement Administration and Bureau of Alcohol, Tobacco, and Firearms with the FBI to achieve financial and administrative efficiencies, political jockeying for and against the idea was quick and intense. Only the most senior people in the government can make the tough, important decisions that such struggles require. According to one study of state and federal re-engineering projects, 92 percent of respondents considered senior executive team involvement as very important (Caudle, 1994).

One other point about the steering team. The choice of words—*team*, not *steering committee*—is deliberate. There is a difference between a team and a committee. Committees typically include representatives from different organizational units. An academic committee will have members from different departments or schools; an agency committee on diversity will have members from different racial and ethnic backgrounds, and so forth. Committee members represent certain groups' points of view, and that point of view is often their major commitment. They are there, first, to *represent*. Thus, the committee may come up with a consensus decision, it may come up with several different options, or it may come up with nothing at all. When the primary purpose is to represent differing perspectives, those are all possible outcomes and may be appropriate.

A team, on the other hand, includes people who have but one objective: achieve the stated task. They represent no constituencies except the organization. Just as a football team cannot win if its members associate first of all with the offensive or defensive unit, an organizational team cannot succeed unless its members have only one mission: to make the best decisions for the entire organization. Re-engineering requires steering teams, not committees.

Design Team

The real re-engineering work is done by the design team. It needs to be small—six to ten members maximum—and should have two types of members: those who work within the current process and those who do not. The team's task is to use the four re-engineering steps to create a new process. They map the current process, start at the end by understanding the end user's needs and expectations, and, beginning with a clean sheet and designing the new process as if no constraints existed, try to meet a large "stretch objective." (These concepts are described in detail in Chapter Six.) The stretch objective is given to them by the project sponsor (see the next section).

To save time in working its way down the learning curve, the team needs some members who understand the current process, how it works and why it works that way. These "internal members" also lend a certain credibility when the team recommends change; their support of the re-engineered process will carry weight with others who may have doubts.

The design team needs to spend time with two key groups: end users of the current process (to learn what works well and what doesn't, from their points of view) and other public and private organizations that have innovative approaches worth learning about. These interviews and benchmarking visits are very time-consuming, as is the whole re-engineering effort. All team members must be given time off from their current departments to give this effort its due.

At least half the team should come from outside the current process. They are in the best position to challenge assumptions and ask "obvious" questions: Why does the process work this way? Why is this department involved? What value do these steps add? What is the time delay at each step? As a re-engineering team leader at the Bureau of Land Management noted, "You need a 'junkyard dog'! You need an iconoclast who won't accept the status quo, who forces people to challenge their assumptions" (E. K. James, personal communication, 1994).

Making waves is important, and it's disruptive. To ensure its ability to work together, the team should go through team-building exercises and receive instruction on process re-engineering principles and steps. A critical factor for keeping the team intact is its facilitator. This person may be selected by the project sponsor or the team itself. In an agency's first re-engineering efforts, it makes more sense for the sponsor to select facilitators; as the agency gains experience and it becomes apparent which types of people make good facilitators, teams should be selecting their own.

Project Sponsor

The project sponsor should be a member of the steering team, with specific responsibilities for setting the overall vision and direction of the re-engineering design team (Carr and others, 1992). The sponsor obtains and allocates resources for the design team; re-engineering efforts can take months, and someone has to decide where the people and funding come from to support the effort. The sponsor sets the specific stretch objective that the team must meet. The sponsor also does "downfield blocking," in the sense that some re-engineering efforts need "advance work" to reduce resistance. For instance, if the design team is going to recommend a new process that would radically change the roles of certain middle managers or reduce one department's perceived power, the sponsor can meet with those affected to help prepare them for the change. This takes a rare combination of skills: the sponsor must be both blunt and tactful, sensitive and task oriented, focused on individual needs as well as organizational imperatives. The sponsor's role is difficult and critical.

The sponsor must be fully informed of the design team's progress and direction, for once the design team makes its recommendations, the sponsor becomes its champion on the steering team. The steering team makes the final decision for each design team recommendation, but it will look carefully at the sponsor's input and arguments. That approach requires the sponsor to be informed of other design team projects, so that she or he can show how the team's recommendations are in sync with other re-engineering efforts, as well as with the agency's overall direction.

The sponsor need not be the agency's most expert person in re-engineering. What she or he must have, however, is a senior and respected position, excellent interpersonal skills, a good conceptual mind for agencywide issues, and the dogged persistence needed to get approval, *as well as implementation,* of the proposed re-engineering. The sponsor is well advised to keep in mind a motto attributed to scientist and educator James Conant: "Behold the turtle, he only makes progress when he sticks his neck out."

Process Owner

The process owner will be responsible for implementing the newly redesigned process. It may or may not be clear who this person is at the start of the re-engineering effort. If the design team truly begins with a clean sheet, with no preconceptions about the new process, then there may be several possible process owners. For instance, in a case described in Chapter Six, there were at least three possible process owners when the City of Charlottesville, Virginia, re-engineered its business license process—the three department heads who were then involved in issuing business licenses. In other instances, the new process owner may simply be the person responsible for the existing process. In general, the process owner has some involvement with the current process, understands the deliverable it produces, and is open to a totally new way of producing it.

While the project sponsor has major responsibility for selling the new process, the process owner has major responsibility for seeing that it works. This person's job is more implementation than conceptualization. He or she should be on the design team and actively involved in all re-engineering efforts; the major task, however, is to make the new process effective. Thus, the process owner is, above all, a doer. As such, the process owner needs the following qualities:

- A thorough understanding of how the new process is to work, its expected outcomes, and how it interrelates with other agency processes
- Good relationships with those involved in the new process
- A reputation as a good implementer
- An ability to inspire those in the new process, since there will be glitches, some resistance, and perhaps hostility from other departments who view themselves as losers in the transaction (Hammer and Champy, 1993)
- A great deal of energy

This last attribute, energy, is often overlooked by those who study effective managers and leaders. John Gardner, who has served six presidents and was secretary of health, education, and welfare during the Johnson Administration, understands this need well. Indeed, he puts physical vitality and stamina at the top of his list of leadership attributes in his excellent book, *On Leadership* (1990). Gardner also notes the impact that effective, positive leaders have on others: "the release of human energy and talent" (p. 136). The process owner will have the same impact on those who work within the new process and on those who use it. By simplifying the work, giving the staff a broad job that taps their skills and creative energies, and offering the end user a seamless experience in using the redesigned process, the process owner adds energy as well as value to others.

The following list summarizes the key roles involved in process re-engineering:

Steering Team

- Coordinates various agency re-engineering projects
- Identifies core processes
- Decides which processes should be re-engineered and timing of projects
- Ensures agencywide learning from each project
- Decides which recommendations to accept
- Manages realignment of agency strategy, systems, and structures
- Settles internal disputes created by re-engineering efforts

Design Team

- Does the actual re-engineering work, from mapping the current process to proposing a new one
- Interviews end users of the current process, to gain their perceptions of problems and positives
- Benchmarks other agencies to learn about alternative ways to meet the stretch objective

- Identifies options for meeting end user needs; documents costs and benefits for each option and its preferred option
- Makes recommendations to the steering team
- Supports the newly designed process with other staff

Project Sponsor

- Is a member of the steering team
- Has responsibility for the overall direction of the design team project
- Obtains and allocates resources
- Sets a specific stretch objective for the design team
- Meets with those who are affected by the design team's recommendations, to reduce resistance and prepare them for new roles
- Supports the design team's recommendations to the steering team

Process Owner

- Is responsible for implementing the new process
- Markets the new process to others affected by it
- Helps the new process team work down its learning curve by identifying end users' reactions to the process and acting on the problems re-engineering creates for others

When senior agency leaders are certain that the necessary conditions for re-engineering exist, when the four key roles have been filled, then the agency is ready to begin the actual re-engineering work itself, the design phase. The steps to follow in the design phase are the subject of the next chapter.

Chapter Six

Re-Engineering Step-by-Step

Chapter Preview

This chapter offers a road map for re-engineering public agencies. It describes the four basic steps in the process and concludes with an example from local government to illustrate how these steps can be managed.

The Steps in Re-Engineering Design

When preconditions for re-engineering are satisfied, senior management launches the re-engineering design phase. As shown in Figure 5.1, it does this via a steering team, which selects a design team that re-engineers the process in question. Relationships among these teams, and their composition, along with the process sponsor and process owner were described in Chapter Five. Our discussion here concerns the nitty-gritty work of the design team—the heart of the re-engineering effort. Although I have broken the design work into steps, only the first (map the process as it currently exists) is sequential; the others can take place concurrently.

The steps offered here will provide ample guidance to those embarking on most re-engineering projects:

1. Map the process as it currently exists.
2. Start at the end and work backward.
3. Set a stretch objective.
4. Begin with a clean sheet.

Map the Process as It Currently Exists

There are several benefits to starting with a map of the current ("as-is") process. A good map shows the basic steps involved, most of which no doubt were created when technology was far more primitive than today. The map of the as-is process may locate certain bottlenecks; it will show redundancies; it also shows what is working well. In addition, the act of trying to understand the current process frequently leads to greater understanding of how certain functions and departments interact or should interact. It also can provide a baseline measure of the cycle time, cost, and quality of the current process.

Several methods for mapping processes are available. Perhaps the most frequently used is a flowchart. Many organizations have offered training in quality management tools, and flowcharts are one of the staples in TQM training. Flowcharts can be as simple as a series of boxes (see Figure 6.1) or can map key functions and departments and show when and where each is involved (see Figure 6.2).

A disadvantage of box charts is that they aren't very detailed and oversimplify the process they depict. That simplicity can also be an advantage, of course, if a team is just learning how to understand processes or if the process is relatively straightforward. In addition, box charts can be used to differentiate between the value-adding and non-value-adding steps, as shown in the Freightliner example in Chapter Four (Figure 4.4).

A somewhat more elaborate flowchart uses certain symbols: ovals for the beginning and ending steps in the process; rectangles for action steps; diamonds for decision steps (see Figure 6.3). The staff at the Hartford IRS office found that this flowchart model gave

Figure 6.1. Simple Box Flowchart.

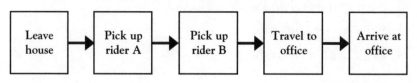

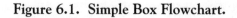

Figure 6.2. Cross-Functional Flowchart.

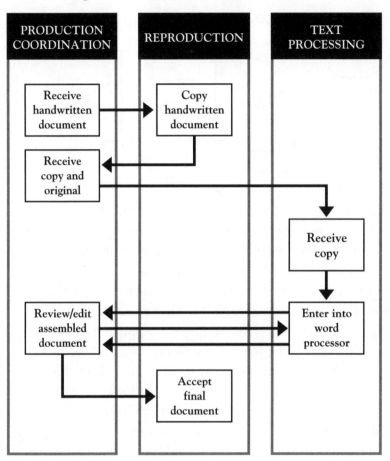

them information to do two types of analysis: understand where the non-value-adding steps were, and identify the time needed for each step in the process.

A creative way to map processes and involve large numbers of employees/customers/vendors is to use a *living flowchart*. In the living flowchart, the entire process is mapped out in one or more rooms. Each step in the process is represented by a table and a flip chart. To understand how the process actually works, where it is user-friendly, and where the delays and bottlenecks occur, employees actually walk through the entire process. At each step they note

Figure 6.3. Flowchart with Symbols.

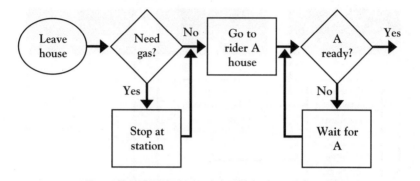

what goes on there, what a customer (external or internal) needs to do, the amount of time it takes, and the output of the process.

Another creative method for mapping out processes uses adhesive-backed, or Post-It, notes. Gather the team in a big room and have them write every step in the process on separate notes. Then place the notes on a large wall so that the entire process is portrayed. Organizations like GE find this approach to be very user-friendly. Putting the whole process on a wall focuses everyone's attention on a common object. It's an enjoyable exercise. Moreover, this approach invites everyone to look for redundancies together and makes it easy to begin streamlining by changing and removing the notes that represent non-value-adding steps.

Finally, some organizations include departments and functions on their flowcharts, in order to understand who has responsibility for each step. Sometimes called *spaghetti charts*, these provide a detailed analysis of the process but are more difficult for staff to understand initially. The Defense Logistics Agency used spaghetti charts to portray its complicated processes (see Chapter Nine, Figures 9.2 and 9.3).

Whether it uses an in-depth, detailed flowchart, a more general map that only indicates the major stages, or a chart that includes organizational functions and departments, a re-engineering team needs to know how the current process works. It needs to be able to document how its proposed change will differ from the current process, what the benefits and costs will be, and how employees will function in the new process. For all these reasons, mapping the current process is the first step in re-engineering.

Start at the End and Work Backward

Like the first re-engineering principle—organize around outcomes—this step comes very naturally to some people. When the stakes are high, starting at the end (with customer needs and expectations) and working backward is usually the method of choice.

The day after Bill Clinton was elected president in November 1992, commentator Mark Shields made an insightful comment on the *MacNeil/Lehrer News Hour*. Shields in effect advised the president-elect to start at the end (of his four-year term). He said Clinton should take out a piece of paper and write down the three things he wants people to associate with him and his presidency when he begins campaigning for reelection in 1996. Then he should take the paper, fold it, put it in his pocket, and keep it for the next three and a half years until he's ready to run again.

Starting at the end and working backward (sometimes referred to as *backward chaining*; AT&T, 1991) seems quite natural, even obvious, to many public officials. It also works very well in the world of sports. After star running back Marcus Allen finished his second year at the University of Southern California, his coach took him aside one day and asked him, "Do you want to win the Heisman Trophy?" Allen replied that of course he did. His coach then sat Allen down, and together they viewed films of his games. By watching himself on film, Allen began to understand what he had to do to reach his goal. The following season he went out and won the Heisman (Bennis and Nanus, 1985).

Retired ITT CEO Harold Geneen looked at business life with the same approach: "A three-sentence course on Business Management: You read a book from the beginning to the end. You run a business the opposite way. You start with the end, and then you do everything you must to reach it" (Davis, 1987, p. 28). Toyota has used this approach for years in setting target prices for its new cars. Unlike the Western, "supplier plus cost" approach to figuring a car's price, at Toyota they start at the end and work backward. Senior executives, working with the design, engineering, and production teams, set a target price for a model being planned. Then they work with the various suppliers and assembly teams to plan backward, figuring out how to make the car at the desired price, while allowing the company and its suppliers to make a profit (K. Nakayama, personal communication, 1993).

The second step in re-engineering, then, is to ask what the end user needs and expects in the service or product to be delivered and work backward to find the leanest, most seamless process for providing that deliverable.

Starting at the end and working backward seems so obvious, why is it not done more often in our organizations?

Most of our organizations simply are not structured to begin at the end. They are structured to begin with one's narrow, fragmented job. Consider Doug Ross's experience after he was appointed commerce director for the state of Michigan. When he wandered around and asked employees what they did, "they invariably described the particular program they were administering. They didn't relate it to an overall goal or organizational objective. . . . they talked about means . . . not ends. It was . . . not an outcome-oriented culture" (Linden, 1990, p. 148). What else could they speak of? They had never been given a larger job, much less any information about how their job connected to the department's overall mission.

Another explanation for why starting at the end isn't the norm for many organizations is that customer needs and expectations aren't always obvious. It sounds fine to say that staff should listen to their customers in order to determine their needs and expectations, then find ways to satisfy them. The problem is that customers (all of us) often don't know exactly what we need in a given situation. For instance, when I told the man who helps me with my computer that I needed a nice graphics program and wanted him to advise me between two I'd read about (each costing about $600), he said he could advise me but wondered why I was about to spend so much money when he could get me a more appropriate one for only $35. In other words, he heard what I wanted but knew enough about my computer use to understand what I really needed. When professionals hear a client or customer say what they want, the appropriate response is to ask questions and get underneath the stated request to find out what basic need the person is trying to meet.

Further, often goods and services are available that consumers don't know exist. As the late W. Edwards Deming liked to point out, no customer asked Edison to create the incandescent light bulb. Nor did anyone ask Edwin Land to come up with the Polaroid Land Camera or Chester Carlson to invent xerography. Who "needed" faxes and beepers before they came out? Now that they're available, most organizations can't imagine functioning without them. So beginning at the end, with the needs and expectations of the consumer or end user, requires discipline. It is an iterative process, in which the staff listen, offer ideas, note reactions, discuss current and future uses of their programs and services, and learn how the world looks to that consumer. In other words, beginning at the end takes a *relationship* with that consumer, one built on mutual trust and confidence.

Finally, some civil servants have difficulty starting at the end with customer needs because they have multiple customers with conflicting needs (such as the Environmental Protection Agency). This problem is addressed in the next chapter, which deals with issues in re-engineering.

Set a Stretch Objective

To understand this step, let's look at two examples, one a missed opportunity to use a stretch objective, the other an appropriate use of stretch objectives.

First, recall the workshop that uncovered the maze of a city's internal utility billing process. This process was a classic, bureaucratic nightmare—nineteen steps, three different departments, outmoded uses of technology, people (literally) writing checks to themselves at one point in the process. The example was dynamite for illustrating the power of flowcharting. Quite often, the very act of mapping the current process can "unfreeze" a group and provide a motivation for change.

After the process was fully charted, I started looking for small, incremental changes. Had this been a workshop on quality management principles, my tactic would have been most appropriate; looking for those incremental steps is at the heart of continuous improvement, one of TQM's basic principles. What I completely failed to realize was the potential for totally re-engineering the process, which requires a giant leap, not small steps. What was required, in fact, was a stretch objective. Fortunately, the city manager attending the session did not miss the opportunity and challenged us to seek major change.

The second example involves a state agency. While planning a retreat for the senior management of this agency, a consultant met with the training and development manager to discuss the retreat's goals (again, starting at the end and working backward). The manager had consulted with the agency head (bringing downstream information upstream) and knew what he was looking for. She and the consultant had fun brainstorming several activities and topics, and then she told him that one decision had already been made.

"We're going to divide the managers into two teams, give each a goal, have them work on their projects before and during the retreat, and end the retreat with their reports. That'll give them something concrete to focus on; otherwise, they'll just treat our information and activities as a bunch of stuff that's beneath them."

The consultant said he liked the concept of giving teams an important project or goal and asked whether she already had some in mind. She did, and she described them both. One team's goal would be to find ways of reducing the time to make purchases within the agency by 25 percent.

He asked, "Why 25 percent?" She said it seemed attainable.

He suggested a stretch objective. "How about a *75 percent* reduction in turnaround time?" She seemed astonished. He explained that it would take something as major as a 75 percent reduction to force the team into truly new thinking. Almost anyone can find 15 percent, 20 percent, even 25 percent worth of waste without too much trouble.

She agreed. The team worked very hard on its goal and amazed everyone by achieving it. And now the nine hundred employees in the state agency are reaping the rewards of their efforts every day.

We have seen stretch objectives work in our national lives. When John Kennedy announced in 1961 the goal of "putting a man on the moon and returning him safely to earth, in this decade," he was setting a stretch objective so large that many in the science and technology community didn't think it could be done. Entire new industries and technologies had to be created, and government would have to work at a pace normally only seen during war. The same dynamic was set in motion when Ronald Reagan announced the Strategic Defense Initiative, an enormous effort designed to create a space shield that would protect our country from incoming missiles. While Reagan's dream wasn't realized, many argue that research on SDI exerted critical pressure on the faltering Soviet bloc and produced important technological benefits, some of which contributed to the U.S.–Coalition victory in the Gulf War.

The use of stretch objectives is increasing in the private sector, for the same reasons we use them in government: demanding a quantum leap in performance forces the organization to change in fundamental ways. It gets people's attention; it jolts them out of their complacency; it challenges accepted wisdom; it makes bureaucratic, fragmented processes totally unacceptable. Most important, it brings organizations closer to their customers and end users.

For instance, when Bell Atlantic learned that its long-distance carriers (Sprint, AT&T, and MCI) weren't satisfied with the time it took Bell to hook up a new customer, it studied its own process and learned about its problem. It was taking from fifteen to thirty days to hook up new residential and business customers to a long-distance carrier. Why? Regis Fritz, the head of Bell Atlantic's carrier access service, described the process: "There were at least thirteen handoffs among different work groups and . . . twenty-seven different information systems. . . . Further study showed that . . . our actual work time was only about ten hours" (Hammer and Champy, pp. 194–195).

Bell Atlantic formed a core team to re-engineer what they realized was a terribly fragmented process. Fritz explained the team's charge: "We gave them a goal. They were to find a way for Bell Atlantic to provide long-distance access services to customers in virtually zero cycle time." Fritz went on to note that only such an ambitious goal would force a genuine change in the existing process, not just a fix (Hammer and Champy, 1993, p. 195). As of 1993, Bell Atlantic had reduced a fifteen-day cycle to a few hours and expected to reduce the interval to a few minutes in some locations before 1995 (Stewart, 1993). Similar stories are reported at Canon, Fuji-Xerox (Takeuchi and Nonaka, 1986), and many other companies.

In *Competing Against Time*, Stalk and Hout (1990) reinforce this point about forcing change in existing processes: "Experience suggests that these [re-engineering] teams must be given radical goals, like collapsing time in half. Otherwise, assumptions aren't challenged" (p. 219). The use of stretch objectives creates a challenge quite similar to the first condition necessary for re-engineering—current or anticipated pain. When an organization experiences real pain, when an organization is confronted with a huge challenge, it creates *tension*, and it is the tension that comes from having to meet demanding goals that forces people to question assumptions and rethink how they do work.

Stretch objectives are important for another reason. They force departments and functions to lower their walls and open up their turf and work together as one unit. The walls and fragmented structure that were created by our mass production bureaucracies could be tolerated as long as the organization felt no particular pain. When a senior agency executive demands that three departments find a way to reduce the time a customer waits for a permit from two days to two *hours*, those three departments suddenly have a real incentive to coordinate. And stretch objectives have a powerful impact on the re-engineering team. As Takeuchi and Nonaka (1986) note, the project team "takes on a self-organizing character as it is driven to a state of 'zero information'—where prior knowledge does not apply" (p. 139).

Examples of stretch objectives include these:

- Reduce response time to citizen requests for income tax status by 90 percent.
- Enable all employees to communicate electronically by the end of the year.
- Attain 99 percent customer satisfaction according to our surveys and phone interviews.
- Issue passports in twenty-four hours.
- Enable all line managers to make purchases under $X directly from any vendor they choose.
- Require job applicants to fill out no more than one piece of paper (internal applicants can apply on-line).

A good example of stretch objectives was stated in the National Performance Review, the Clinton Administration's plan to reinvent government. It states that the U.S. Postal Service will display several standards in post offices, including first-class mail will be delivered anywhere in the United States within three days, local first-class mail will be delivered overnight, and customers will receive service at post office counters within five minutes.

How to Determine Appropriate Stretch Objectives

Setting an arbitrary and inappropriate stretch objective can be harmful for the organization. There are at least three ways to determine appropriate objectives.

Start with Important Customer Needs or Complaints. This point follows from the second re-engineering step: start at the end and work backward. For instance, when Secretary of Labor Robert Reich announced a plan to totally revamp the U.S. government's unemployment insurance system, he noted that one key aspect of the new system would be the one-stop career centers discussed in Chapter Four. Reich was posing a stretch objective that will affect several government departments and services. He obviously understood there would be a constituency for this objective—the eight million or more unemployed people in our country, plus their families. He understood that nobody likes waiting in three or four long lines to obtain basic services. He was starting with a clear customer concern, one that can and should be corrected.

It is important to keep in mind that Reich, like Bell Atlantic, wasn't focusing on the internal structure of the organization. Setting goals of reducing the number of steps in a process, moving to self-managing teams, and reducing the number of management layers may be laudable, but they say nothing about how the end user or customer benefits. It's the end result that is the important focus of a stretch objective. If the U.S. Postal Service follows through on its 1993 pledge of serving all customers within five minutes, it will achieve a stretch objective that virtually all customers care about.

Benchmark. A second way to determine appropriate stretch objectives is to engage in benchmarking—a fast-growing trend in both the public and private sectors. Benchmarking has been defined by former Xerox CEO David Kerns as "the continuous process of measuring product, services, and practices against the toughest competitors, or those companies recognized as industry leaders" (Carr and others, 1992, p. 60). Benchmarking provides a powerful incentive for change in most organizations, creating the pain and challenge needed for re-engineering. When a world-class organization like the National Geographic Society learns that other high-quality organizations can fill customer orders in one to five days, compared to its own one- to two-*month* customer fulfillment cycle time, it realizes it has a major problem, and it has an incentive to change.

We may fairly ask why any organization as well positioned as the National Geographic Society would care that other organizations can deliver products to customers faster than it does. After all, those organizations—companies like L. L. Bean, Motorola, General Electric—are not in direct competition with National Geographic. The answer is that, in a global consumer-driven economy, everyone is being compared with everyone else. When a citizen can contact the IRS using her computer and find out the status of her tax return, she naturally wonders why the city hall forces her to stand in long lines or wait on hold when she calls to find out about her state and local tax status. We're using our "mental report cards" all the time to make comparisons, and we usually don't care that one organization is private and another public. We expect convenience, speed, quality, and customization from everyone. Because consumers make comparisons with the best, leading organizations do too.

When it's clear that customers or end users are dissatisfied with a particular service or product, that's an excellent time to learn what the competition offers. When Chrysler studied the Honda Corporation in the late 1980s, it learned that Honda could design and build a new model in about forty-eight months, which gave it many advantages over car makers that required the more typical sixty months. Chrysler learned how Honda had managed to compress time in its new product development cycle and became competitive with its new LH series, which took thirty-nine months from concept to showroom.

Some organizations look for others in the same industry to benchmark against—as in the Chrysler and Honda example. I prefer the approach used by the civilian personnel office at the Norfolk Naval Shipyard. When the head of the personnel office wanted his staff to stretch their thinking and compare themselves to the very best, he didn't limit them to other defense department personnel shops. He didn't limit them to government agencies, in fact. Rather, he told them to identify the best personnel outfits they could find, visit them, and determine what they could learn from such offices. He thus gave them tremendous freedom of choice in the benchmarking process. The staff came back with wide eyes and several ideas that were implemented (Linden, 1990).

A couple of caveats are in order. First, it's easy to visit several leading organizations and come back fired up with a dozen ideas for improvement, with specific targets for stretch objectives. However, the fact that someone else is faster or better at something than you are doesn't mean that this is the process most in need of re-engineering. Again, the place to start is at the end—with the customer's needs and expectations. (See Chapter Seven for more on selecting processes to re-engineer.)

A county human resources specialist called me some months ago, excited about self-managing teams. She and her boss had visited another county that was making excellent use of such teams. Would I help them learn how to reorganize around the self-managing team concept?

I asked why they would want to go that route. Were customers unhappy with the current service approach? No. Were customers complaining that service delivery was too slow? No. Were customer needs and expectations changing, such that only self-managing work teams could fill their emerging needs? Again, no. So why the change? Embarrassed pause. . . . "We just thought that the approach looked good, and the county that is using it is considered an innovative organization."

That isn't a good enough reason to make a major change. In

fact, it's usually a poor reason, since such a change will not be in alignment with the organization's other major systems and processes. Employees will see it for what it is—a trendy response with no context or clear purpose.

The second caveat in benchmarking has to do with the difference between learning from others and imitating others. Benchmarking, when done well, helps identify the best standards in some area (response time to requests, quality level of products and services, how user-friendly it is to interact with the organization, and the like). When an organization like the National Geographic Society discovers it's way behind the curve in the area of customer fulfillment, it can use the best standards to set its own internal stretch objectives. Then, it needs to build on its own strengths and unique culture to find ways to meet that standard. When Chrysler benchmarked against Honda, the goal wasn't to become an American Honda but rather to learn from Honda, set targets against Honda's performance standards, then use its own core competencies and cultural strengths to meet or beat those standards.

Organizations that benchmark against their leading competitors, then try to become just like those competitors, will lose their identity in the process. I sometimes wonder whether one reason for the incredibly high divorce rate in the United States is that a lot of spouses, unhappy with their marriage, look around and "benchmark" against the most attractive potential mates they know. That doesn't lead to learning; it usually leads to losing. In a totally different context, Harry Truman once noted the dangers of imitating your competition. Unhappy that many Democrats were behaving like Republicans in their election campaigns, Truman remarked, "When the American people are given the choice between a Republican and a 'Republican,' they'll choose the Republican every time!"

Learn from Your Own Best Performance. This might be called "internal benchmarking." To set an appropriate stretch objective concerning, say, the time it should take to screen, interview, and hire for a new position, ask yourself, "What is the fastest we've done this? When, how did it happen?" The fact that, when faced with pressure to move very quickly, your agency was able to cut through the forms and sign-offs and red tape and complete the entire cycle in ten days indicates that ten days is a doable target.

"But that can't be," some will protest. "We could only complete this hiring cycle in ten days because it was an emergency. We had to move heaven and earth to get it done that fast. We can't go through that every time."

No, of course, you can't. And yes, of course, you can. You cannot go through the same pressure-packed, exhausting process each time you hire someone, but you certainly can re-engineer the process so that ten days becomes standard. The fact that it was painful and difficult only indicates that you aren't currently organized to move quickly, which proves the point. If you can screen, interview, make a hiring decision, offer the position, go through some negotiation, get a response, and complete all of the documentation in ten working days, using a rigid, hierarchical system, you certainly can move that fast on a routine basis using a re-engineered, streamlined system. Using the organization's exceptional response as a stretch objective isn't unrealistic—it's very realistic. It says, let's set our standard by the best we've ever done, then re-engineer the process so that our best doesn't require a herculean effort and tremendous political pressure.

When Vice President Gore visited the Interior Department on May 17, 1993, he was told that a department employee named Edythe Ferguson had saved the department $331 during an out-of-town trip on agency business. Her agency was part of a frequent fliers club, and she was able to save the agency money by volunteering to extend her out-of-town stay one day over a Saturday night. However, when Ferguson filed for her per diem allowance of $38 to cover the extra day, her claim was rejected. Some bureaucrat was acting on some regulation (rather than on the basis of the end user's need and basic common sense), and since Ferguson had not originally been approved for travel past Friday, she saved the government money but lost $38 in the process (Barr, 1993a).

The vice president turned to Interior Secretary Bruce Babbitt and asked him to look into it. Since the episode came up at a town hall meeting for hundreds of department employees, since it received prominent press coverage, and since it came up during the vice president's active involvement in the 1993 National Performance Review, it's highly likely that Ferguson got her $38 back, fast. At any rate, let's assume that Ferguson did, indeed, get her money back, within three days. Isn't it a reasonable stretch objective that anyone who loses money in the process of saving the government more money should receive his or her money back that fast? Certainly, huge government bureaucracies that are passing out on-the-spot awards of $50 (and many are) can find a seamless way to reimburse those who are efficient, without the intervention of the country's vice president.

Stretch objectives are essential to re-engineering. A study of a hundred re-engineering efforts found that setting an "aggressive performance target" was consistently associated with successful efforts (Hall, Rosenthal, and Wade, 1993).

Begin with a Clean Sheet

About ten years ago, two foresters returned from a hard day in the field to make plans for the coming week. They found themselves overwhelmed by voluminous editions of policy manuals, reports, and binders filled with thousands of directives. One of the foresters recalled the very first Forest Service manual—small enough to fit into every ranger's shirt pocket, yet containing everything foresters needed to know to do their jobs.

"Why is it that when we have a problem," the other forester asked, "the solution is always to add something—a report, a system, a policy—but never take something away?"

The first replied, "What if . . . we could just start over?" (U.S. Department of Agriculture, 1987, p. 1).

This step—beginning with a "clean sheet," inaugurating re-engineering with no givens, no assumptions about what should be kept from the current process—is somewhat controversial. Some re-engineering enthusiasts insist that it's the only way to go; radical change requires cleaning the slate and beginning anew (Davenport, 1993). Indeed, Hammer and Champy (1993) write that their quick definition of business re-engineering is "starting over." They argue forcefully that our assumptions about what takes time and what can't be done are so deeply imbedded in our organizations and us that we must take the radical steps of using a clean sheet approach. Carr and coauthors (1992) argue just as strongly that redesign can only take place after careful analysis of customer preferences and strategic options. Start from strategy, they state, not from scratch.

The point in favor of starting from strategy, not from scratch, is an important one and cannot be dismissed. If the overall strategy, direction, and culture of the organization aren't considered by the re-engineering design team, the result can be a hodgepodge of processes and innovations that don't begin to fit together. In fact, Chapter Eight is devoted entirely to this question of how to get an organization in alignment, once it has begun the re-engineering process.

There is also much to be said for forcing people to rethink the basic assumptions of how they run their operations by starting with a clean sheet. We all "know" that certain processes (procurement, hiring, new product and program development) take time, a lot of time. Any government veteran has seen his or her colleagues shrug when a piece of new equipment goes down after one week and mutter, "Must have been bought from the lowest bidder." And, in the organizational cliché that makes me angriest of all, both civil servants and private contractors doing work with the government are all too willing to chuckle after some imperfection is found and say, "Close enough for government work." (I was told by a manager at the EPA that the phrase "close enough for government work" originated with government contractors who were making uniforms for the military 150 years ago. Because government standards for uniforms were so *high* at that time, saying that something was "close enough" meant that it was genuinely first-rate quality. How far we've come!) It's all too easy to let the "can't do" types in the office beat down our optimism and desire for change. Starting with a clean sheet challenges assumptions about how work is done and how it might be changed.

I believe the argument between start from scratch (clean sheet) and start from strategy is an interesting but false debate. The two statements are compatible. Re-engineering loses its power if it doesn't require staff to begin with a clean sheet. Starting with a clean sheet forces the staff to challenge fundamental assumptions. It allows them to focus on the deliverable, the end user needs, rather than on current procedures and regulations. And it liberates them to push for truly radical change. Without a clean sheet, it's too easy to begin making trade-offs and compromises before any creative thinking takes place.

At the same time, one of the necessary conditions for re-engineering is the presence of a clear plan to deal with the organization's pain or problems. That plan must be based on an explicit or implicit strategy. It may be as simple as "Become a customer-driven agency," or "Empower the staff to use their creativity in solving problems and improving performance," or "Leverage other community resources by forming partnerships with them." Such general strategies don't tie the hands of the staff, they provide general guidance. They make the second re-engineering step—start at the end and work backward—more meaningful, because that "end" is now placed in a context. Thus, beginning with a clean sheet and beginning with strategy address two different but related questions. The clean sheet approach helps staff deal with the question of *how*: how do we redesign this process? The begin-with-strategy approach informs staff on the question of *what*: what is the overall goal?

Let's return to an example cited earlier in this chapter, the state agency management team that was planning a retreat. After the consultant convinced the training and development manager to "raise the ante" and give one of the teams the goal of decreasing purchasing turnaround time by 75 percent, the consultant sat in on that team's deliberations. The team was given no constraints to work within—they had a true clean sheet, with the exception of the state's procurement law, much of which covered large purchases. Here is a sample of the dialogue:

Member A: What if we just give all line managers the ability to purchase everything under $500, with no higher clearance needed?

Member B: We can't do that; you know all managers have to comply with certain regulations governing phone bids, written bids, diversity in terms of small vendors, and so on.

Member C: Right, that's true *now*, but whose regs are those?

Member B: Well, those are ours.

Member C: They're ours; we wrote them, so we can change them, right?

Member B: No, I don't think so, because they were written to keep us in line with the state law on procurement.

Member A: Let's check that law and see what it actually requires on purchases below $500....

(A check reveals very few requirements in the law.)

Member C: So like I said, we wrote those regs, we can change them. We *were* given the task of streamlining this process, right? So let's not assume that we have to do anything more than what's written into the law. I'll accept that we can't get the legislature to change the state code, at least not during our two-day retreat! Beyond the law, let's get rid of any assumptions, any regs, and just create a process that cuts turnaround by 75 percent. Let the rest of the senior managers tell us we've gone too far.

That argument won the day. The group agreed to decentralize purchasing decisions under $500 (the majority of purchases made in the department), give each manager and supervisor training in the state law, provide them with information on approved vendors, and offer backup consultation on complex purchasing decisions. This approach worked, and it reduced turnaround by more than their 75 percent target.

But note how hard it was to help every member let go of the status quo. No doubt, member B was thinking that those department regulations were written for a reason and that it was unwise to toss out the regs without understanding the reasoning behind them. That's a sensible argument. My own experience with such teams is that one or a few people can do some research on the current regulations and guidelines governing the existing process, while the rest move on and look for creative, streamlined approaches. Becoming concerned with history can lead to the "rear-view mirror" approach that prevents innovation. It's also important to note that this state agency had been discussing customer needs and expectations for over two years. Middle and senior managers had held lengthy debates trying to identify their customers, both external and internal, and the deliverables that those customers expected. While there was no explicit strategic plan on the books, the director had articulated an overall vision of becoming customer driven. Without ever mentioning that vision during the team exercise, it was clearly an influence on the discussions. Back to the argument that re-engineering must start from strategy, not from scratch: Did this team start from scratch? Clearly. From strategy? Implicitly.

One last note on beginning with a clean sheet. James Fallows, in his book *More Like Us* (1989), makes an insightful observation when he discusses the great American desire for starting over. He shows what an important part of our history and national psyche it is to start over: immigrants who fled from religious and political persecution have come here by the tens of millions to start over. Those who didn't like the crowded eastern cities started over by heading west. We've celebrated our land as a place where upward mobility is valued highly, where anyone can become president, anyone can start a new business, and (slowly but steadily) anyone can live, go to school, be paid equally for equal work, and eat and sleep anywhere, regardless of race or gender. This openness and constant yearning to start over is captured from time to time by our national leaders: FDR's New Deal, JFK's New Frontier. It gets captured in many popular books: *Reinventing the Corporation* (Naisbitt and Aburdene, 1985), *Reinventing Government* (Osborne and Gaebler, 1992), *Reinventing Home* (Abraham and others, 1991), and the like.

This belief in the ability to start over is a national myth (in the sense that a myth is the way we want to see ourselves), one that Fallows believes is very important to our success in competing internationally. I believe re-engineering efforts that begin with a clean sheet are myths in the same sense. Of course, certain laws will not change, and we must take those into account. Of course, we aren't going to fire half the work force, at least not in government. Of course, some changes will be phased in over time. But if we begin with the *presumption* that we have a clean sheet, if we act *as if* we can take any approach that meets the goal and accept current laws and givens as exceptions to be grudgingly admitted one at a time, then our chances of real breakthrough thinking and radical change are much greater. That's the whole point of starting at the end and working backward. Look for the leanest, most seamless and natural way to meet an end user's need, draw it up, and only then deal with constraints. That's the essence of re-engineering. (For more on the problems of beginning with a clean sheet in government, see Chapter Seven).

Case Example: Obtaining Business Licenses

To understand how the conditions and steps for re-engineering all come together, let's look at one simple and highly successful example.

In 1993, three department heads in Charlottesville, Virginia, city government gathered to discuss a need they had often talked about in the past: the process for obtaining business licenses. The process was time-consuming, a real "bureaucratic triathlon." Citizens wanting to open a business had to have a license. In Charlottesville, that required customers to go through three different departments, up and down several flights of stairs, and often return home for information they didn't know they needed.

The Old Process

Applicants stopped first at the commissioner of revenue's office, where they filled out a form (with three carbon copies). Then it was up two flights of stairs to Building and Life Safety, to see whether their business was approved for the building to be used and to check for handicapped access and a certificate of occupancy. Then, two floors down to the Department of Community Development, where staff asked about use of a sign; if one was needed, that was another application and payment. They also determined whether the building was in the city's historic district (which might require a review by the Board of Architectural Review); checked the zoning; decided whether the required number of parking spaces were provided; and noted whether a house was being used for the business. Applicants wanting to use a house had to fill out an affidavit with the homeowner's signature, which required a trip to the owner if different from the applicant.

Finally (!), the applicant took all of the forms and licenses back to the commissioner of the revenue's office, where all signatures were checked. When everything was in order, the applicant paid a fee and received the business license. Because three different departments were involved, because they were scattered around City Hall, and because only one or two people were authorized to sign the licenses and application forms needed in two of those departments, the process took two days, on the average—if everything went smoothly.

The Premeeting Meetings

The department head who took the lead knew there might be resistance, and he wisely decided to smoke it out before the re-engineering meeting took place. Knowing that a key staffer in one department worried about technological problems if they tried to automate the system, he upgraded her computer and got her the tools she said she needed, so that she was more open to listening. For a fellow department head who said she was ready for a major change but was unsure about doing it when the city was downsizing, he explained that streamlining the tedious process would help everyone maintain current operations with fewer people. When staff at a third department expressed concerns about the one-stop shopping approach and whether any one department could learn all the steps in the process, the department head felt they were really saying that they were indispensable and wanted to hold on to their turf. He listened and suggested that perhaps these staff could play a major role in teaching others what they'd learned to do so well. Finally, the information systems department was consulted; a one-stop approach would require automating certain functions, and the computer experts were asked what was possible in the short and long run. Once all the bases were touched, the lead department head invited his colleagues and several of their staff to meet and discuss the possibility of streamlining the process.

The Re-Engineering Meeting

The three department heads had discussed this tedious mess several times in the past, but nobody had gotten hold of it to change it. This time was different. The group already understood the current process but quickly reviewed it to be sure everyone understood the problem. They had no trouble identifying the customer's need and expectation: the person applying for a business license wants just that, a license, as quickly and cheaply as possible. The creative challenge was to figure out a way to meet this need and still give the city the information and accountability it needed. One thing was clear to the group: it didn't take three departments to gather and process the information for each applicant. In fact, it was as poor a use of each department's time as it was for the applicant.

The group quickly agreed that the process needed to be simpler, which led to the idea of naming one department that would handle all aspects of the application. Working backward, that required a consolidation of the various application forms into one and a good deal of training for the lead department's staff, who would now become generalists and deal with the entire application process, start to finish. That, in turn, put the other two departments' staff in the roles of trainers, consultants, and resources when the lead department got questions that their staff could not answer. By beginning at the end (a simple, quick, one-stop process for applicants needing business licenses) and working backward, the pieces fell into place. The group also discussed ways of using technology to get rid of the multiple forms and speed up response time, and they identified the information that applicants needed when they first walked into the lead department's office (or, better, would be given on the phone when they called to learn where to apply). Thus, downstream information would be brought upstream.

After the meeting, the department head who had organized it found one more area of resistance—within his own staff. The person who had been the point man for business licenses in his department was having trouble letting go. Even though he frequently complained about being overworked, he didn't want to give his part of the process to another department. The department head handled that by giving his staffer an important task—he had to teach those in the commissioner of revenue's office how to do the job he'd been doing. The department head pointed out that the new design would only work if he played the important role of teacher and consultant. He also made it clear that the change *was* going to happen. This combination of appealing to ego and pointing out the realities worked.

The New Process

After more detailed discussions and separate meetings within their own departments, the department heads agreed on the newly designed process. Within three months they were able to provide the one-stop shopping they had been seeking.

Now, applicants go to the commissioner of revenue's office, where an employee helps the applicant fill out a simple one-page form. The employee calls the other two offices to verify zoning, sign usage, parking, handicapped accessibility, and so on, while the applicant is there. There is no waiting because several staff in this office have been cross-trained; there are no surprises, because the employee tells the applicant everything he or she will need to complete the process, up front; there are no carbons to carry around. Once the other two departments have verified the applicant's eligibility by phone, they send their verification to the commissioner of revenue's office by E-mail.

Result: What used to take up to two days or more now takes less than half an hour. The applicant has a simple, quick system, and the staff saves considerable time (only one person fills out a one-page form). And there is only one employee to deal with, so the applicant's needs are understood and dealt with in a streamlined, seamless way. Figure 6.4 illustrates the contrast between the two systems.

I like this example because it reflects most of the necessary conditions, steps, and principles involved in re-engineering an organizational process. All four of the conditions were present, to a greater or lesser degree. The "pain" caused by the current process came from two sources: customers didn't like it, nor did the staff who had to implement it. One department head, known as a strong manager and innovator, got especially interested in changing the process, and he voiced this interest to his colleagues. He had a general approach in mind (one-stop shopping), although he didn't know exactly how that would work. He maintained an active and visible involvement throughout.

Figure 6.4. Old and New Systems for Business License Applications in the Charlottesville City Government.

The Old System

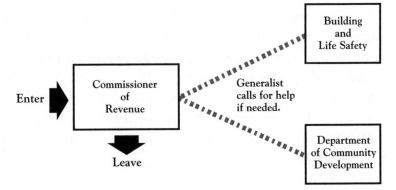

	Building and Life Safety	Handicapped Accessibility	Certificate of Occupancy
Commissioner of Revenue			
			Department of Community Development
			Sign Application
Zoning Application	Parking Spaces Application	House-as-Business Application	Board of Architectural Review

Start → ← Finish

Time to obtain license: 2 days.

The New System

Enter → Commissioner of Revenue → Leave

Building and Life Safety

Generalist calls for help if needed.

Department of Community Development

Time to obtain license: 15 to 30 minutes.

The team followed the re-engineering steps noted here. They discussed the current process, and they understood the customers' needs and began with those as their overall goal. They didn't set an explicit stretch objective (such as, "Reduce average time to obtain business licenses from two days to x minutes"), but they had an implicit objective of forcing a major simplification of the existing process. And they were quite willing to start with a clean sheet.

Finally, the team used several re-engineering principles. They organized around outcomes, focusing on the customer's need to get a business license, easily. They brought downstream information upstream, by telling the customers everything that they would need at the front end. They captured information once, at the source, when they collapsed several forms into one. They maintained a continuous flow of the main sequence by giving applicants a single point of contact (one-stop shopping at the commissioner of revenue's office), eliminating several non-value-adding steps (such as going from office to office), and cross-training several staff to eliminate waiting in that office. They substituted parallel for sequential steps—two departments now verify applicant eligibility by phone, then send official verification via E-mail, *after* the applicant leaves the commissioner of revenue's office. And they avoided "paving cowpaths." Rather than automate the outmoded process, they brought in advanced technology to speed up the streamlined one.

In this chapter, a four-step process for re-engineering agency processes has been described, as well as a case example. The re-engineering of business licenses is notable for its relative simplicity. Indeed, simplicity is an important characteristic of seamless organizations. *Simple*, however, should not be confused with *simplistic* or *easy*. Re-engineering is rarely easy, and it raises important issues, especially when attempted in the public sector. We turn to those issues next.

Chapter Seven

Overcoming Public Sector Constraints

Chapter Preview

In the previous chapter, we walked through four basic re-engineering design steps. Civil servants who have used this re-engineering model tell me that it makes sense, that they like it for its simplicity and clarity. They also have raised certain practical questions and issues as they worked with the model. In this chapter, we will look at three issues frequently raised by government practitioners: Can you really begin with a clean sheet in government, where funding bodies, oversight commissions, and staff agencies micromanage you to death? How can you begin at the end with the "customer's" needs, given that government agencies have multiple customers and stakeholders who frequently have divergent and even opposing needs and expectations? And which processes should be re-engineered first?

How Do You Begin with a Clean Sheet in Government?

This is one of the biggest challenges to process re-engineering in the public sector. Many government innovations have been stopped, or severely limited, by oversight and regulatory bodies that focused more on the slight chance that some abuse might occur than on the much greater probability of positive results. Too many instances of fraud, too many well-publicized $600 toilet seats have led to oversight and regulations that have public support.

To take just one example: The U.S. Forest Service experimented with a "lump sum" budget as part of its pilot study in the 1980s. Forest Service managers in the pilot units were given their

budgets in one lump sum—no budget codes or line items attached—
so that they could get out of the bean-counter mode and spend
their time looking for the most productive ways to spend their
funds. The experiment worked well; pilot managers spent far less
time documenting where they *might* need money and had much
greater flexibility to spend their funds where they were actually
needed. The General Accounting Office (GAO) studied the Forest
Service's use of the lump sum approach and supported it, but when
the GAO presented its findings to a committee of Congress, the
reaction was far from enthusiastic. The lump sum approach ran
directly against the way most members of Congress see their role;
they believe people want Congress, not civil servants, to exercise
strict oversight of how and where federal money is spent. The Forest Service soon dropped the lump sum approach, realizing that
there was no possibility of expanding it to other units. How can we
expect civil servants to think creatively and without restrictive
assumptions, which is the whole point of the clean sheet approach,
when the regulations and regulators simply do not go away?

This fact—the overregulation of government by government—
is perhaps the greatest barrier to effective process re-engineering in
the public sector. Is there any way government agencies can get
beyond the grasp of regulators and micromanagers to truly begin
re-engineering with a clean sheet?

The long-term answer to this dilemma requires educating the
public about the *costs* of overregulating the public's business.
Unfortunately, it is far easier to get the public's attention when the
government screws up in the other direction. Any public official
can gain the media spotlight by doing so, as former Senator
William Proxmire did with his Golden Fleece Awards. Such allegations get quick press and are good "photo opportunities"; unfortunately, they also lead to more layers of control and oversight. Less
attractive to the media, but more important, are the ongoing and
unseen costs of requiring fourteen people to sign off on the pur-

chase of a $100 item, for example, or nine people to agree to a hiring decision. It will take an ongoing educational campaign to reverse this trend. High-level government officials and those who once served in government, such as the eight hundred members of the nonpartisan Council on Excellence in Government, will have to educate the nation about the cost-benefit ratio of such rules and regulations.

In the short run, here are some steps would-be re-engineers can take to reduce the number of rules and regulations cluttering their otherwise clean sheet.

Sell the Benefits of Starting with a Clean Sheet

You must show the key constituencies who can block or help you the advantages of starting with a clean sheet. That was one reason for the success Connecticut's Department of Labor enjoyed, when it transformed its culture (see Chapter Nine). Senior department officials spent time with key members of the legislature, labor leaders, all members of the department, and senior people in some other state departments. The process was exhaustive and exhausting but created a constituency for change. The Hartford IRS office used a similar inclusive strategy.

Find Someone in a Powerful Position Who Will Champion the Change

This person should be able to point out the outrageous nature of current rules and the real costs they impose on end users. Vice President Gore did an excellent job of playing such a role during the six months of the Clinton administration's National Performance Review in 1993. The National Performance Review was the eleventh major effort to reform the federal bureaucracy since Teddy Roosevelt's presidency. It outlined four major goals: (1) cut red tape,

(2) make government customer oriented, (3) empower federal workers to improve productivity, and (4) eliminate obsolete programs
and update government technology. It sets the ambitious goal of cutting federal employment by 252,000 jobs over five years and saving
$108 billion during that period.

Virtually every week, Gore gave well-publicized speeches or
held meetings with various agencies, pointing out absurdities in our
present system. He hammered away at some of the biggest barriers
to reform and did so in clear, simple examples that were reminis-
cent of the great communicator, Ronald Reagan: the need to junk
the 1,600 pages in the Federal Acquisition Regulations (with the
2,900 pages of agency supplements that accompany it); the fact that,
in 1991, the Navy's Human Resources Office processed enough
forms "to create a monument 3,100 feet tall, six times the height
of the Washington Monument" (Gore, 1993, p. 21).

One of Gore's most persuasive examples came during a talk he
gave to the National Governors' Association. Gore held up an ashtray to the group and recited the General Service Administration's
federal specifications governing ashtrays:

- They run 9 pages, with two pages of drawings.
- For Type I, square, $4^1/2"$ glass ashtrays, GSA lists five
  optional design requirements and concludes that "a
  minimum of four cigarette rests, spaced equidistant around
  the periphery and aimed at the center of the receiver, shall
  be molded into the top. The cigarette rests shall be sloped
  toward the center of the ash receiver. . . . All surfaces shall
  be smooth."
- The rules cite exact dimensions for the cigarette rests:
  minimum length, $^7/8$ inch (22.3 mm).
- GSA even regulates the tests for potential ashtray defects.
  Paragraph 4.5.2 states that the ashtray should be struck with
  a hammer "in successive blows of increasing severity until
  breakage occurs. The specimen should break into a small

number of irregular shaped pieces not greater in number than 35, and it must not dice. Any piece, $1/4$ inch (6.4 mm) or more on any three of its adjacent edges (excluding the thickness dimension) shall be included in the number counted. Smaller fragments shall not be counted (see 3.4.1)." For metal ashtrays, the specs require a shock test, in which the ashtray is dropped three times from a height of 30" (762 mm) to a concrete floor [Barr, 1993b, p. A18].

As humorist Dave Barry would say, Gore's not making this up!

Gore's stories, of course, emphasized the surrealistic world our regulations create. Seemingly bright adults are reduced to green-eyeshade types, conjuring up images of school principals in the 1960s using rulers to measure the height of girls' miniskirts, ensuring that they followed the dress codes. What on earth, Gore is asking, does any of this have to do with effectively delivering government services? Nobody has to answer. The point is obvious.

These absurd rules have been denounced for decades, of course. But when someone with the first name "Vice President" points them out, does so continuously (and visibly) for months in order to educate people about the real nature of the problem, and concludes with a detailed plan for eliminating the outdated rules (as well as layers of bureaucracy), then a constituency for change is created. The pain of the status quo is clear.

Remember That Many Onerous Regulations Were Created to Prevent Problems and Abuses

Before a solid constituency for change can be maintained, re-engineers must learn why the regulations were first instituted. As described in Chapter Two, the major reason for the growth of bureaucratic controls in government was to prevent mistakes, fraud, and abuse. If the purchasing process is being re-engineered and the current procurement law requires mountains of paperwork and tedious bid procedures, then the proposed change must address the ever-present danger of fraud and abuse. The present regulations may be absurd, but they won't be eliminated out of hand. They will only be *replaced* by other controls, and that is where process re-engineers have an opportunity.

In the low-tech ages of the Reform Era and the 1940s and 1950s, when many government regulations and oversight bodies were created, bureaucracy was the control mechanism of choice; no alternative to preventing abuse and fraud was apparent. Today, advanced technology and an increasingly well-educated work force offer good alternatives. Modern information systems can check and transfer information in nanoseconds. There is no need for managers to check other managers, when well-trained and accountable employees are perfectly capable of checking their own work.

Employees' minds and advanced technology can substitute for bureaucratic controls. Another useful replacement is a unit's reputation and demonstrated competence. Many civil servants have been begging for the power to determine the appropriate job classifications of their employees. Typically, this function is performed by a central personnel shop. When personnel does classification studies and controls the outcomes, it often leads to bickering, appeals, charges of empire building, and turf guarding. Personnelists reply, with some justification, that line managers are not equipped or trained to do classification, that they would have a conflict of interest in doing so, and that they sometimes refuse the responsibility that would come with their desired authority.

Line managers can put the lie to these understandable concerns by getting training, accepting responsibility for their actions, and taking on the classification function. Better yet, they can enlist personnelists in the cause of replacing outmoded, narrow pay grade schedules with a few, broad pay bands, as is being done successfully in an Office of Personnel Management (OPM) demonstration project (informally called the China Lake Experiment) and by the City of Hampton, Virginia, with its self-managing teams (see Chapter Eight). At the Naval Weapons Center, China Lake, California, and the Naval Ocean Systems Center in San Diego, the demonstration project allows line managers greater authority over assigning, promoting, and rewarding subordinates. There are five broad career paths and four, five, or six broad pay bands, depending on the path. Managers and line staff have been enthusiastic about the new approach, and an OPM evaluation of the demo sites and two similar labs on the East Coast found many positive outcomes in the experiment.

Finally, professional associations and employee unions can help find substitutes for stifling regulations. Many professional associations provide training and set standards for their members' performance. If a member of the International City/County Management Association (ICMA) violates the association's code of ethics, for instance, the person could face public censure and loss of membership, both of which harm one's career. And many public unions are willing to work with agency leaders to streamline processes, as the National Performance Review has demonstrated. The key: involve union leaders early in the process.

Begin As If You Had a Clean Sheet

Irrespective of the agency's success in warding off oversight bodies and pointing out the absurdity of current regulations, those on the design team should act "as if" they had a clean sheet. More than anything, re-engineering is about challenging fundamental assumptions. Design team members will find it almost impossible to challenge assumptions if they begin the re-engineering process with a list of constraints. Breakthrough thinking is what's required, and that occurs "outside the box" of limitations we so willingly put ourselves in.

Beginning the redesign process as if the team had a clean sheet may sound impractical, but it needn't be. The point is to unleash as much creativity as possible and allow seemingly outlandish ideas to flourish. Many groups find that it takes time and some truly bizarre ideas to create the kind of climate in which innovative ideas come out. If the design team can brainstorm in the most freewheeling and playful way possible, it will find breakthrough ideas lurking within apparently ludicrous ones.

Once the design team has challenged the assumptions under-lying the current process and explored a variety of new approaches, then it is time to allow unforgiving constraints back into the room. Even as the team does this, it should check out how rigid each con-straint is. "Where is this written in the law?" is a good initial ques-tion. Other questions include "Where did that regulation originate? Did this agency create it, or was it imposed by an oversight body?" During its pilot study, the Forest Service found that more than 50 percent of the rules and regulations limiting its action were *inter-nally created*. In order to stay on the safe side of the OMB, GSA, and other agencies, Forest Service staff had regulated themselves far beyond what was required.

Beginning with a clean sheet is not as easy in the fishbowl of public life as it is in the private sector. However, many civil ser-vants are finding that some of the biggest barriers to our creativity lie within our own minds and actions. Redesign as if you had a clean sheet and then, but only then, allow external constraints back into the room, grudgingly.

How Can Government Staff "Begin at the End" with Customer Needs?

When agencies have multiple customers and stakeholders with fre-quently divergent and even opposing needs, beginning with cus-tomer needs and expectations as the first step may appear a daunting task. Many civil servants tend to discount management innovations: "But we're different, we are not like business, we have different missions, no bottom line, a micromanaging funding body . . ." and so on. While there is truth in such statements, I generally see more similarities than differences between the public and pri-vate sectors when it comes to management. It is simply too easy to hide behind the statement "But we're different"—it removes the responsibility to learn and change.

When it comes to customers, however, there is an important difference. The simplistic notions of "Meet the customers' needs" and "The customer is always right" aren't helpful in government. Consider: if you make cars, the task is clear. You segment the market, determine the desires and needs of each segment, and produce different products for each. That job is not always easy, but it's relatively straightforward. To say "Meet customer needs" in such a business makes all the sense in the world.

If you are the principal for a public school, on the other hand, are the students customers? If so, are they "right" when ninth graders say they want less math and more recess? If you run a group home for the retarded funded by a local government, who are the customers? The residents? The residents' families? The agencies that referred the residents? Or are they the local, state, and/or federal agencies that fund the program? Perhaps it is those who live in the neighborhood surrounding the group home. Each has a claim to being a "customer," and each would have different, and at times conflicting, needs and expectations. Unlike the automaker who can produce a different model for each customer segment, the group home is expected to somehow satisfy all of its differing "customers" with just one product. When civil servants complain that "meeting customer needs" doesn't necessarily fit their reality, I am most sympathetic. Furthermore, as James Swiss (1992) has written, "government organizations have obligations to more than their immediate clients. Sometimes the agency's most important customers—the general public—are not only absent but totally inattentive" to the agency's actions. Yet the general public, what Swiss terms a "hidden customer" of government, has important (and often contradictory) needs and demands that must be acknowledged by all agencies (p. 358).

To deal with this dilemma, some agencies find it helpful to divide their various stakeholders into what I call the *three Cs:*

customers, consumers, and constituents (Linden, 1992–93). Each of these Cs has its own needs and relationships with the agency:

- Customer—Who pays
- Consumer—Who uses
- Constituent—Who cares

In this model, *customers* are the individuals and groups that fund the agency or program—city council, state legislature, Congress, and various congressional committees. They are also the individuals who pay directly for the services they receive. Their needs usually have to do with the use of their funds: efficiency, fiscal integrity, avoidance of embarrassing errors, responsiveness to legislative intent. *Consumers* are the end users of the program or service (usually termed customers in TQM language). Consumers generally seek quality, timeliness, user-friendly services, convenience. And *constituents* are those who have a vested interest in the agency's mission; their needs relate to policy and political matters, who gets served by the agency, how it affects their members' interests.

When a good deal of overlap is apparent among the needs of an agency's three Cs, the agency's task is far easier. For example, the Marines and the Centers for Disease Control are successful organizations for several reasons. One important reason is the consensus among their various Cs as to mission and program direction. For the hypothetical group home mentioned earlier, things can get much dicier. The customers (funding bodies) want to keep costs down and controversy out of sight. The consumers (residents) may want many things (flexible hours, freedom to come and go as they like, frequent visits from friends) that certain constituents (family members, neighbors) do not agree with. And some consumer needs and demands will cost far more than the customers are willing to pay. Whose needs are to be met?

For agency staff to make sense out of the second re-engineering step, start at the end and work backward, they can use the three Cs model when end user needs are in conflict. First, look for overlap: is there consensus on any needs? In the group home example, some areas of consensus would be safety, development of the residents, and good relations with neighbors. Second, where there are apparent conflicts among the various needs, look for ways to "reframe" certain needs in order to gain a consensus. Group home residents want flexible curfew hours (or none at all); their families and neighbors may want very strict hours. One way to reframe the issue is to seek criteria on which all can agree: for example, curfew hours should respect the need to be a good neighbor while giving residents the maximum responsibility that they can handle. To translate such criteria into specifics would require negotiations, of course, but at least the group home staff know how to define the need they are trying to meet—curfew hours that meet agreed-on criteria. Some state and federal law enforcement agencies, for example, have wrestled with the problem of meeting customer (consumer) needs. One way to reframe these customer needs is to "develop a process that respects the rights of criminal suspects." Criminals will never be "delighted customers" of the police, but it's possible to ensure a process that guarantees their due process needs.

Finally, government agencies can add a fourth C to this model—coalitions. When a consensus doesn't exist as to goals and programs, the agency can try to create one by forging coalitions among some of its more important Cs. That is what community policing attempts to do. By getting police back into the neighborhoods, forming relationships with residents, and working with area businesses and local agencies to solve neighborhood problems, the police expand their base. Their consumers now include many residents, not just criminals. Their constituents (who used to show up only when they were angry with the police) now number many active members working with the police to prevent and solve problems. This expanded consumer and constituent base has many interests and needs in common, and they will stand with the police when the department seeks additional funding from its customer, City Hall.

It takes creativity, good communications and consensus-building skills to forge coalitions among groups that are frequently at each others' throats. But for civil servants, those are the skills they must master as they attempt to start at the end and work backward. Even at agencies that don't re-engineer, seeking consensus and forging coalitions is the name of the game today. There simply is no other way to pursue the mission effectively unless some consensus is gained. The three Cs model is one tool to identify common and differing needs, to begin building consensus.

Which Processes Should Be Re-Engineered First?

Three major criteria determine the priority of a re-engineering process: (1) impact on customers/consumers/constituents, (2) impact on overall organization performance, and (3) feasibility. Of the three, the first and second are most important. Re-engineering begins as a top-down process; building confidence in it depends less on starting with sure-fire winners (feasibility) than on selecting the processes that will have a material benefit for the consumers/customers/constituents and the organization.

When determining which process improvements would most benefit the organization's performance, staff should look for potential improvements in financial savings, public image, ability to achieve goals, ability to attract and keep talented staff, cycle times, responsiveness to important mandates, and competitive position. "Competitive position" isn't a phrase in common usage among civil servants, but public agencies do compete. They compete for budgets, important missions, talented people, and the public's support. In the early 1990s, the San Diego Zoo began redesigning its exhibits around bioclimatic zones (such as an Asian jungle environment) rather than taxonomy. The change excited many staff and allowed the zoo to cut some costs and keep its admission price less than half of a chief competitor, Disneyland. During a deep recession, the zoo enjoyed a 20 percent increase in attendance

(Stewart, 1992). It redesigned a process (exhibiting animal and plant life) with a major impact on organizational performance.

Re-engineering should begin with processes that are of special interest to the consumer. The fact that some processes can be easily fixed is irrelevant if your consumer has more important things on his mind. For instance, I frequently teach courses for the Navy Department and sometimes spend the night in the Bachelor Officers' Quarters (BOQ) on base. A few years ago, a BOQ I have stayed in was making major efforts to streamline its check-in/check-out process, and succeeded. It used to take about five minutes to register, get a room, get a key, and be on my way, and they got that down to about a minute. I was impressed, until I realized the registration procedures weren't my major concern at the BOQ. What has always irked me about this place is the fact that they issue paper-thin towels and little bars of soap that have half-lives measured in seconds! Further, they take hours to respond when my room has a plumbing or air conditioning problem. *They did a beautiful job of "fixing" the wrong process.* What this BOQ needs to do is identify the processes and products that are most important to its consumers and to its overall success.

To apply these three criteria, you can construct a simple grid to graph impacts on your agency's three Cs, along with a scale to chart feasibility (see Figure 7.1). We can apply the grid to some of the government re-engineering examples already mentioned:

- *Sheffield Ranger District* (Chapter Three). The Sheffield staff replaced its functional structure with one organized around process teams: design, operations, and information management. The change improved planning and communications, affecting organizational performance. Consumer impact was indirect. The change wasn't costly but required specialists to adopt generalist roles, which has taken time.

- *Hartford IRS Office* (Chapter Four). Staff re-engineered the

Figure 7.1. Determining Which Process to Re-Engineer:
How Case Examples Fit Criteria.

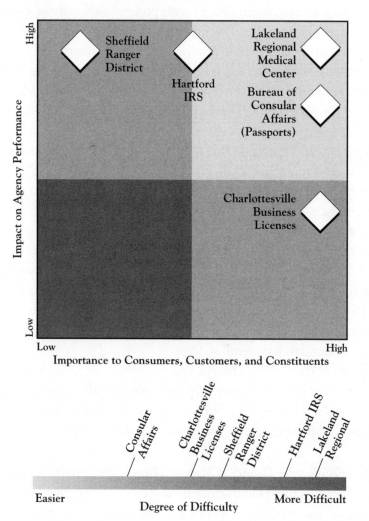

process for determining a case was "noncollectible," reducing process cycle time from 14.7 to 1.4 days, saving staff time. It also eliminated tedious management reviews of staff work and provided state-of-the-art technology. This approach enabled front-line staff to provide one-stop service to taxpayers, which benefited them both and increased collections of delinquent taxes. Changing roles, adapting to new technology, and giving up some control took time, patience, and money.

- *Lakeland Regional Medical Center* (Chapter Three). The key process change was the delivery of patient services. The use of multiskilled teams has had a major impact on the organization (money savings, longer staff tenures, faster turnaround on test results), its patients (who love the new system), and other constituents. Degree of difficulty: high—virtually every process and system has to change to align with the care pair/trio model.

- *Bureau of Consular Affairs—Passports* (Chapter Four). The use of a triage system streamlined the process for renewing passports, greatly pleasing customers (waiting time cut in half) and improving organizational performance (25 percent increase in volume, handled by fewer staff and resources). Re-engineering this one key process was not difficult and proved to be a win-win for staff and consumers.

- *Charlottesville Business Licenses* (Chapter Six). Streamlining a multistop, two-day journey into simple one-stop shopping was technically easy and not expensive. The consumers love it. Organizational performance is not affected significantly, except that the city received highly favorable media coverage, pleasing an important customer—the city council.

This analysis is done after the fact, of course, but managers who want to begin re-engineering can use this grid in the assessment phase to determine which processes are the best re-engineering candidates. Occasionally, a single process produces a win-win for staff and agency and is relatively easy, as in the passport example. Such "win-win-wins" aren't common. The IRS office had to overcome decades of tradition and change deeply held attitudes; Lakeland Regional has invested $5 million and had to convince doctors that their turf was not going to be stolen by the nurses. In other words, public managers will have to consider *trade-offs* when deciding which processes to re-engineer. But, in the public sector, dealing with trade-offs comes with the job.

Thus, of the three major criteria for selecting re-engineering candidates, the impacts on the consumer and agency performance are the most significant. Feasibility is important, but not so much to gain staff confidence as to avoid wasting time and energies. Some processes are governed by rigid laws that aren't about to change; others are micromanaged by governing bodies and become highly political (hiring senior officials); others are slow and tedious because of important organizational values (such as intellectual freedom in universities, which requires abundant time and consultation before making any decision affecting academic policies). Such processes are terribly difficult to streamline and may not be worth the effort.

In this chapter, we have looked at three important issues that staff must confront as they go through the re-engineering steps. For those who successfully re-engineer a process to provide more seamless service, the good news is that their end users will be delighted. The challenging news is that the staff have only just begun. In the next chapter we will examine a critical organizational issue, one all too often ignored in the popular management literature: how to gain *alignment* among the various processes, systems, strategy, and structure.

Chapter Eight

Aligning Systems to Support Seamless Work

Chapter Preview

The previous two chapters have described re-engineering design steps and issues they raise. But once agencies make the shift from functional to process orientation, they must then align internal systems and structures with the new culture. In this chapter, we will look at a model for achieving organizational alignment. Then we'll examine three innovative organizations that are attempting to align their systems and processes with fundamental changes they have made in their organizational design and structure—the city of Hampton, Virginia, the U.S. Forest Service Region 9 Office, and the Lakeland (Florida) Regional Medical Center. Finally, we'll use the alignment model to analyze their stories.

The Absence of Alignment: An Example

The Charlottesville, Virginia, Social Services Department has experienced a wrenching decade. Since the recession of 1981–82, claims for food stamps, Medicaid, and Aid to Families with Dependent Children (AFDC) have skyrocketed, while staffing levels have remained the same. The crunch has hit the department's Benefits Division especially hard. In 1991 that division began re-engineering its process for handling benefits claims.

Under the old system, an applicant had to see a different program specialist for each benefit sought. An applicant needing three benefits would make three appointments with three different specialists, fill out three different forms, and wait days or weeks to learn whether he or she was eligible.

The new system resembles the one-stop shopping approach used by Connecticut's Department of Labor. The staff have been cross-trained. Applicants come for one interview and fill out one application, and one worker determines eligibility in much less time. In 1994, the division helped pilot a new software system that will allow for an interactive interview, which will give clients information about their eligibility within an hour or two.

The change was dramatic; the division had worked hard to make it succeed. Despite having only eighteen workers for a caseload that by state standards requires twenty-eight, the staff took on the challenge and created a new system that successfully streamlined the process for applicants.

The only problem was, the staff were miserable.

They brought in a consultant for team-building sessions. They learned more about each other and openly discussed their hopes and concerns for the new system. They even held their own version of a "wake," mourning the old approach and formally letting go of it. They went through the stages of death and dying, got to a point of acceptance, and tried to embrace the new system in the interest of their clients. But still they were miserable. And with their misery came a good deal of finger pointing. Workers blamed supervisors for micromanaging, supervisors felt the workers were whining, there was a general breakdown of trust and confidence . . . and the consultant was asked to come back and lead a session on stress management.

The Benefits Division didn't need stress management, although they surely had their share of stress. Nor did they need additional team building. Their problem stemmed from the fact that their unit was out of alignment. They had made one major change in the workers' jobs, which transformed them from narrow, specialized positions to broad, generalist roles. But nothing else had changed. Supervisors' roles hadn't changed; they were still expected to catch and correct worker mistakes. The evaluation system hadn't changed; it was still based on the number of errors detected. The pay and decision-making systems were still the same. The result was that capable and dedicated staff, who had the courage to make a major change to benefit their clients, were working in two different worlds. Their expanded jobs were highly professional, but the surrounding systems and processes were based on an industrial model. Stress management would have been a Band-Aid. They needed to complete the job they had started and get the rest of their division in alignment with their new generalist roles. Fortunately, the staff understood the need when it was pointed out to them and formed two teams to work on aligning systems and processes. As they did so, staff began to experience a greater sense of consistency in their work. Morale improved, as did performance.

The Problem of Alignment

Alignment refers to *the degree of congruence or consistency within an agency's culture:* how well the various systems, structures, messages (both spoken and unspoken), and styles support and reinforce each other on an everyday basis. A leader who preaches the importance of candor, then shoots the first messenger who brings bad news, is not creating alignment. An agency that creates self-managing teams but continues to hire, promote, evaluate, and reward staff based solely on individual accomplishments is not creating alignment.

When your car is out of alignment, it pulls to one side. The tires wear unevenly, and the ride gets bumpy. When it gets really bad, you have to hold tightly to the wheel just to keep the car on the road. That is what it's like to lead an organization that is out of alignment. The leader has to hold on tight. The ride is rough. Different units are pulling in opposite directions. You may get where you need to go, but it's a lot bumpier, more costly, and more time-consuming than it needs to be. And sometimes you can't get where you need to go.

Most government agencies are out of alignment. They don't send consistent signals to the staff. No wonder employees roll their eyes and give each other knowing looks when their managers come back from conferences and workshops proselytizing for the latest management trend or fad. The staff have seen too many of these things come and go to get excited. They assume the boss will "get over it," as though "it" were some sort of disease. And even if the boss is genuinely committed to a new approach, the staff understand full well that the cards are stacked against change. How can we move toward empowerment, or quality management, or self-managing teams, they wonder, when the personnel system is antiquated, the purchasing system is still impossible, the information systems people insist on controlling everything, the budget process rewards waste, and the same old empire builders control what really goes on every day? How, indeed.

Compare this with the life of Toyota salespeople. At Toyota in Japan, they don't have to talk about teamwork, because every aspect of the sales team's life is geared in that direction. Salespeople, typically college trained, work in teams of seven or eight. They have been trained in every aspect of the sales transaction, from product information and order taking to financing and insurance. They are paid on a group commission; a salesperson has no incentive to jump at the customer walking in the door, because they all gain equally when a customer buys a car. They begin and end each day with a team meeting, at which they compare notes on current trends, problems, opportunities. Since they work on a team incentive basis, they have an interest in sharing, not hoarding, information.

The sales team spends one full day each month in the office, working as a quality improvement team. They analyze the month's results, look for ways to solve problems that cropped up, and focus on future issues. Because their goal is to make customers part of the Toyota family, they rarely haggle over price. Their concern is long-term relationships, with their customers and with each other. Thus, the sales team at Toyota works in a system that is very much in alignment. From initial cross-training and group incentives to the nature of each day's work, they receive consistent signals over and over (Womack, Jones, and Roos, 1991).

Once an agency has successfully re-engineered its processes, the next critical step is to align the rest of the agency accordingly. The benefits of a successful re-engineering effort can be quickly lost if nothing else changes. As James Q. Wilson (1989) has pointed out, the structure of a government agency is not the most important influence on the staff's behaviors. Rather, most employees respond to the more *immediate* cues they receive from the agency's systems, their supervisor and their peers, the formal and informal reward systems, the specific work situations they find themselves in, and the work culture, its attitudes and norms. As the social services supervisors in our example learned, improvement does not automatically come from redesigning roles and structure. That structure needs to be supported by all the other systems and signals influencing staff behavior.

The 7-S Framework: An Analytical Approach to Creating Alignment

In the late 1970s, McKinsey and Co. developed the "7-S Framework" as a model for understanding and improving organizational performance. (For more, see Peters and Waterman, 1982; Pascale and Athos, 1981; Waterman, Peters, and Phillips, 1980; Waterman, 1987.) Dubbed the "happy atom" (see Figure 8.1), the McKinsey researchers identified seven key organizational variables that require consistency: three "hard Ss"—structure, strategy and systems, and four "soft Ss"—staff, symbolic behavior, shared values, and skills. Definitions of the Ss are as follows:

The "Hard" Ss

- *Structure*—The organization chart, job descriptions, who reports to whom, and how the units relate to each other
- *Strategy*—The organization's plan for allocating resources to achieve its goals
- *Systems*—The procedures, processes, and routines that characterize how important work gets done

Figure 8.1. The 7-S Framework.

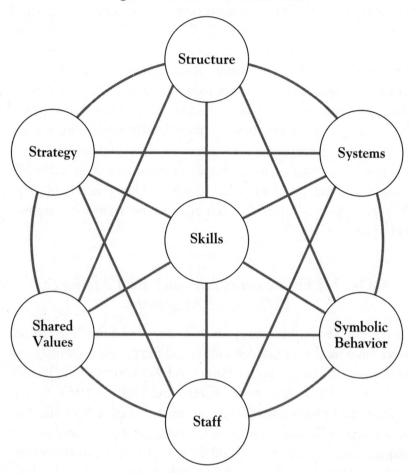

Source: From *The Renewal Factor,* by Robert H. Waterman, Jr. Copyright © 1987 by Robert H. Waterman, Jr. Used by permission of Bantam Books, a division of Bantam Doubleday Dell Publishing Group, Inc.

The "Soft" Ss

- *Staff*—The kinds of people in the organization, their demographics, experience, and education
- *Shared values*—What the organization stands for, its overarching purpose
- *Symbolic behavior*—Managerial actions and styles and the organization's culture (originally termed style)
- *Skills*—The distinctive capabilities of the organization and its key staff

They put skills in the middle to suggest that organizations are skilled to the extent that the other six Ss support those skills. Skills becomes the dependent variable, reflecting the consistency and strength of the other variables.

The 7-S Framework can be a useful tool for managers who want some guidance as they try to align their organizations, but I believe it needs one change. Rather than the "happy atom" configuration, which suggests that the six Ss are equally important and together determine the organization's Skills, I suggest giving priority to Strategy and Structure. The three cases described in this chapter, and the examples of private-sector firms like GE that are successfully aligning themselves, show the importance of beginning with a clear strategy, then altering the structure to support it. Once those two Ss are in place, the other five can be changed in whatever order fits the organization's needs and resources.

The 7-S Framework offers a useful analytical tool for understanding the efforts of the organizations described in this chapter.

Hampton, Virginia: Alignment Around Self-Managing Teams

When the city council of Hampton (population: 133,780) selected Bob O'Neill as city manager in 1984, O'Neill inherited a fairly

typical local government structure (see Figure 8.2). He reported
to an elected city council, and his assistant city managers reported
to him. Few department heads had much leeway to run their
departments as they saw fit, even though they were competent and
capable of doing so.

O'Neill began by asking his council to assess the city government's performance. The council found several positive and a few
negative aspects; more important, O'Neill learned that council
members agreed on the overall direction and goals the city needed
to set. O'Neill also asked his department heads to assess city gov-

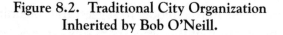

**Figure 8.2. Traditional City Organization
Inherited by Bob O'Neill.**

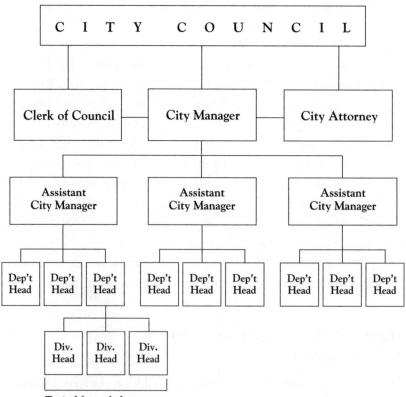

ernment and their roles in it. They told him that they had confidence in their ability to run their departments and didn't need much oversight in the day-to-day running of the city. Further, they had experienced staff with good technical skills who knew what to do. One thing that the department heads did want was more information about, and input into, the overall picture of where Hampton was going.

O'Neill decided that he and his senior staff had to refocus their attention, from daily minutiae to the big picture. After extensive discussions with department heads, he changed the organization structure, grouping the thirty-seven department heads into four task forces: public safety, citizen services, infrastructure, and management resources (see Figure 8.3). He assigned one department head (who rotates annually) to serve as a task force leader for each.

The task forces are self-managing; the concept is to create much more lateral communication and coordination, to break down walls that had separated department heads and get them working together on issues of common concern. Amazingly, all thirty-seven department heads report to O'Neill, who believes our traditional notions about span of control are obsolete in an era of self-managing teams and flat organizations. Task forces serve to pool expertise and generate interdependence. They develop their own agendas, determine their priorities, and take on a corporate leadership role in helping to run the city. The task force chairs meet weekly with O'Neill and the assistant city managers to keep everyone informed of their directions and issues. The assistant city managers were taken out of day-to-day line responsibilities and given broad policy areas to oversee, such as economic development and quality of life. O'Neill and his department heads were trying to position themselves to focus on big-picture and future issues and learn to work as a team.

They instituted several other innovations, including self-managing teams, annual surveys of citizen perceptions of city government effectiveness, extensive employee involvement programs,

Figure 8.3. Hampton's New Organization.

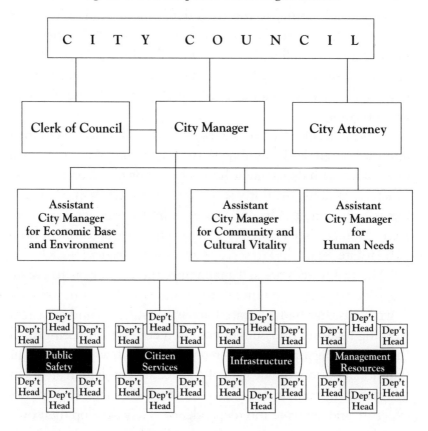

department head peer input on their performance evaluations, and a strategic planning process that leads directly to annual city and managerial goals. The city council works with staff and citizens to set strategic five-year goals, then it sets annual goals within that larger context. O'Neill and his department heads establish their own annual goals and strategies in support of the city's one-year and long-term targets.

In 1990, when the council determined that city government had to grow smaller, O'Neill led a downsizing that included extensive staff involvement. The result was a cut of over ninety positions. To guide this painful process, the staff developed two criteria for determining which positions add least value and should be eliminated. Positions that (1) primarily serve to check up on others and (2) move information through the organization would be among the first to go. The two-year downsizing process reduced the work force to 1,500, the smallest work force per capita in the large Tidewater, Virginia, region.

The government's culture was being slowly transformed and citizens were responding positively. Annual citizen surveys showed that over 90 percent of Hampton's residents gave City Hall good grades on its performance. But every organizational change pointed up the need to change something else. For instance, several departments began using self-managing teams after the Human Resources Department (HRD) pioneered the first one in 1985, and by 1993 over two hundred city employees worked on self-managing teams. The team concept worked well in most departments, but it wasn't in alignment with the rest of the infrastructure; the appraisal system, the training program, hiring and promotion, pay scale, and career paths were all geared to narrow, individual positions, not the generalist, team-oriented work that self-managing team members were doing. The changes discussed in the following sections are aligning the culture with a team approach.

Performance Contracts

Each year, Bob O'Neill works out a performance contract with the council, targeted to the city's overall strategic goals and annual goals. Then each department head works out a contract with O'Neill, with specific goals that support his goals and those of the city. In the HRD, the team helps department head Tharon Greene write her contract with O'Neill. Then she asks her staff to recommend performance standards and goals for their performance contracts with her, aligning their goals with her own. The contracts include training plans and specific strategies to achieve the desired standards.

Performance Review

Six months after her contract is written, Greene meets with her teams in a coaching session. There is no formal evaluation. Rather, they look at feedback from department customers. When the HRD went to the self-managing team concept, her team took on day-to-day operating decisions and replaced the narrow, functional job descriptions (training, employee relations, and so on) with customer-based positions. Each HRD team member meets all personnel-related needs of a particular city department, and department employees give written feedback on HRD services twice a year. Greene and the team also discuss overall team performance relative to their goals and standards.

At the end of the twelve-month review period, team members write a self-assessment of progress toward goals. They also write their assessment of one another's contributions to the team and their customers. The written comments go to Greene. Under a new team-based pay system going into effect in 1995, she and the team will review the team's performance in managing their budget, again review customer feedback, and compare the team's performance with stated goals. The review will lead to an overall evaluation that translates into a pay increase for the team. It's important to note that the entire team will receive the same percentage increase. "No matter what their individual salaries are, everyone will go up the same percent," Greene noted. There is also a provision for individual bonuses, which allows recognition for team members who made outstanding contributions on particular projects.

In the performance review, Greene and her department head colleagues must model what they preach to their teams. When Bob O'Neill evaluates his department heads, he takes into account the peer feedback he has received on them. He also looks at their performance relative to certain stretch objectives set for each one—O'Neill wants to know what his senior managers did during the year to move their department to the next plateau. "How many hits did they make, and how many swings did they take?" as he puts it. Two important features of Hampton's evaluation system for department heads reflect its emphasis on teamwork and big-picture action: They are assessed on their contributions to other departments and their efforts to help the community at large. All of this, plus their achievements relative to certain bottom-line performance standards, go into a performance evaluation system that people take seriously. It's taken seriously because it's used. Each quarter, the council is briefed by several department heads on their progress toward their annual goals. And their annual salary adjustment and the possibility of bonuses directly reflects that progress.

Broad Pay Bands

For self-managing teams, the city is replacing its former system of narrow pay grades with a few broad pay bands. The old system rewarded survival; hang on another year, move up 5 percent. The new system is intended to reward multifunction members of teams by identifying the competencies needed for progress. "It's not pay for knowledge," emphasized Greene. "We looked at companies like Siemens, where they pay for knowledge, but that is not what we wanted. We needed a system that pays for *demonstrated skills and results*."

At the HRD, there are four levels—trainee, entry, mid, and senior—defined by the degree of independence and scope of work. *Entry level* means the ability to handle all of the basic HRD functions and do more complex tasks (such as dismissal, grievance, pay studies) with the help of more senior people. A *mid-level* HRD staffer can do the complex tasks independently, and a senior-level person must be able to manage citywide issues and demands, such as developing a training program for all staff middle managers.

Staff now know what is expected of them and what they must do to advance, in terms of demonstrated competence. Thus, the reward system has been fundamentally transformed from reinforcing survival and guarding narrowly defined jobs, to learning, growth, and increasing competence in several disciplines.

Selection and Orientation

When openings occur the self-managing team recruits and reviews applications, interviews the most promising, and gives their recommendation to Tharon Greene. She almost always goes along with their choice. Because the team does the interviewing and knows the kind of person it is looking for, it has a good record of selecting people who fit into the generalist, team approach (team members report that they put more emphasis on their own intuitive reactions than on the applicant's formal references and qualifications). Occasionally the choice has proven to be a poor one. Some people can't handle the generalist roles required by the team; thus far when that's been the case, the person and team both realized it and the person left on his or her own.

New members of the department are oriented through the use of a "buddy" system. To learn the technical aspects of the job, they're paired up with senior members who have particular expertise in one or more functional areas. The experienced buddies also help new members learn the informal rules of the department and provide a kind of on-the-job training.

Training

Each performance contract includes a training plan geared to the staff member's goals. Team members utilize the same kinds of formal training activities that most government employees use: classes, conferences, workshops, and the like. Given the large and growing number of self-managing teams in Hampton, the city provides classes on problem-solving models, teamwork skills, and skills in leading teams and participating on self-managing teams. Perhaps more significant than such formal training is the informal training and education that comes from the buddy system, from the generalist role that requires knowledge in all functional areas, and from training others in the organization in various aspects of human resources.

Other Examples of Alignment

As the self-managing team concept takes hold in Hampton, it's leading to fascinating changes in the culture and the sense of alignment with overall city goals. One example is the Consolidated Procurement Department, which handles both city government and Hampton schools' purchasing needs. The department recently organized its staff into four teams of two—a buyer and a clerk. These teams handle all purchasing needs for certain city departments and schools. Procurement assigns one buyer-clerk team to each of the city's four task force groups. Under the former system, buyers specialized in purchasing certain commodities—vehicles, paper supplies, computers, and so forth. In the new approach, the buyer-clerk teams specialize in their client task force's needs, whatever those needs may be.

To streamline purchasing, Procurement allows department heads to purchase items up to $500 with no prior approvals. There is no approved list of vendors for such purchases, no long paper trail. "We tell them to just go where you have to go, get what you have to get, and we'll deal with the paper afterward," said Bo Parker, head of the Procurement Department. Department heads may share this purchasing authority with as many of their staff as they choose.

The procurement teams get feedback each year from their department customers. They also give each other peer feedback, and their department head rates them. Bo Parker wants these evaluations to mean something, so he attaches money to them. If the department hasn't spent its entire budget by the end of the fiscal year, Parker gives half of the unexpended funds to his four teams as a one-time bonus, dividing the money according to their relative performance evaluations. The system thus rewards efficiency, customer service, and teamwork (peer ratings being an important part of the overall evaluation process).

Hampton in Perspective

The Hampton story is a classic in how to strive for alignment. The formula could be termed consensus, strategy, structure.

Bob O'Neill began by learning—he learned how his council viewed the city and city government and how his department heads saw their roles and their departmental staff. Since there was a general consensus that city government was working well and that city leaders needed to give more attention to future issues and strategic planning, he got the council's agreement to an overall strategy for the city. Next, he changed the structure of city government, emphasizing lateral communications and coordination, teamwork, continuing customer feedback, and a focus on future issues and opportunities.

With the new strategy and structure in place, O'Neill's more innovative department heads and managers seized opportunities for change and began aligning their units with the emerging direction. Self-managing teams, new performance appraisal systems, broad pay bands, creative training, and other changes *resulted from* the initial changes in strategy and structure. O'Neill demonstrated a very important marketing principle: some changes are best achieved through pull rather than push. Many leaders try to push change; they announce a new direction, gather their senior managers, and give them directions for implementing the change. O'Neill realized that bright, competent people often respond better to "pull." He gave his department heads what they wanted—autonomy to run their departments—then changed the structure to reward teamwork, creativity, and customer service. The direction is clear, rewards for change are there, and managers are free to adopt the direction in their own way, at their own speed.

The results of all this creativity have shown up on the bottom line. The city has revitalized its downtown waterfront; employee suggestions saved nearly $3.5 million over a six-year period; and the city's tax rate, one of the state's highest when O'Neill arrived in 1984, is now one of the Tidewater region's lowest.

U.S. Forest Service Region 9: Transformed Roles, Lateral Leadership, Integrated Management

Like most large state and federal agencies, the U.S. Forest Service divides its various field sites into regions and uses regional offices to perform oversight functions. Civil servants who work in the field often find their regional offices to be more hassle than help. They typically play a controlling role: monitor performance, control budgets, and require multiple forms to be filled out each month. Job descriptions for regional workers contain terms like *regulate, control, establish uniformity, oversee, demand accountability*. It's no wonder that regional staff are often disliked; they play the distasteful function of policing the front-line workers who do the agency's work. Region 9 of the Forest Service was in this typical "command and control" mode before it began to transform itself in the mid to late 1980s.

In 1985 the Forest Service initiated a national pilot study, trying to loosen up the culture and tap the creativity and innovation of its 40,000-member work force. Under the leadership of Dale Robertson, the Forest Service chief, it began with four pilot sites, which were given great flexibility in their operations—personnel ceiling controls were eliminated, requests to waive onerous regulations were regularly approved, budgets were given in a lump sum rather than by traditional line items.

The pilot was highly successful, and several other units requested the same flexibility and autonomy. In addition, Robertson refined the vision and philosophy of the pilot into a formal charter given to all Forest Service units. The charter emphasized creativity, innovation, and risk taking; it preached the importance of quality results, not bureaucratic rules. In a statement resembling the "policy" given to all Phoenix police officers, the charter concludes that "We have dedicated and hardworking people. . . . We trust them. . . . Our people should use common sense and their best judgment, and then go ahead" (U.S. Forest Service, 1989).

Project Spirit

In 1987, Floyd J. "Butch" Marita, the regional forester and head of the Region 9 office, requested and was granted pilot status for all of Region 9 (covering twenty states in the Northeast and Upper Midwest with nearly half of the U.S. population). Ideas began to blossom in what the region called "Project Spirit." The core idea of Project Spirit was to loosen up the traditional top-down management style and give staff at all levels freedom to make changes. A streamlined suggestion system was put into place. The response was overwhelming; in the first five years of Project Spirit, over twelve thousand ideas and proposals were submitted. One idea that streamlined a procurement process for paying vendors worked so well it was implemented throughout the entire Forest Service, saving half a million dollars annually.

Project Spirit was a good start, but it was just a start. As the culture began to loosen up, Marita and his senior staff realized that their office had to change the nature of its leadership, role, size, and use of resources. "We had a foot in each of two worlds," recalled Karl Mettke, a member of the human resources team whose business card reads "Creative Consultant." "Our leadership team was moving into a new mode of behavior, but the rest of us were still in the old structure." Marita decided to do things that supposedly aren't done by the power-grabbing, turf-controlling bureaucrats so often portrayed in the media. He capped growth of the regional office budget in order to make more funding available to the local forest units it supervised. The regional office's budget had been rising faster than those of the forest units, and Marita determined that they had to reverse that trend. The result was redistribution of about $2.7 million to the forest units during the following three years. The Region 9 office now uses only about 8 percent of the total budget allocated to the entire region, the lowest regional office allocation in the Forest Service.

Downsizing

In another departure from the norm, the leadership team decided to reduce the size of the office *without being directed to do so from headquarters*. To implement its decision to cap its budget, the regional office set a target of reducing its staffing level by 30 percent as of 1995, from approximately 220 full-time equivalent positions (FTEs) to 150. By the end of 1993 it was down to 170 FTEs, all the reduction having been achieved through attrition.

Shared Leadership

In 1988 the regional office took another step considered unprecedented among civil servants. Marita and his senior team decided that they needed to adopt a shared leadership style rather than the traditional top-down mode. Many organizations talk about sharing leadership, of course, but in very few does the top leader actually share power in a meaningful way. Marita decided that it didn't make sense to have one boss on top, so he *informally promoted* his two top deputies to create a "three regional forester" model. Since then, the three have shared the leadership responsibilities and power that formerly were Marita's alone.

Beyond that structural and power change, the leadership team wanted everyone in the regional office to feel like and act like a leader. So they opened up their leadership team meetings; all office staff members are welcome to attend and join in the discussion. It's not unusual for sixty or more staff members to participate in a leadership team meeting, at which decisions are usually reached through consensus! They also gave the staff a very clear message about the true nature of leadership: they are all leaders in their own units and are expected to act as leaders for the office. For instance, the leadership team gave everyone the authority to write and sign letters in the name of the regional office.

Other structural changes further reinforced the leader concept. Decisions formerly made at the "top" are now routinely given to the various units, where they try to seek a group consensus. Cross-functional teams are frequently formed to deal with officewide issues and challenges. And beginning in 1992, the numerous functional units were combined into five operational teams: human resources, natural resources, capital resources, information resources, and public and cooperative relations. The change was more than cosmetic. The teams oversee broad areas: where there had been several individual units dealing with such areas as recreation, wildlife, fisheries, and timber, there was now a broad-based team, natural resources. Similarly, the work of fiscal, property, procurement, and engineering functions were brought together in the capital resources team.

"It's not a one-size-fits-all approach," noted John Locke, culture and environment team leader. "Each team has to work out its own style and approach. They have to deal with issues of power and information and control. But we see it working every day. And that's largely because the leadership and strategy teams do such a good job of emphasizing the new culture and modeling what they want all of us to do."

Integration

Some of the steps already noted helped to create a greater sense of integration in the office. Like many government agencies, the Region 9 office had suffered from compartmentalization: too many narrowly defined jobs in an office with too many functional departments led by too many control-oriented middle managers. Creating the five broad-based operational teams and the officewide strategy team (discussed later) brought together staff that in the past had protected turf. It also reduced operating costs.

Money is a powerful factor when it comes to teamwork and efforts at integration. Leaders can make impassioned speeches about the need to think and act as one large team, but when the dollars come to individuals and small units, the result only reinforces fragmentation. The Region 9 office staff changed their budgeting system to emphasize the need for integration. The practice of budgeting for each unit was abolished. Today there is only one budget, a regional office budget. An ad hoc budget team (made up of staff from each operational team) makes recommendations on expenditures after reviewing requests from the operational teams, and the final decisions are made by the strategy team. Thus, if an opening occurs on, say, the human resources team, that team doesn't automatically retain the position. If the budget and strategy teams determine that another team needs the slot more than human resources, that position will be transferred. The emphasis is always on the needs of the entire office in fulfilling its mission. This budgeting approach gives the office flexibility to respond quickly to change.

Strategy

The leadership team realized that they could get caught up in daily crises, as could the rest of the staff, if they didn't force themselves to focus on broader issues. So they created a strategy team, composed of the three regional foresters, and one staffer each from four other operating teams. They defined their roles as providing leadership, vision, strategy, and overall guidance (meaning coaching and facilitating, not controlling) to the rest of the staff.

The strategy team often focuses on specific, strategic issues that could have a major impact on the office's ability to achieve its mission and vision. This team also has to anticipate trends and seek out opportunities. The strategy team took the leadership team's vision and engaged the entire staff in developing a regional strategic plan.

The strategy team isn't a leisurely, meet-once-a-quarter type of group that conjures up grand visions and writes long documents. It meets *everyday* to deal with the cross-cutting issues that affect the whole office. They also bring in specialists and supervisors from their regional forest units to brief them on current problems and trends.

Roles

One of the most profound changes in the regional office has to do with its role. Its mission is to provide accountability for the results of the forest units within the region. It must demonstrate to the Forest Service chief and members of Congress that its units met the program and budgetary intent of Congress, that they carried out environmentally sensitive land practices in accord with agreed-on forest plans, and that they were responsive to the public's needs.

In a word, the regional office must provide oversight. That goal easily puts the office in a potentially adversarial relationship with the ninety-plus units it supervises. The office staff decided to change the relationship to one of partnership. The staff now see their roles in terms of encouraging, facilitating, offering information, and providing overall vision and integration of activities. They view the forest units within the region as their customers and partners in a joint venture, not their direct reports.

For instance, the regional office staff look for ways to streamline processes, reduce paperwork requirements, and provide quick and flexible guidance when it's sought. They have replaced detailed procedures and process-oriented management reviews with result-oriented strategies and standards. The staff organize several-week-long "Changing Culture Visits," which are trips to the local units at which they listen, exchange information and ideas about cultural change, discuss experiments and innovations, and think through issues related to expanding the management philosophy to every level of the Forest Service. Unlike traditional visits to field sites, nothing is documented during these trips. They are unstructured, interactive sessions focused on mutual exchange and learning. The region's new roles are consistent with those of a seamless organization. Cross-functional teams focus on outcomes (not inputs or outputs); they emphasize fast, customized responses to their customers' (units') needs; and they emphasize broad, generalist roles.

Information Management

This is one of the most exciting aspects of the region's alignment efforts. Supported by a national Forest Service team that developed a strategic information management plan for the entire agency, the Region 9 staff are viewing information technology as a key to their efforts at integrating all office functions.

In the past, the decentralized regional structure rewarded a functional approach to information management. If a wildlife staffer collected information on a specific project, the information went into his or her computer. Other staff working on a similar project collected their own data, some of it overlapping, none of it easily shared. Different staff and units used different databases, each supporting their own local, functional program. The result was a great deal of wasted effort: the same data were collected numerous times by different staff; the data were incompatible and couldn't be brought together for quality decision making or timely response to questions. And retrieval costs were high. This situation encouraged criticisms of Forest Service management and its decentralized approach.

The new Forest Service and Region 9 approach to information management is based on principles that support the region's integrated team philosophy and the needs of a seamless organization:

- Information is a critical resource to the organization's success.
- The goal is to provide quality information in the right form to the right people at the right time.

- Data will be captured once, at the source, and used often.
- A shared data environment is being built, consisting of databases that can be integrated.
- Those who develop and manage information are stewards of the information, not owners of it.
- Widely used, commonly understood, and persistent data are standardized.
- All data are shared and available to all users and are systematically integrated with Forest Service plans and programs.

The new approach doesn't envision a single, agencywide database. Rather, it involves easy and rapid sharing between databases. Flexibility must be maintained, without the cost of the old, functionally separate systems. In its former information management approach, a group of three scientists coming to a meeting to plan an interdisciplinary project would have to spend much of their time clarifying their data requirements and definitions before they could begin to discuss the project itself. In the new system, the scientists can immediately begin discussing their project because their shared, integrated information means they already have a common understanding of the data. All staff will have access to such information, in real time.

Region 9 in Perspective

As a regional office in a huge federal bureaucracy, Region 9 has less control over its destiny than a city government like Hampton. Thus, in areas such as pay grades and compensation, it can't make the kinds of changes that we saw in Hampton. What is intriguing about Region 9 is that its leadership doesn't see its seeming lack of control as an obstacle. Butch Marita "promoted" his two deputies, even though he had no formal power to make them his equivalent. His leadership team has found creative ways to make dozens of employees feel and act like organizational leaders, getting them involved in making top-level decisions. Marita led the office through a downsizing exercise without being told to do so by headquarters. Marita and his team demonstrate a very significant, and unusual, approach to public-sector leadership. To achieve alignment with the overall vision when lacking full control, they act *as if* they were in control. Because of Marita's demonstrated commitment to the vision and because of the office's demonstrated competence in meeting headquarter's and Congressional requirements, the staff has been given the leeway to chart its own course.

Lakeland Regional Medical Center: Aligning Around the Patient's Needs

Lakeland Regional Medical Center (LRMC), the hospital described in Chapter Three, is located in the geographical center of Florida. It's also located right in the middle of a new revolution in the delivery of health care—organizing around the patient's needs rather than the bureaucracy's. Concerned about its ability to remain financially sound but rejecting the downsizing and efficiency-enhancing strategies typically used by hospitals, LRMC helped light the fires of medical change when it began restructuring to develop patient-focused units in April 1989. Since its first patient-focused unit became operational in August of that year, three other units have been redesigned using the same principles. The LRMC story is complex, but its approach to alignment is simple: organize around the patient's needs.

The patient-focused units at LRMC aim to provide 90 percent of the patient's services as close to the patient as possible, as I will describe. Most services are delivered by an eight- to twelve-person team made up of multiskilled nurses and technicians who work in "care pairs" and "care trios" and coordinate the care of patients across shifts. The team includes care pairs or trios for the day shift, evening shift, and weekend days, as well as a multiskilled individual or pair for the night and weekend evening and night shifts. Since any given pair or trio sees the patient for no more than one-third of the patient's stay, the entire team is given responsibility for the patient's care.

"It's a self-directed team in the true sense of the term," said Phyllis Watson, LRMC vice president for nursing. "A self-directed team must be accountable for its work, but you can't hold a team accountable unless it has control over its work. Those working on a single shift can't be fully responsible for patient outcomes; only the entire team working with the patient twenty-four hours a day can. So we consider the entire set of pairs and trios to be a team. They schedule their work, manage their time, and are accountable for patient outcomes."

Several elements contribute to Lakeland's alignment with the patient-focused concept. We'll take a closer look at each.

Team Coordination

Teams are coordinated by a team leader, who is selected by the administration. The leader for a newly forming team then selects the rest of the team members, always looking first to current hospital staff. Thus, the team leader has ownership in the team members. Physicians, who are each assigned to a primary and secondary team, refer their patients to those teams and coordinate closely with them and with the hospital's master scheduler.

Reduced Number of Service Providers for Each Patient

Lakeland's strategy is to keep the number of providers per patient as low as possible. In the patient-focused units, patients interact with an average of thirteen personnel during a typical hospital stay, compared to fifty-three in the hospital's traditional units. Watson put it this way: "We want to reduce the number of people in the patient's parade."

Services Provided as Close to the Patient as Possible

The staff have developed an analytical model to determine who should deliver which services to patients, conceptualized through the use of concentric circles (see Figure 8.4) to represent the following levels of service:

- *Level 1: Self.* What services can a given patient provide for him- or herself? Many can do self-medication, for example.
- *Level 2: Family/significant others.* Is there a significant other who can deliver services that the patient can't self-administer? Patients with memory deficits, for instance, may need family members to administer drugs or remind the patient to do exercises.
- *Level 3: Patient-focused team.* The great majority of services

**Figure 8.4.   Levels of Service in Lakeland's Model
for Patient-Focused Care.**

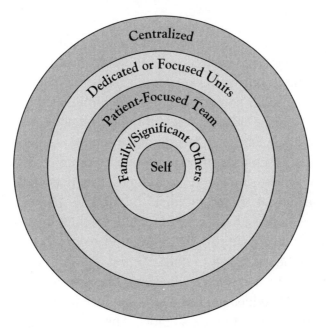

that the patient and family can't provide are given by members of the multiskilled team. Because of their intensive training, the teams are capable of doing most services required in the hospital, and they form the primary care givers for those in the patient-focused units.

- *Level 4: Dedicated or focused units.* Some tasks belong close to the patient but aren't appropriate for the multiskilled teams. Hospital pharmacy services, for instance, can't be provided by the teams. Pharmacists must provide them. To keep the patient focus, however, each pharmacy is dedicated to the patients of certain teams, and those teams only.

- *Level 5: Centralized.* Even at Lakeland, some services can't be provided locally. The archival function for records, emergency room services, and others that for reasons of cost, usage, or expertise can't be provided by the unit-based teams are delivered by a central staff in one location.

Focused Training

Nurses and technicians who form the care pairs and trios go through an intensive six-week education program, taught by clinical specialists within the hospital, to broaden their skills. To develop the classes, competencies were determined for each clinical area: electrocardiogram, respiratory care, rehabilitative service, physical therapy, laboratory testing, and diagnostic radiological procedures. The teaching methodology includes classroom instruction, interactive video, simulations, and clinical experiences; to demonstrate mastery of the required skills, students take a pre- and posttest. And the educational process continues on the patient-focused unit until each participant is considered competent enough to perform the wide array of skills.

Training also includes team building. Teams are more than a collection of multiskilled professionals. They need chemistry to hold them together in highly stressful jobs. The team-building sessions give staff a deeper understanding of the background and vision for patient-focused care, as well as a better understanding of each other and the expectations and competencies they bring to the team.

Technology for Local Scheduling and Team Control of Patient Services

Computer terminals in each patient-focused room link that patient and team to the hospital's mainframe. This allows for decentralized admitting, charging and discharging, and bed control. A specially developed software, Carelink, allows the hospital master scheduler to assign patients to units and rooms much like a hotel reservation system.

Physicians who send patients to Lakeland are assigned a primary and secondary team within designated units. When physicians want a patient admitted, one of their staff calls the hospital's master scheduler, who coordinates a conference call with the patient-focused team requested by the doctor. Based on the patient's anticipated length of stay, the scheduler either places the patient with that team or repeats the process with the physician's secondary team.

The software plays a key role in maintaining a reasonable workload throughout the teams. It also gives teams the information they need to coordinate the patient's overall care. When a physician comes to the patient's room, a patient-focused team member can provide immediate information on the patient's status. There are no handoffs. Physicians get real-time information that ensures continuity of care through a seamless service system.

Reduced Handoffs, Seamless Processing

One of the more unpleasant aspects of a patient's hospital experience is the initial contact. At LRMC, they have streamlined the process to provide a virtually seamless entry process.

During a preadmission visit, the patient is met by a multiskilled support person (MSSP), who works on the unit to which the patient is assigned. The MSSP has been cross-trained and understands the unit's various services and the kinds of treatment the patient may be needing. At the preadmission visit, the MSSP does any lab work, X ray, and paperwork needed. The MSSP introduces the patient to members of the patient-focused team that will be managing the patient's services, and they take care of any additional assessments. Finally, the MSSP schedules an admission date. On that date, the patient goes right to the hospital room; no waiting room delays, no paperwork, no surprises.

Compensation and Career Advancement

This is a very important, and tricky, area for organizations that are transforming specialists into multiskilled generalists and teams. While many staff at Lakeland were eager to join the new patient-focused units, there was an understandable concern about losing their professional identities. As Phyllis Watson put it, "Many individuals use the compartmentalized departmental structure of hospitals . . . to further protect their territory . . . and eliminate the real professional thought and problem solving that might occur when individuals from different backgrounds are brought together" (Phyllis Watson, personal communication, 1993).

At LRMC, the staff has developed a two-part approach to compensation. Part A is driven by education and skills. A new member of a patient-focused team can "challenge" her or his existing compensation level by demonstrating a level of skills meriting a higher salary. While all team members have the same job title—multiskilled practitioner (MSP)—there is a clear recognition that different people bring different competencies to the job. When an MSP challenges the compensation level, she or he is tested on both demonstrated skills and knowledge. The test can result in a higher base salary. The formula for determining salary is based 60 percent on demonstrated skills, 40 percent on formal education.

Part B of the plan consists of a bonus system. Once the base salary is determined, MSPs may receive one-time increases, determined by their leadership, cross-training, and professional development. Leadership counts for 45 percent, cross-training 35 percent, and professional development 20 percent in figuring bonuses. In addition, the hospital does a market assessment and market adjustment each year, to determine how its pay structure compares with its competitors.

Greater Professional Responsibility

The word *empowerment* is in good currency these days, but it's often misunderstood. I often work with professionals who believe the word means, "Let me do what I want to do." That's a misuse of the term and has led to tremendous anger and disappointment in many organizations.

At LRMC, they understand the true meaning of empowerment. It means greater authority and control, *with greater responsibility for results*. For instance, MSPs now have full information about their unit's budget. They have more control over expenditures. They feel ownership in the budget, as they should: their evaluations include two items on managing the budget. In addition, the full team is responsible and accountable for patient outcomes. And the goals for the next five years include major changes in the physical design of the hospital and in its governance. In both instances, MSPs will be expected to play very active roles.

Lakeland in Perspective

"Once you initiate a patient-focused approach, even in one pilot unit, you start uncovering issues and principles and the process keeps on going," commented Darlene Starling, who was manager for the first patient-focused unit. She was talking about a basic systems principle: in social systems, you can't do just one thing. The staff at Lakeland seem to understand and even relish that principle. They look forward to a hospital that is totally transformed to patient-focused teams by 1999. They work on tough, knotty issues like compensation and evaluation at the same time that they remain sensitive to the concerns of well-trained professionals who worry about losing their technical "edge" as they move into multiskilled roles. And they are very sensitive to the needs and perceptions of physicians, a group that carries immense clout. They continually assess patient and professional reactions to the changes. Surveys thus far show very favorable results, and cost per occupied bed is lower in the patient-focused units than the rest of the hospital.

They have years to go and issues not yet dealt with, but the organizing principle for alignment at Lakeland isn't changing, nor is it complicated. *They organize around patient needs.* That's it. A simple, powerful concept around which all health care professionals can rally. And the beauty of it is, it works for everyone.

Case Analysis and the 7-S Framework

Similarities as well as differences are apparent in the three approaches to alignment described in this chapter. Among the similarities: clear performance standards, which provide a basis for clear accountability; training geared to the specific skills and knowledge needed for the job; job-based learning, which is valued at least as much as classroom-based learning; structural change, which generally precedes other changes; broad generalist roles and multiskilled teams. Among the differences: whether pay for performance is necessary for alignment, whether the most important changes occur from the formal structure and systems or in the informal culture of attitudes and values, and whether a person or a team leads the change process.

Let's return to the 7-S Framework introduced earlier in this chapter. Each S helps us understand what these agencies did to gain alignment.

Strategy

Each began with a sense of direction or strategy, either to deal with existing problems or to capture future opportunities. Bob O'Neill and Butch Marita knew they wanted a more customer-oriented, entrepreneurial, team-based culture. The leadership at Lakeland had a vision of seamless, client-focused service.

Structure

To pursue their strategy, each changed the structure in major ways. O'Neill put his department heads on self-managing task forces and gave his assistant city managers specific citywide issues on which to act. Marita first downsized, then collapsed a large number of functional units into six broad-based teams. And Lakeland transformed the staffing for certain units, eliminating narrow specialist roles and creating multiskilled teams.

Systems

Some of the most creative work in these agencies went into aligning systems with a new strategy and structure. Performance appraisal systems changed in each one. Information systems were revolutionized, giving multiskilled individuals and teams needed information at their fingertips and connecting them with other parts of the agency. Entire pay systems, career ladders, performance management, and the budgeting process were altered to correspond with the new culture.

Staff

Staff composition in agencies that re-engineer themselves poses a dilemma. Even when top leadership makes it clear that nobody will lose a job because of the change, many are threatened and some typically leave. That was the case in Hampton, as staff members who could not handle the demands of a self-managing team chose to go. If organizations provide counseling and assistance in such cases, it can retain the loyalty and good will of the staff who stay.

Shared Values

These are articulated in many different ways. More important than formal values statements are the actions that managers take. One reason Bob O'Neill has solid credibility with his staff, for instance, is that everyone knows he will support them if they take risks that result in mistakes. Region 9 staff knew that teamwork wasn't just a trendy slogan because they saw their leaders act as a team and invite any staff to their leadership team meetings. This area is probably the biggest challenge for those who want to re-engineer their agencies. Their actions will be scrutinized by staff who want to know if the leader is willing to take the same risks being asked of them.

Symbolic Behavior

Related to shared values, these behaviors also have to do with the ways the organization honors those who make exceptional contributions. Region 9's peer awards reflect its lateral, team-oriented culture; its openness to unusual titles (such as creative consultant) reinforces its desire for entrepreneurial behavior. The use of a generic job title at Lakeland, multiskilled practitioner, also conveyed a message about the new roles being formed and rewarded.

Skills

One of the most prominent features of these agencies' alignment efforts was the clear, high standards they created for staff competencies. The rigor that went into the training and testing of staff applying for multiskilled practitioner positions at Lakeland is indicative of the accountability and performance measurement the public is demanding from its government.

These agencies provide excellent examples of alignment. They also demonstrate several important re-engineering principles. Most important, they each organized around desired outcomes (seamless patient care; quick, customized customer service). Their self-managing teams brought downstream information upstream as they eliminated useless handoffs. They captured information once, directly from the customer. And two of them utilized advanced technology *after* redesigning their processes. They aligned around principles of simplicity and seamless service.

The Sense of Alignment

The 7-S Framework is one model for achieving alignment. What is critical is not the model but rather the awareness that alignment is a fundamental requirement of any re-engineering process. As Hall, Rosenthal, and Wade (1993) have written, "The redesign must penetrate to the . . . core," fundamentally changing the roles, measurements, structure, values, and skills (p. 119). Without paying attention to alignment, staff members receive mixed signals and are confused about the direction to take. And in today's environment, a lack of direction leads to mediocrity and failure.

When an agency has a sense of alignment, it engages and releases people's energies and talents in at least two ways. First, it encourages lower-level employees to take initiative without fear of reprisal. Second, it reduces the amount of turf fighting, because the overall priorities are clear and there are strong rewards for pursuing them (Kotter, 1990). When an agency has a sense of alignment, working there is much like dining in a fine restaurant. Every element is in sync—the decor, menu choices, food quality, behavior of the servers and maître d', table setting, lighting, and (unfortunately) the price. It's all of a piece, it fits together, you know why you're there, and how to get the most from it. That's how an aligned organization feels to its staff—and its customers.

Part Three

Pulling It All Together

Chapter Nine

Re-Engineering Lessons
from Two Agencies

Chapter Preview

The principles and steps outlined in the previous chapters are guide-lines for would-be process re-engineers. There is no exact formula, no cookbook solution for every instance. Each manager and team should apply the principles and steps according to their agency's particular circumstances. In this chapter we will look at two cases in detail in order to illustrate both the unique nature of each agency's re-engineering needs and typical challenges that re-engineers encounter.

The first case is about re-engineering, and more. The leaders of Connecticut's Department of Labor re-engineered the process for delivering employment services as part of a much larger cultural transformation of the agency. The effort included a radical reduction in management positions, redefinition of all 1,400 positions, introduction of quality management principles and tools, and a streamlined, one-stop-shopping approach for citizens needing services.

The second case is a classic process re-engineering example. Faced with a changing world order and a need to respond more quickly to sudden threats, the Department of Defense re-engineered the major processes at its giant logistics center, the Defense Logistics Agency. Costs were reduced, functional "stovepipes" were replaced by multifunctional teams, and lead times were reduced from months to days.

The Transformation of Connecticut's Department of Labor

In 1990, Connecticut's Department of Labor faced a challenge, and its leaders knew it. The department had been functioning as most bureaucracies do—slowly, methodically, carefully. Staff worked in specialized jobs in one of three discrete program areas—unemployment benefits, training, and job-matching services—and the training and reward systems affecting their behavior ensured a control-oriented culture. They weren't equipped to handle the complex, cross-functional problems that now challenged them. The fragmented system was especially onerous for the department's customers, unemployed citizens who had to wait in long lines to apply for unemployment compensation, then go to a second line for job information, and a third for job training. These factors, plus the possibility that another agency was going to take them over, generated a good deal of pain and energy for change.

The problem was that only those at the top felt the impetus to change. "We knew that we couldn't create the kind of customer-focused, high-performance organization we needed in the current structure," recalled Larry Fox, former deputy commissioner of the department. "That's why we didn't begin with a TQM effort. The old 'functional stovepipe' structure wasn't capable of forging a new culture for the agency. We needed a paradigm shift before continuous improvement could help us. If we were to fulfill our mission of helping the working men and women of the state find and keep good jobs, we had to help stimulate the development of a high-performance work economy. We decided that the best way to do that was to model what we wanted for the rest of the state. Problem was, we had to find a way for all of the 1,400 employees in the department to feel this."

First Phase: "Unfreezing" from the Present

To understand how Fox and his colleagues helped transform the department's culture, it helps to recall a theory of change articulated by the one of the founders of organization development, Kurt Lewin (1951). Essentially, Lewin taught that the change process in social systems involves three stages: unfreezing, changing, and refreezing. Some change efforts fail because they begin with the second stage, the change itself. But organizations, like all social systems, maintain the status quo until something creates an imbalance that forces change. That's where unfreezing comes in. The unfreezing process forces members of the organization to accept the need for change, by helping them see the dysfunctional aspects of their current approach. Approaches such as customer contact and feedback, comparison with peer organizations, internal surveys, structured face-to-face sessions between subordinates and supervisors (like GE's Work Out program), or the threat of a takeover create a sense of tension that makes people uncomfortable with the status quo. The first phase of Lewin's process fosters what he called a "felt need" for change by showing staff that the organization is broken, or at least in need of major repair.

Fox did several things to unfreeze the agency. He spent hundreds of hours over several months in small- and large-group meetings with all 1,400 staff, asking them what they thought of the current organizational structure and systems and what they thought was needed to succeed in the future. He did formal surveys of the employees, asking whether there was a need to change (overwhelmingly they said there was) and what sorts of changes would be needed. He met with union leaders to get their input and seek support. He and his top assistant, Ann Nichols, led educational sessions that detailed the nature of a high-performance organization. And, in one of his more creative steps, he had certain employees videotaped as they discussed what they thought of their agency. Their comments, some positive and many negative, were played back to employees and managers, upsetting many and creating the kind of tension that Fox knew would be needed to re-engineer the agency. He also worked with the governor's office and key legislative officials, which ensured that they knew what was going on and were supportive.

Second Phase: Envisioning the Change

Ann Nichols facilitated a retreat of the department's supervisors and managers, where they developed a vision of the new organization and culture. The new model and structure were radical departures from the past. The vision of a customer-focused, rather than rule- and control-focused, agency would be achieved by first streamlining the structure. They decided to reduce the number of management layers from nine to four. That meant a radical reduction in senior management positions from twenty-three to eight and in middle managers from seventy to eighteen. The emphasis would be on empowering front-line employees to meet all needs of their customers, by re-engineering their jobs and the support for their jobs. Rather than the old narrow, specialized positions, the 408 direct service employees would be trained to deliver all services that the department offered. To help employees visualize the change and prepare for it, the department provided many training sessions describing the nature of a customer-driven organization, what the terms *external customer* and *internal customer* mean, how to determine customer needs, how to get customer feedback, what "impeccable" customer service might look like, and so on.

Changing the structure and envisioning the future were only part of the battle, of course. They had to give people new skills and help them adopt new attitudes about their jobs and roles. One of Fox's key steps was to guarantee that no layoffs would result from the massive change. "I told them that there were going to be lots of leadership roles to play in the new organization. For the managers, that meant many opportunities to help and lead, though not necessarily as managers. We guaranteed nobody would lose their job, but we never assured anyone that they would have the same job."

Nichols knew that the model made sense but also that it needed to be fleshed out in detail. She and Fox also concluded that ongoing involvement of employees and unions was critical to their success. They organized six pilot projects involving some twenty-one offices in the department, each trying out one or more of the model's concepts. The idea was to have several offices experimenting with parts of the new model in order to refine and gain experience with it before full implementation.

The pilots gave Fox's team information about the best way to develop the innovative services they wanted. Moreover, pilots were early signals to the entire work force that this change would be implemented by *them*. To be selected for a pilot project, units had to include a good deal of staff input and involvement in their pilot proposal. Nichols led classes on the principles that pilots had to reflect, such as staff empowerment and quality service.

At the same time that pilots were being run, the agency began reducing the numbers of managers and management levels. *All managers were told they had to apply for their positions.* Since there were far fewer management slots available, managers had to assume there was a good possibility they wouldn't be in a similar position after the change. The department brought in first-rate career counselors to help managers think about the types of positions they wanted to pursue in the new organization, help them adapt to the change, and prepare for new jobs and even different careers. Most stayed and used the counseling, while some took early retirement.

To select the top five career managers, Nichols involved the department's three appointed officials. Together, they wrote an exam for the senior management positions. They based the exam on the vision, values, and concepts embedded in the new organizational model: entrepreneurship, customer focus, quality service, empowerment, and the like. The exam was tough; it required the applicants to think on their feet and demonstrate both knowledge and skills about the new culture they were to help build. Nichols and the three officials made the selections for the top five positions. Once chosen, the five senior managers replicated the same process for the eighteen middle manager openings. They identified the criteria for the new positions and developed an exam for those who wanted to apply. Many of the seventy former middle managers competed for the slots and went through the same grueling process of preparing for and taking the exam. The five senior managers graded the exams and helped make the selections for the middle management slots. Then, the eighteen who got the middle management positions helped create the exam for the hundred first-line supervisors to be named and made selections based on the exams.

The process was challenging for all involved. People had to learn how to design an exam that reflected values not yet in place. They had to learn something about tests and measurements, the values themselves, the kinds of competencies needed in the new culture, and ways to challenge people in a test situation to show those competencies.

"Most people hated the whole process!" Nichols commented. "We were going through a massive amount of change, and it challenged people's assumptions. The old 'ceiling' of what was expected—hard work—was becoming the 'floor' as we kept raising the standards." In spite of that, the intensive staff involvement built a tremendous amount of staff ownership of the whole process. It was becoming *their* organization and model now, not someone else's.

The Conceptual Leap: Re-Engineering Jobs from Narrow Specialists to Multiskilled Generalists

For front-line workers, the biggest challenge came from redesigned roles. Each of the 408 staff had to learn whole new areas of work. Again, unions were involved in the deliberations and difficult decisions: How do we train the workers to be generalists? How do we define their new jobs? How do we evaluate them, and how do we reward them?

The front-line staff themselves were heavily involved in designing the new positions. A cross-functional staff team was formed to work on a draft of the job duties, performance standards, methods for evaluation, and best methods for teaching staff about their new jobs. They had to determine the specifics of the new jobs: What does it mean to take a new claim? How long does it take, and how long should it take? What is an acceptable level of performance?

The team shared this draft with all of the affected employees, used their feedback to make changes, then designed a curriculum for a three-week course that would prepare them for their new duties. Nichols and her staff then led a training-the-trainer session for the unit coordinators (first-level supervisors), helping them develop some basic presentation skills, so that they could teach the course to all 408 staff. She rarely missed an opportunity to involve the people who had to live in the new structure.

"It was a major leap, making these changes in the service workers' jobs," Nichols recalled. "We were changing so many things at once. We had to switch from 'pay for another year of living' to 'pay for skills,' and that ran counter to the way the state operated. It meant getting support from state administrative and personnel departments, and it was a battle. Larry Fox helped by keeping the governor and legislators well informed. He held several well-publicized meetings to keep the concepts on the front burner, educate people, and sell the new approach. He 'ran interference' with agencies that might have fought us otherwise. Without his incredible energy, guts, and leadership, we wouldn't have done it. In addition, the staff worked hard to make the changes succeed."

To provide an incentive for front-line workers to go through the training and stress of learning their new jobs, the department got special dispensation to use the pay-for-skills approach as a state experiment. Fox's background as a former union official was especially helpful here, since many unions oppose pay-for-skills as a thinly disguised attempt to weed out workers whom management doesn't like. To help get union and worker support, Fox got permission to give the 408 workers a raise, *before* they had learned and demonstrated their new skills. This was a virtual revolution in state government, and it was a key move. The raises gave these workers an incentive to learn the requirements of their re-engineered jobs, and learn fast, because they knew that after their training, they would be tested on the new skills and concepts and would have to pass the tests to retain their raises.

The tests for front-line workers were designed to capture both the technical, quantitative aspects of the job as well as the behavioral, qualitative requirements. For instance, the workers were put in a simulated interview with a "claimant," reviewing requests for services and demonstrating that they could answer all pertinent questions and had the interpersonal skills needed. The unit coordinators administered the paper-and-pencil aspects of the test as well as the simulated portions. Again, the staff were involved in all aspects of the redesign effort.

"We learned so much from the staff involvement," Fox reflected. "One of the main learnings is that training must be done within the context of the work group itself. The work group must coordinate and help design the actual training. Going off to outside classes won't do it, not when you're transforming your agency as we did. The staff must own the training, the design, the change itself." He estimated that 75 percent of the ongoing staff training is OJT, and only 25 percent comes from the classroom.

"We also had to demonstrate, to the unions and the employees, that we wanted everyone to succeed. This wasn't an attempt to get rid of people. In addition to the 'no layoffs' pledge, we got rid of the bell-shaped curve for evaluation. We said that performance is a *learning issue*, not a disciplinary issue. Those who weren't demonstrating the necessary skills needed support and training, not punishment. So the whole evaluation system had to be learning-focused, and performance-focused, and that means that the next challenge is to establish benchmark standards for performance. They have a long way to go, but they know the path now."

Third Phase: "Refreezing" by Aligning Systems with the New Structure and Culture

To support front-line workers in their new generalist roles, a $20 million information system is coming on board. The expanded role is far more demanding than the former narrow jobs, and the staff need mountains of information at their fingertips. The new software and PCs will streamline the intake process, helping front-line staff handle whatever service the customer requests. Beyond that, unit coordinators will be developing a test for front-line staff who have mastered the basic skills and want to be promoted. A new performance appraisal system has been developed for all managers and supervisors, requiring them to demonstrate knowledge and competence on principles and behaviors of quality management.

The department is also starting to use multilevel feedback for managers. This system, very popular with innovative private and public organizations, gives managers feedback from subordinates and peers through anonymous, computer-analyzed questionnaires. The department began using the process for the senior managers, and, as they learn how to tailor it to their new culture, will expand it to middle managers and first-level supervisors.

Feedback from external customers is a key to the transformation this agency has made. One of the twenty-one pilots experimented with customer surveys and focus groups and found the information extremely useful. The department has extended this feedback system to several other offices and plans to bring it to all offices in the future. Other innovations are being phased in as resources permit: touch-screen kiosks with job listings and training opportunities; voice response technology for filing unemployment insurance claims and inquiries; and dial-up access via modem to other department databases.

Figure 9.1 presents a timeline for the department's transformation process.

Questions and Issues

The basic re-engineering step in the Department of Labor story was the transformation of the front-line staff positions, from control-oriented jobs focused on one specific program, such as unemployment benefits, to multiskilled professional positions aimed at

Figure 9.1. Major Milestones, Connecticut Department of Labor.

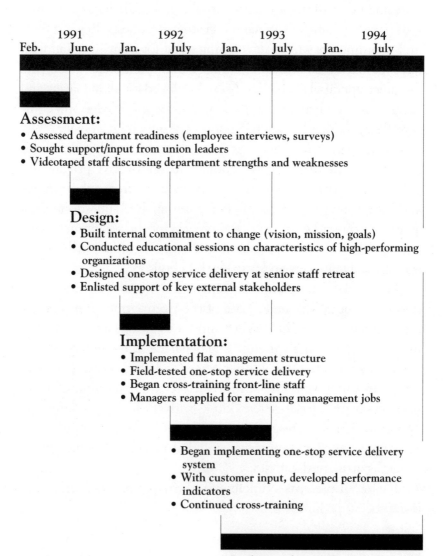

	1991		1992		1993		1994
Feb.	June	Jan.	July	Jan.	July	Jan.	July

Assessment:
• Assessed department readiness (employee interviews, surveys)
• Sought support/input from union leaders
• Videotaped staff discussing department strengths and weaknesses

Design:
• Built internal commitment to change (vision, mission, goals)
• Conducted educational sessions on characteristics of high-performing organizations
• Designed one-stop service delivery at senior staff retreat
• Enlisted support of key external stakeholders

Implementation:
• Implemented flat management structure
• Field-tested one-stop service delivery
• Began cross-training front-line staff
• Managers reapplied for remaining management jobs

• Began implementing one-stop service delivery system
• With customer input, developed performance indicators
• Continued cross-training

• Implemented new information systems:
  • New network with client server architecture
  • Touch screen kiosks with job listings and training opportunities
  • Voice response technology

helping applicants obtain all needed services. But the story is about far more than a redesigned position. It is about a sea change in the corporate culture. As Larry Fox noted, they could have focused on some specific projects, and those projects could have succeeded without any real change in the culture and nature of the department. While many quality management efforts rightly focus on gaining some small wins at the outset in order to gain staff confidence and build momentum, Fox knew that his department needed a paradigm shift, one aimed at changing people's assumptions about their work, changing their roles from cop to enabler.

Making such a vast change raises a leadership issue. In a government agency, led by political appointees who often have no more than two years to make their mark, does the leadership have the courage to focus on real cultural change? Such change takes many years, the leaders may be gone before any tangible benefits are reaped, yet in the political world you are judged by what transpired on your watch. Are the leaders willing to begin change at the foundations of the agency, even if they will not be around to enjoy its successes?

That point raises a related question. To go through the turbulence and resistance created by a massive re-engineering and cultural change, the leadership has to shield the agency from outside influences as much as possible. Fox played that role by gaining the support of the governor and legislators. And many others made major contributions, such as Bennett Pudlin, the department's executive director, who kept its basic services and programs operating smoothly during and after the reorganization. Does the leadership have the relationships with its key sponsors to build the power base needed for major change? Can it keep the control-oriented types in the central administrative departments from pulling the rug out? Alternatively, can it gain the wiggle room to experiment, as the Labor Department did when it got permission to give its front-line staff raises before they had demonstrated their competence in the soon-to-be-re-engineered positions? And does it have a strong, respected senior manager like Pudlin to keep basic programs operating amid the chaos of change?

Finally, a personal issue. Larry Fox is an energetic, colorful, competent, and confident man who seems ideally suited to forge the kind of change he and his top team created. His background as a union official helped immeasurably; so did his savvy with the media and with the state's highest officials. His willingness to play hardball, to cajole and threaten when necessary, plus his desire to form consensus, meet with people through countless sessions, listen and learn as he sold the concepts, were exemplary. While he and Ann Nichols had tremendous staff involvement throughout, Fox was clearly the catalyst who got the ball rolling. It's fair to ask whether the transformation of an old-line, bureaucratic agency requires the unique skills and background of a Larry Fox. Or can any government manager adapt his or her style to the situation and find a formula that works in that particular agency?

Re-Engineering the Purchasing Process at the Defense Logistics Agency

The Defense Logistics Agency (DLA) is a huge bureaucracy with an annual budget exceeding $17 billion. Begun in 1962, it was one of former Defense Secretary Robert S. McNamara's efforts to save money by consolidating functions. Rather than have each one of the armed forces do its own purchasing of common commodities, McNamara sought savings through a consolidated procurement agency.

DLA handles all aspects of material management, including distribution, customer service, contract management, and most inventory management functions for its customers—other Department of Defense (DoD) agencies. It manages approximately four million of the five million secondary items managed by DoD. These items are stored in over sixty locations. DLA receives roughly 28 million customer requests annually, which results in over 18 million billing transactions and 1.3 million procurement actions. DLA is a very big business by any definition.

To handle the volume, DLA was organized by functions: procurement, engineering, quality, technical support, and the like. This structure led to a rigidity and rule orientation that created a good deal of turf protection. Staff in each functional area saw themselves as specialized experts, receiving data from the previous function, processing it, then "throwing it over the wall" to the next. The result: many functions acted on the same data, recorded it in separate files, and duplicated each other's work. Worse, no one function had overall responsibility for the agency's mission: to get the customer agency what it needed, when needed, at the right quality and price. Rather, they worked toward their own individual goals, which at times were in conflict. They also worked in a reactive fashion. Most important, the rigid functional approach created delays for the customer. And when that customer is maintaining an F-18 jet, delays can be costly, to say the least.

DLA's Need to Change

In 1989, when the Berlin Wall fell and communist regimes began crumbling in Eastern Europe, DoD's leadership realized its size and mission would be changing rapidly. The Soviet empire had been a formidable but predictable enemy for over four decades. Now the United States was looking at a far more turbulent world scene, and Pentagon planners knew they would have to create a leaner and quicker military. The logistics area became critical, and the planners didn't like what they knew about their logistics capabilities. Lead times for purchasing certain large items were as long as three years. Further, there were no modern systems to streamline these processes for a scaled-down military.

In 1989, DoD Comptroller Don Shycoff made an important change in the department's budgeting approach. He introduced the Defense Business Operating Fund (DBOF), which gave managers the tools to see the real cost of doing business. Unlike traditional functional budgeting, which shows the amount spent on items like travel and salaries for individual functions and departments, DBOF details the costs of specific processes and outcomes. That is, it shows the full cost of managing material, which includes the costs of operating a supply center, and transporting and distributing material, which gives managers the cost for each unit of material. When DLA managers began to understand their real unit costs, the results were astounding. Most change is pain driven, and the unit costs created real pain.

"We looked at the numbers and learned for the first time what it took us to manage the business," recalled retired Navy Captain Tom Malsack, then deputy commander of the Defense Industrial Supply Center (DISC), one of five supply centers overseen by DLA. "And the numbers were huge. A full 35 percent of our costs went to overhead. That's enormous. A business with a 35 percent overhead cost for inventory management would go belly-up. The new budgeting system made us aware of how much we needed to change. It got our attention."

The numbers also got Don Shycoff's attention. He knew something had to change, quickly. Shycoff issued his own version of a stretch objective, directing DLA to reduce the cost of managing its inventory. He did it by instructing the agency to work with an 80 percent replacement factor. That is, for each dollar of material they sold to another DoD agency, they could only spend $0.80. Then, after Desert Storm, Shycoff went further, limiting DLA to a 50 percent replacement factor. These limitations created a howl of protest, but Shycoff was betting that DLA managers would learn to make up for the revenue losses by cutting costs.

The leadership at DISC didn't join the protest. Malsack and his staff thought they could live with the 50 percent rule. Not only that, they saw it as an opportunity to streamline and reduce lengthy lead times. "We didn't know the term 're-engineering' at the time, but in retrospect that's exactly what we decided to do," Malsack noted. And they proceeded in a straightforward re-engineering effort.

Mapping Current Processes: The "As-Is" Model

Because of his success at leading DISC, Malsack was given an additional task: to work with a team charged with redesigning inventory management for all of DLA. First, they looked at how they were doing business, mapping out the current process. They used a sophisticated mapping tool called IDEF (for Integrated Definition), part of the Integrated Computer-Aided Manufacturing program (ICAM), developed in the mid 1970s by the Air Force. IDEF uses models to provide a structured analysis of all business activities and relationships in a functional business process, identifying inputs, outputs, controls, and mechanisms for each activity. Malsack's team studied every activity associated with inventory management. His team represented all five supply centers and every function. They studied the process of acquiring material for both large items (defined as over $25,000) and small.

Figure 9.2 shows the diagram for making large buys at DLA. This "spaghetti chart" may appear designed to make one's eyes glaze over; in fact, the re-engineering team found it very helpful in viewing the existing process.

The chart shows four major functions, listed from left to right under "Manage Consumable Items": Manage Resources (A1), Provide for Market Requirements (A2), Provide Technical and Quality Support (A3), and Procure Matériel and Service (A4). Under each function are listed the key activities involved in it. For instance, under Manage Resources are listed four key activities (numbers A11 through A14).

After the team laid out the functions and key activities, they mapped the process of making a large buy in order to show when

Figure 9.2. The As-Is Model for Large Purchases at DLA: Organized by Function.

Manage Consumable Items (As-Is Model)

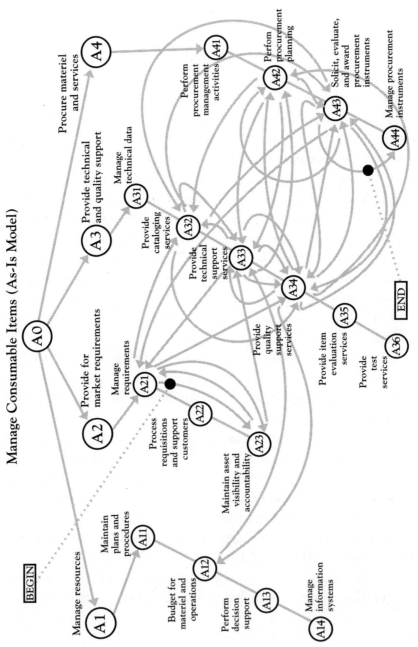

Source: Defense Logistics Agency (1992).

different functional activities were involved in that process, beginning with A21, Manage Requirements, and ending with A44, Manage Procurement Instruments. (To understand the chart, follow the line that begins closest to each arrow's end—from A21 to A23, back to A21, to A23 again, then to A33, A34, A33, back to A21, and so on.)

Next, the team took its process flow diagrams and collected data. They did a value-added analysis of each major step and sought ways to reduce or eliminate the non-value-adding steps. They were especially interested in lead time data and cost data. The data provided some immediate targets for streamlining. They found, for instance, that 92 percent of their contracts with suppliers were written for five or fewer items, which resulted in a huge amount of administrative time and paperwork. Certain high-cost processes were redesigned quickly and fairly easily.

Setting a Stretch Objective: Beginning with a Clean Sheet

Other processes took more time and required more radical surgery. "When we saw some approaches that obviously needed major overhauls," Malsack recalled, "we tried to step back and ask, 'If we started from scratch, how would we design this?'" Malsack added to Shycoff's challenge—of reducing expenditures by 50 percent—and gave his team an even tougher stretch objective: to reduce administrative lead time by 95 percent on 70 percent of their purchases. Malsack was challenging his team to begin with a clean sheet.

"Most of us had spent a lot of our careers in the government," he said, "and we weren't sure how we'd do it if we could start over. So we decided we needed to get out of [the] DLA and see how the very best outfits managed their inventory. To use the current jargon, we benchmarked. We went to K-Mart and Price Club and studied Wal-Mart. And we found a whole new way to organize. At Price Club, for instance, we estimated that they put items on the floor for about a quarter of our cost, and we were charging cost plus 35 percent or more.

"We also looked at previous studies made of DLA that pointed out ways to streamline, and we found excellent ideas for change; only problem was, few had ever been acted on. For instance, an '86 study described a vision that emphasized shared databases. Well, [the] DLA was organized in a traditional, functional stovepipe fashion with an information system that reinforced the functional approach. Shared databases would have been a major improvement . . . except that the idea wasn't implemented. So, between the benchmarking visits and previous studies, we were getting lots of ideas on how the agency might change."

Next, Malsack's team met with a core team of staff—leaders of eight teams that were working in parallel on the redesign effort—and they brainstormed how DLA should look by the year 2000. They reviewed all kinds of data and impressions, from their initial process mapping efforts, from the data analysis, from the visits and the previous reports. "Some of the data analysis really shocked us. We learned, for instance, that our administrative lead time for large buys was 203 days. It was 109 days for small buys. Compare that with Wal-Mart and Price Club, which use EDI to connect them with their suppliers and operate with virtually no administrative lead time. Again we realized that there's a world of difference in how organizations can operate these days."

It's important to note that when Malsack refers to "administrative lead time," he isn't talking about the number of days between receiving a customer's order and filling that order. He is only talking about the period from forecasting a need for an item, to placing an order for it. The time was spent determining the order quantity, reviewing the order, adding technical data, moving it up through as many as five levels of review, and obtaining multiple sign-offs. The order went to procurement, which did several levels of review before receiving bids and awarding a contract for the item. Just printing and mailing the award to the winning bidder took up to *one month*.

The benchmarking visits were particularly helpful to the

redesign teams. They learned that organizations like Price Club and Wal-Mart typically ordered against huge, multiyear contracts they had with their major suppliers. Taking a page from the Japanese system of just-in-time management, these organizations were making frequent small orders, not the huge, occasional purchases that DLA procurement people were used to. "We found a strange world out there," Malsack recalled, "and we liked what we saw."

Designing the "To-Be" Model

The core team used many of their findings to craft a "to-be" model, a new design for DLA. The team made over sixty recommendations. Some of the key changes:

- They set a target of making about two-thirds of their purchases from long-term, indefinite delivery contracts. These contracts would run for three to five years or more, covering hundreds of items and multiple purchases of those items at fixed prices, which would radically reduce administrative lead time.
- They eliminated quality assurance (QA) as a separate function and embedded it in the engineering and procurement function. In the past, engineers designed quality tests for inspections, then gave the test procedures to QA, which did the administrative work with the test requirements and test results. In the redesigned process, engineers will put the data into a shared database.
- They decided to create a standard for suppliers to meet. To become a quality supplier to DLA, the vendor must do its own statistical process control, assuring the quality of the items being sold. This step reduced the need for after-the-fact inspection.
- They suggested a major reorganization of DLA. Implemented in January 1993, the new design replaced the old functional approach with commodity business units. These units are made up of small, multifunctional teams representing all the functions involved in handling a particular order or stocking an item. This

one change required the move of 1,800 employees at DISC alone.

• They also began allowing their end user customers to make certain orders directly, without going through DLA. They also went to a system of direct vendor delivery, which means that the item ordered goes directly to the DoD customer that needs it rather than stopping first at DLA. "This created lots of resistance from some of the supply center folks, who want to inspect the purchased item first, collect data on it, maintain their own QA," Malsack said.

Figure 9.3 shows the to-be model the team mapped for making large buys, based on the new structure organized around multi-functional units. Each of these units has staff from the various functions (A1 through A4) identified in the as-is model in Figure 9.2. The new structure is focused on cross-cutting processes: Support Corporate Environment (A1), Market the Business (A2), Provide for Matériel Requirements (A3), and Provide Engineering and Technical Services (A4).

The new model for making large purchases begins at A21, Identify Customers and Address Their Needs. It ends at A33, Ensure Product Delivery. Unlike the as-is model, which is primarily internally focused, the new model is externally focused on customer needs. And, as this comparison shows, it's vastly simpler and leaner than the former process: The old model required thirty-four steps; the new, just nine.

Results

Some of the recommendations have been put into effect; others are being implemented more slowly. As Malsack noted, old ways of thinking and acting do not die quickly. However, the results to date are impressive. For instance, at DISC, budget and staff level were reduced substantially, while the volume of orders remained constant:

• The time to obtain certain orders not in stock, like steel, has been reduced by 87 percent.

Figure 9.3. The To-Be Model for Large Purchases at DLA: Organized by Process.

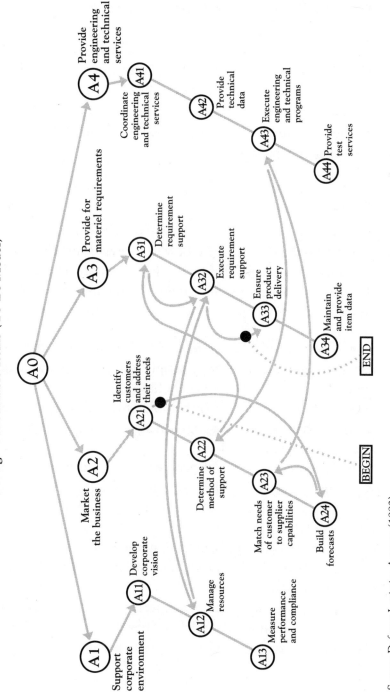

Manage Consumable Items (To-Be Model)

Source: Defense Logistics Agency (1992).

- The number of items on back order has gone from 220,000 to 170,000 in two years, which lowered costs substantially.
- Despite reduced staff and budget, availability of materials has remained constant at about 89 percent (meaning that 89 percent of their customer orders can be satisfied quickly from items in stock).
- They accomplished this with only 60 percent of their previous matériel budget.

Lessons Learned

Tom Malsack retired from the Navy to help government organizations around the country learn how to re-engineer their processes. What he and his team did at DLA offers important lessons to those who want to re-engineer large, rigid, and tradition-bound organizations:

- They advanced in stages and bit off only what they could manage at any one time (for example, some changes were made immediately, and others are being phased in).
- They made the pain of their old system clear by communicating the true cost of managing each aspect of it. Making the costs visible got people's attention.
- They understood that people would wait them out unless they demonstrated that they were serious and had the clout to make change. The move to the multifunction, commodity business units served that purpose.
- Rather than limit themselves to their own experience, they made themselves think "outside the box" by benchmarking innovative organizations.
- They read their culture very well. To convince the powers that be in the Pentagon and DLA, they documented every step along the way, using over 115 diagrams to portray the as-is and to-

be models. They also used sophisticated modeling procedures to document financial benefits of their to-be model.

• They had an ample supply of the key innovator ingredient: *persistence*. "We had three false starts," Malsack later recalled. "It wasn't easy getting people to let go of their 'functional silo' mentalities." He's right, which is not a criticism of government employees. Like corporate employees, civil servants see many energetic "idea people" come and go. It can become very painful to get excited about a leader's idea, try to implement it, then see that person get diverted to some other project (or leave for another organization). Thus, the wait 'em out game is often protection against having one's expectations raised and dashed.

Because process re-engineering promises such major change, it can be especially threatening. The onus is therefore on the leadership to show their determination by taking on the bureaucratic battles. By doing so and by making the easier changes quickly as Malsack's team did, leaders help their followers let go of old mental models and take the risk of trying on new ones.

Re-Engineering Principles Used in These Cases

The Connecticut Department of Labor and Defense Logistics Agency both ensured a continuous flow of the main sequence (getting unemployment assistance, procuring needed matériel), they provided a single point of contact for customers, they streamlined their processes before automating, and the Department of Labor captured information once through its generalist front-line staff who provided one-stop service. Most important, they both organized around outcomes, not functions. Connecticut organized around its customers; DLA, around its processes.

This chapter has described two cases that involved fundamental changes in agency systems, structures, cultures, and basic assumptions about work. The fact that both efforts were successful should not mask the difficulties and enormous amount of hard work involved. Both efforts extended over two years simply to assess, redesign, and begin implementing the new designs. There were false starts and mistakes along the way. Implementing all of their changes will require several more years.

Implementing new models isn't as exciting as designing them, but, as a highly successful public manager once stated, "Implementation . . . is, ultimately, what government is all about" (Chase and Reveal, 1983, p. 13). The next chapter identifies further strategies for effective implementation.

Chapter Ten

Getting Started on Re-Engineering

Chapter Preview

A story is told about Harry S Truman, probably apocryphal, but consistent with the popular image of plain-spoken Harry.

One day the president was being briefed by his senior economic team. Each economist took a turn analyzing current trends and forecasting the future. Unfortunately for Truman, each chose to hedge his bets, saying things like "On the one hand, Mr. President, if interest rates continue at present levels, then we expect . . . but, on the other hand, if there's an increase, then we're looking at. . . ." After several of these "on the one hand, but on the other hand" presentations, the president slammed his hand down on his huge desk.

"Damn it!" he exclaimed. "I wish I could find a one-handed economist!"

Many people in government react to new management trends with an "on the one hand, but on the other hand" frame of mind. The opportunities appear wonderful, but—on the other hand—many questions and apparent barriers remain: How do you implement re-engineering when staff are tired of "flavor of the month" management fads? How do you deal with resistance from staff who disagree with the direction or have a lot to lose? And what about turf protection and empire builders? Good questions, requiring practical answers.

This chapter deals further with the issue of implementation. We will look at the barriers and challenges to re-engineering and offer practical tips for those trying to create seamless service for their customers.

What Doesn't Work: Pilots, Trickle-Down, Tell and Sell

Re-engineering, by definition, challenges people's fundamental assumptions. *Of course*, staff get upset when told they need to change from specialists to generalists, from cops to coaches, from individualists with great visibility and authority to members of teams with shared responsibility. Such changes go directly against the assumptions many people have about their jobs, careers, and agencies. Why wouldn't they get upset? Indeed, as a consultant I get most worried when I *don't* hear any resistance or resentment. I'm sure it's out there, and if it doesn't surface sooner, it will come back and bite me later.

The question isn't, Why will some people resist re-engineering? The question to be faced first is, Are you doing anything that creates more resistance than necessary? Re-engineers should keep in mind the Hippocratic oath taken by medical students when they receive their M.D.: *"In the first place, do no harm."* The following approaches often create more harm than good.

Pilots

Most experienced civil servants know that it pays to call a new approach a pilot. It lowers initial resistance and makes funding more likely. The problem is, pilot projects are often rejected by the rest of the organization much as the human body tries to reject a transplant. Why? It's all too easy for the 99 percent of the staff not involved to discount the pilot's successes: "Anybody could succeed with the hand-picked group they put on that project; it was loaded for success." People also discount pilots by suggesting that any experiment can work in the short run, but it's the long run that counts (in other words, "If it still looks good in ten years, we'll consider learning from its lessons then"). And some worry that a pilot's success reflects poorly on the rest of the staff ("Maybe we should have been doing this all along"), especially if some staff came out against the ideas tried in the pilot. Thus, many will have a vested interest in the pilot's failure and will not want to learn from it.

In addition, the very word *pilot* suggests an experiment, a way to test the waters to see if they are warm. Re-engineering isn't an experiment; it cannot be started in a tentative manner. It must be studied carefully before implemented, because it's not for everyone. If an agency is committed to change and uses a pilot to learn how its changes will work (as Connecticut's Department of Labor did), that approach can succeed, but first the agency must make a clear and firm commitment, and it needs to involve many people, not just those in a pilot. As master consultant Marvin Weisbord has said, "To change an organization, the more people you can involve, and the faster you can help them understand how the system works and how to take responsibility for making it work better, the faster will be the change. It doesn't happen through isolated pilot projects" (Galagan, 1992, p. 33).

Trickle-Down

This approach is quite popular with many TQM consultants, who like to train the top team, then have the next level trained, then the next, and so on. There are two problems in using trickle-down for re-engineering.

First, training is irrelevant if the staff members have no way to apply the training soon after the session ends. In other words, adults need just-in-time training (Gilbert, 1993); they need to learn concepts and skills that can be applied quickly on the job. Some organizations have spent small fortunes training tens of thousands of workers, with little or nothing to show in terms of results (Schaffer and Thomson, 1992). For training to be done on a just-in-time basis, the team trained needs to be able to apply it to a project, and that needn't be done on a trickle-down basis. Once senior leadership has bought into re-engineering, any team with an important process to manage can get started.

The second problem with trickle-down implementation is that it suggests there is something important that can be done within each level of the agency. In fact, re-engineering cuts *across* levels and functions. Re-engineering isn't done by a group of middle managers or first-level supervisors or any other homogeneous group. It requires a cross-diagonal slice of the agency to form a re-engineering team. The trickle-down method isn't in alignment with fundamental re-engineering principles.

Tell and Sell

As a study done for the Kettering Foundation noted, tell and sell is the method used by many policy makers to gain public support for their ideas. In their fascinating report entitled *Meaningful Chaos: How People Form Relationships with Public Concerns* (The Harwood Group, 1993), the authors looked at the ways Americans make up their minds about public policy issues (health care proposals, gun control bans, educational reform ideas, and so on) and the methods used by national leaders to promote policy initiatives.

Tell and sell works like this:

1. Break the problem into small, manageable bits, fragmented from other issues.
2. Bring in experts to lend credibility to your solution.
3. Marshal facts favorable to your solution.
4. Appeal to people's immediate self interest.
5. Polarize the debate—"ours is the only reasonable approach; the others make no sense."
6. Finally, "win over" people by continually repeating your solution.

Focus group participants told the Kettering researchers that they get turned off by this approach. I have seen many organizational leaders use the same approach to sell a new management initiative (TQM, empowerment, creativity), usually with minimal success. Civil servants, like the public at large, are not convinced by tell and sell.

What Does Work: Meaningful Chaos, Control, Involvement, Phased Implementation

In Chapter Five we discussed the preconditions for re-engineering: felt pain with the status quo, which is articulated in a way all can understand, a game plan for dealing with the problem, and active commitment at the top. Once these are in place and re-engineering begins, there are four useful themes to keep in mind.

Meaningful Chaos

This term, used by the authors of the Kettering report noted earlier, characterizes the way citizens make decisions about public policy issues. In my experience, it beautifully captures the ways most staff go about deciding whether to buy into a new management initiative in their agency.

By meaningful chaos, the authors mean that the American people do not make up their minds about complex issues in a mechanistic, straightforward, linear fashion (as the tell-and-sell approach presumes). Rather, we think things through in a messier way, characterized by dialogue (not polarized debate) with friends and co-workers (not experts).

Specifically, people need time, space, shades of gray, and discussion with those who have credibility, as they decide whether to support a given solution. We want to be actively involved not passively sold. We want to interact with others like ourselves. And we want to hear all sides of the issue, not be subjected to super sales pitches.

Several implications prevail for leaders about to begin a re-engineering process. First, keep in mind that you have no greater asset than your credibility (Kouzes and Posner, 1987). Thus, don't oversell re-engineering. Be straight about the difficulties as well as the benefits. Don't suggest that it's the only approach or that the agency will go belly-up tomorrow without it.

In addition, staff need all the information you can give them as to what the problem is, why it's so important to address it, why this approach appears better than others, and which other approaches were considered but not adopted. Further, meaningful chaos implies that people have time and space to talk with others about the new approach; informal organizational leaders will have more influence on staff members' thinking than will formal leaders at this point, which means that informal leaders (including union representatives) need to be involved in discussions leading up to the decision to re-engineer.

And meaningful chaos suggests that staff need to see connections; to understand if and how re-engineering affects agency mission, staff roles, career ladders, the way work is done. In a word, staff need to see the *context* in order to decide whether to actively support the initiative.

Control and Involvement

Any stress management workshop worth its price will focus on people's need for some control during stressful situations. A major re-engineering project will raise the stress level, and staff need some levers for control. Moreover, they need a variety of ways to become involved, not as passive consumers but as active participants. There are different ways to foster control and involvement.

One approach is to learn from the Connecticut Department of Labor experience. Of all the re-engineering cases in this book, that may well have been the most disruptive: from nine management layers to four, from ninety-three managers to twenty-six, which required managers to compete in order to retain a management role. How did the leadership team pull it off? Extensive staff involvement was a key. Managers and front-line staff were asked to do everything from write new job descriptions and performance review systems to train one another and assess each other's capabilities.

A second approach was being used by a U.S. Forest Service team charged with literally reinventing that agency for the coming decade. The team members agreed on many of the changes that the Forest Service must make in the future. Rather than write up their report and send it in, the team started by using what one member called a "process of discovery." The idea was to take all the information they had gathered about the agency, its systems and programs, its customers and their perceptions of the agency, its future challenges and opportunities and threats, then give it to groups of Forest Service employees around the country. Those groups were asked to review and discuss the information and determine what changes they believed were necessary to meet the future challenges they envision.

The risk of this approach, of course, is that different groups would come up with wildly differing conclusions. However, if the information includes a clear statement of the agency's mission and the team's task, if staff groups are given a clear set of criteria within which to work, and if they understand that their reactions are input for a senior team (so that expectations aren't raised to impossible levels), it's interesting how often such staff groups come to similar conclusions on their own. The discovery process has many advantages, if managed well. The most important advantage is that staff members will be convincing each other of the changes needed. Just as happy car owners are the most persuasive marketers of their model to potential buyers, the discovery process can transform hundreds of staff into an internal constituency for change.

Finally, staff can gain a sense of control and involvement by forming what I call "re-engineering user's groups." Once the re-engineering principles and steps have been learned, staff at all levels can become energized and committed to their use through informal user groups. The results of the meaningful chaos study showed that change and commitment are not linear processes. People need their own space and time to think and explore proposals with those they respect. User's groups provide the ingredients for involvement, control, and meaningful chaos.

Re-engineering, by definition, is about radical change. Such change doesn't take place in one swift act. Rather, it needs to be phased in over time, as was the case with the Department of Labor and DLA cases described in Chapter Nine. The overall plan should be in place at the start, so that everyone knows what to expect. However, most major re-engineering projects proceed in stages.

In the first stage, managers frequently implement steps that can be taken within the existing budget and culture. These won't necessarily lead to a quantum leap in performance, but they can be taken quickly and signal the leadership's commitment to change.

Here are some examples of steps that can be taken quickly, within existing budget and culture:

- Eliminating non-value-adding steps in the process
- Training staff in skills needed for new roles
- Making procedural changes
- Changing position descriptions
- Using pilots to test and learn from certain parts of the model
- Forming multi-functional teams

In the second stage, managers can take steps that require additional resources and that begin to change the agency culture. These usually involve more far-reaching changes, and often a good deal of disruption, as the old process is replaced by the new.

Examples of steps that require additional resources and that change the culture include

- Moving from a functional to a process orientation and structure
- Migrating to new information technologies

- Forming close working partnerships with suppliers and customers
- Using activity-based costing to identify costs associated with activities and processes
- Doing ongoing measurement of the new processes: cost, time, quality, and customer satisfaction

How Do You Deal with Resistance?

Let's assume that you've followed the above guidelines. There still will be some staff who will resist the change. Chances are, resistance will come from three sources:

- Managers who fear losing their turf, power, and even their jobs
- Staff who like their technical specialist role and do not want to become generalists
- Those who work in central staff departments (planning, finance, accounting, human resources, purchasing, and the like) whose jobs may evaporate, be transferred, or change from a control orientation to a consulting role

Managers Who Resist Change and Fear Loss

The loss and changing role of management jobs isn't new, of course. It has been going on since the 1981–82 recession and shows no sign of letting up. The trend will only grow, as middle managers everywhere know. In fact, middle manager ranks were the prime targets for cuts identified in Vice President Gore's National Performance Review. The task force's recommendations on downsizing noted that roughly 700,000 federal employees "manage, control, check up on or audit others." These positions, it emphasized, usually add little value, and quite often subtract value (Gore, 1993, p. 14). The administration estimated that of 252,000 positions to be abolished,

140,000 would come from the management ranks (Barr, 1993a).

Re-engineering typically requires change at the middle-manager level, and that is where much of the resistance to change can be expected. According to a National Academy of Public Administration survey of state and federal managers engaged in re-engineering projects, turf battles by functional officials was the most frequently-cited barrier to success (noted by 51 percent of the respondents). The major barriers identified by the NAPA study (Caudle, 1994) included

- Turf battles (51 percent)
- Resistance to change (45 percent)
- Lack of someone with authority to push the project (42 percent)
- Lack of incentives (41 percent)
- Difficulty in thinking "out of the box" (41 percent)
- Resources tied up in legacy systems (41 percent)
- Lack of top management commitment (38 percent)
- Skepticism about another management change effort (38 percent)

Most managers who remain in changing organizations will be taking on new and challenging roles. Some will find these changes to be exciting opportunities; many will find them painful. "It's gut wrenching," according to Xerox CEO Paul Allaire. "The hardest person to change is the line manager. After he's worked like a dog for five or ten years to get promoted, we have to say to him or her, 'All those reasons you wanted to be a manager? Wrong. . . . You have to be a facilitator or a coach and, by the way, we're still going to hold you to the bottom line" (Davidow and Malone, 1992, p. 177). What can managers do who fear, rightly or wrongly, that they will be losers in any re-engineering effort?

First, they need to do what all major changes require: *accept the fact of change*. Our organizations aren't going back to the top-down, one-size-fits-all, traditional bureaucratic designs that most of us grew up in; those days are gone. A second step is to *look for opportunities*. Opportunities abound to grow and learn, and many organizations going through wrenching changes are providing excellent career counseling and training services to their affected employees (the Defense Department is an excellent federal example). There are opportunities to try out new roles. Many managers tell me they have wanted to get out of their controlling mode but didn't know how. And there are opportunities to go "back" to a direct service or technical role. Some managers miss the immediacy and satisfaction they had in earlier jobs. Technical and direct service jobs provide real-time feedback, a sense of accomplishment that something tangible has happened.

And the final step for managers is to *choose*. Once they have accepted the inevitable and have explored their new options, they need to make honest choices that reflect their abilities, hopes, and personal situations. Some will opt to leave. Some, unfortunately, will find their jobs gone and will try to stay while fighting the change. Those who stay must be very realistic about the future. It will be both exciting and painful. Exciting, because the new processes and systems can delight external and internal customers alike. Painful, because the skills and behaviors rewarded by the old system won't be rewarded by the new one. In addition, the changes won't come in one neat and tidy bundle. Rather, they can continue for months or years. Like the marathon runner who climbs a long hill at the twentieth mile, only to find at the top that the road continues upward, managers will find their journeys long, often uphill runs.

Those who choose to stay provide the organization an invaluable resource—they have credibility, they contain knowledge of the agency history, and they know where the processes break down. Those who choose to stay and learn how re-engineering can transform an agency will have chosen the wisest career strategy available today, the strategy of remaining employable.

Technical Specialists Who Fear Taking on Generalist Positions

This situation is a serious problem in government. Many government agencies are "technocracies" in the sense that they hire people who are well trained in one technical specialty, then promote them because of their technical contributions. Our agencies are filled with engineers, scientists, lawyers, social workers, extension agents, accountants, auditors and the like. The Senior Executive Service (SES), established in the federal government in 1978 by the Civil Service Reform Act, was supposed to foster the creation of a corps of senior generalists who would rotate, take sabbaticals, and learn how the entire federal system worked. It was a noble idea; it didn't work. And little wonder. The systems didn't change to reward generalist perspectives.

Contrast our government model with that used at Honda. There, an engineer spends the first three months working on an assembly line. Then he or she works in marketing for three months. The next year is spent rotating through the various engineering departments before settling into a technical area. But that isn't all. Honda continues to rotate its engineers; even the most senior ones spend one month a year in a totally different department to gain broader exposure to the whole company (Womack, Jones, and Roos, 1990). It's said that in Japan, a manager specializes in a company, not a functional area. Few federal employees have any experience with this sort of rotation and cross-training, military personnel being the one major exception.

The best option for an agency's technical specialists during re-engineering is to look for opportunities to learn. Like their managerial colleagues, their roles will change, and gaining new skills is the best strategy for dealing with this change. As government agencies downsize, they won't be able to support large numbers of narrowly trained specialists. They will need more generalists, and the remaining specialists will frequently find themselves working with staff from different technical areas.

To support these changes, government agencies must provide intensive training and education. In this respect, many agencies have a tremendous gap to fill. Leading private companies going through similar realignments are investing enormous amounts in training and retraining their workers. Motorola, a Malcolm Baldridge Award winner, is a leading example. *Every* one of Motorola's 104,000 employees is required to spend at least forty hours a year in job-related training. This costs Motorola about $200 million a year—and the company is planning to increase training requirements (Porter, 1993). Other corporate leaders like Levi Strauss and Intel make similar investments in their employees.

According to the National Commission on the Public Service (1989), leading private organizations spend 3 to 5 percent of their budgets on training, retraining, and upgrading employee skills. By contrast, *the federal government spends less than 1 percent on training,* and the largest amount of the training dollar goes to educating managers, not technical or support staff. A few agencies can boast of genuine investment in ongoing training (one such is the Family Housing Office at the Naval Public Works Center in Yokosuka, Japan, where they close the office to external customers a half day a week for ongoing staff development training), but they are, by definition, major exceptions. The area of education and training should be the largest growth area for our public sector institutions during the coming decade.

Central Staff Specialists Whose Roles Are Being Eliminated

These staff may face the toughest challenge in re-engineered agencies, for their very reason for being is at the heart of our agencies' problems. Most central staff functions—personnel and civil service, finance, planning, management and budgeting, purchasing, contract specialists, auditing—were created to prevent abuses in government. Some, like civil service, go back to the 1880s. These staff, as well as oversight boards and commissions, were given a very explicit mission: oversee the work of the line departments, and prevent fraud and abuse. Thus, they were given the "white hats" to wear in government; they were the virtuous ones, sent to weed out graft and wrongdoing (Barzelay and Armajani, 1990).

The tensions that frequently exist between these central staffers and the line managers they monitor are not primarily a function of different personalities or turf fighting, although those are part of the problem. The fundamental issue is totally differing missions. Line departments, established to perform the agency's mission, are rewarded for implementation. Central staff departments, on the other hand, are rewarded for catching the implementers doing something wrong. Thus, it's no wonder that many staffers see their role in very bureaucratic, rule-bound ways (what reward is there for making exceptions?), while the line people wear the Nikes in the agency, wanting to "just do it."

As government agencies map current processes and look for non-value-adding steps, they will continually point to the central staff functions as major barriers to change. It's not that these staff functions add no value; they *subtract* value if they maintain a control mentality. The folks with the white hats are suddenly seen as villains.

The future for central staffers is clear. Their units will become smaller as many of them are farmed out to line departments. Whether they remain in their unit or go to line departments, most central staffers will switch from cop to consultant. They will teach line managers and staff how to do what the central staff once did for—or to—them. A model is the Hampton, Virginia, Human Resources Department, where staff "specialize" in their client departments, not in the various personnel functions. A typical day for a member of Hampton's HRD self-managing team might involve advising a police lieutenant on an EEO question, leading a workshop for middle managers on how to develop a pool of qualified applicants for supervisory positions, training a group of employees in the Americans with Disabilities Act (ADA), and counseling a secretary who wants to appeal a performance evaluation.

Notice the nature of these tasks: information sharing, educating, consulting, helping, counseling. These roles have no power in the formal sense of the term. And that's the point. The central staffers will lose their formal power to check, control, police, say no, and cite for violations. Their new, informal power will be generated by the value they add as enablers. For many central staffers, this will take a totally new mind-set.

Their challenge will be twofold. First, they must confront their vastly changed *role* and reason for existing. That means viewing line managers as customers, not as potential wrongdoers. Second, they must develop the *skills* needed to be helpful consultants. They will learn better how to listen, assess others' underlying needs, and use consensus-building skills. Moreover, they will need to learn how to think strategically. Staffers will need to understand those departments' direction, vision, comparative advantages, strategies, shortcomings, and formula for success. Even more important, they will have to learn how to help their customer departments do such thinking for themselves.

The changes for central staff represent a whole new world. It will be an incredibly exciting world for those who want the challenge. Staff in the information systems shop will help customer departments hook into networks and create paperless offices, as the Forest Service is doing. Former purchasing czars will be rewarded for taking themselves out of the loop, equipping departments with on-line systems giving them real-time information on prices, availability, and service. Personnelists will be leading train-the-trainer sessions to build a cadre of employee trainers who deliver personnel information. They will also facilitate employee teams that design new evaluation systems. Finance people will be helping line managers learn how to use activity-based costing, a method for tracking costs to the work processes performed (see the next chapter), and they will organize workshops on the latest available financial software packages. Accountants will help reduce the paper flow by replacing invoices and purchase orders with electronic data interchange (EDI) systems that link the agency's computers with those of its suppliers and customers.

It will happen; some of it is happening now. It won't be easy, and it will be painful to some who sincerely try to get with the new program. For, as Davidow and Malone note (1992), "[i]t will be one of the sad ironies of the new business revolution . . . that many of the workers and managers who worked so hard to bring that revolution about will find themselves unable, by personality or sensibility, to cross over into the Promised Land. It will be the task of management and labor, working together in a shared task, to help the group of disenfranchised workers succeed" (p. 216). Corporate America's current love affair with downsizing shows no sign of letting up, and the trend is spreading to government. The wise advice of journalist Ronald Henkoff (1990), to "eliminate work, not necessarily workers" (p. 40), isn't being heeded today.

And What About Those Who Still Don't Get the Message?

What do you do with empire builders who simply won't let go? I am a fierce believer in one of the central tenets of the quality management movement: most mistakes come from management and systems problems, not from the front-line employees. The late W. Edwards Deming was right when he made that statement, and the Japanese have shown the value in bending over backward to find new slots for staff who aren't performing well.

Having said that, I have no sympathy for the individual who insists on holding his or her turf when the agency needs to move away from a control orientation and toward process teams. These empire builders know how to tie the agency up in knots. And that, of course, is exactly what happens all too often, because nobody is able or willing to challenge them. I don't believe in lifetime employment for such individuals—they have no right to hold the agency back, and leaders are responsible for dealing with them directly. Some empire builders are adept at *appearing* to go along with the new approach while still holding tightly onto the controls. Once such individuals have been counseled, listened to, given opportunities for involvement, and so on, only one practical step is left (assuming they cannot be fired): eliminate their job.

Whether you can fire such individuals or not, it may not be in the agency's interest to do so. They may have many talents you don't want to lose, they may have fine performance appraisals that leave you no firm basis to terminate them, and they may have an important network of colleagues whom you cannot afford to totally alienate. On the other hand, you cannot afford to keep them where they are. People who stubbornly sit on their empires leave you few options. The requirements of a seamless agency leave you only one, which is to change the job. Find or create another job for this person, but don't allow a control-oriented position to remain when the rest of the agency is moving away from control and toward outcome-based processes.

When you have the luxury of time, you can try the "pull" method used so well by Bob O'Neill in Hampton. He allowed department heads to make changes at their own speed, as long as they met their performance contracts with him each year. This approach created some tension and anger, but far less than the radical surgery used in Connecticut, where dozens of control-oriented management jobs were eliminated. Among the assumptions challenged by re-engineering is the turf-oriented managers' belief that they have the power and savvy to wait you out. It's up to you to demonstrate that that assumption no longer holds water. It's not easy, and it certainly isn't fun, but it's essential. And when leaders demonstrate that empire builders and "control artists" will no longer be allowed to hold the rest of the staff back, it sends a powerful, even inspiring message to those who support the transformation. The message: This change is for real.

This chapter has focused on implementation strategies for managers eager to re-engineer their agencies. For managers to be successful over the long run, an infrastructure supportive of seamless organizing must replace the walls that have supported our government's fragmented bureaucracy, as discussed in the next chapter.

Conclusion

Working Without Walls

The Best of Times, the Worst of Times: A Tale of Two Governments

Most people have little difficulty recalling an example of government fouling up the works. Here is one of my all-time favorite stories.

In New York City, on May 28, 1986, Donald Trump made an offer that New York couldn't refuse. He offered to reconstruct the ice skating rink in Central Park, complete the job in less than six months, at a cost of $3 million, with any cost overruns coming out of Trump's pocket. The offer was irresistible because the city had spent six years and almost $13 million trying to rebuild the rink, with no success. The city's failure was due to several factors, including a refrigeration system that did not work, requirements to go with the lowest bidder (irrespective of past performance), and bureaucratic requirements forcing the city to renegotiate the contract for *every single change* it wanted to make. Mayor Ed Koch agreed to Trump's offer one week later, and the city quickly appropriated money for the project. On October 28, one month ahead of schedule and $750,000 under budget, the renovation was complete. Two weeks later skaters were using the rink (Wilson, 1989).

Unfortunately, it isn't as easy for people to cite examples of streamlined, innovative government. But here is one of the most important examples: the Internal Revenue Service.

At certain sites around the country, taxpayers are benefiting from one of the federal government's most innovative and ambitious projects, the transformation of the IRS. Today, some taxpayers can file their returns electronically, getting faster refunds that can be deposited directly into their bank accounts. Another innovation that is expanding in use is TeleFile, which allows tax-payers to do all of their filing using Touch-Tone phones. Some tax-payers can now file state and federal returns in one transaction; a single electronic transmission of their tax information satisfies both state and federal requirements, instantaneously. And in the near future taxpayers will be able to make payments, enter into installment agreements, file for extensions, and perform other transactions twenty-four hours a day through their phones, using a voice response system. These and other innovations will be avail-able to all citizens before the year 2000 (U.S. Department of the Treasury, 1993).

Which of these scenarios will characterize the coming decade? Will we continue to be plagued with bureaucracies that cannot perform the most basic of government services (like fixing an ice rink)? Will our elected officials continue to micromanage agencies, hampering streamlining efforts through their financial controls? Or will they have the foresight to give their agencies greater flex-ibility in return for more accountability? Will they have the will to make the investments that seamless government requires? (The IRS alone is spending $7.8 billion to restructure and bring in new systems over the next fifteen years to achieve its vision.) Will civil servants find ways to cut through the red tape and turf battles that made it impossible for our nation's largest city to fix its most visi-ble skating rink?

A Seamless, "Anytime, Anyplace" Government? Structural Requirements and Hopeful Signs

This book has described how some agencies are transforming them-selves, how they are tearing down the functional walls separating staff from their colleagues, consumers, and constituents in order to provide seamless service. But what will replace those walls? In almost all organizations, the functional walls are "load bearing," which means that they provide the only structure the staff know.

If we tear the walls down, what do we put in their place? How do we avoid chaos?

One important answer has been detailed throughout this book. We are replacing rigid functional departments with flexible process teams accountable for achieving specific customer outcomes. For those process teams to succeed, however, more will be needed. First, we must create *new mechanisms* to support the process teams. Second, we must create an *infrastructure* that supports these new mechanisms. Finally, we need to change the *micromanaging role* that elected officials often play as they carry out their oversight function. Fortunately, there are reasons to be optimistic about each of these changes. In this chapter, we will look at these three challenges and at trends and tools that can help civil servants meet these challenges as they re-engineer their agencies for seamless service.

New Mechanisms

It is one thing to temporarily remove walls between departments or between an agency and its customers/constituents, for a specific project. It's quite another to remove them permanently. Like bamboo, they tend to grow back every time they're cut down. Organizational gurus like David Nadler believe that information will provide the "load-bearing" material of the future (Stewart, 1993). In the public sector, however, information won't be enough. To ensure that special interests, the media, and elected officials don't create more walls, new mechanisms are needed. The following measures can ensure that the old walls stay down, permanently.

Alternative Dispute Resolution

The legal profession has been slow to recognize the value of alternative dispute resolution (ADR), but many government agencies have embraced it as a godsend. This approach includes mediation, arbitration, minitrials, and fact finding. It has been used to resolve a variety of disputes in the rule-making process, contracts, enforce-ment actions, equal employment suits, and a wide range of per-sonnel disputes.

Alternative dispute resolution keeps problems out of courts, avoids polarization of issues, and reduces delays and costs of griev-ances. Those costs run high: the Labor Department employs 530 full-time attorneys and 220 support staff who handle 24,000 litiga-tion cases each year (Gore, 1993); the Air Force estimates that it costs $80,000 to take a discrimination case through the entire for-mal complaint process (Hoffman and Wagner, 1993). Federal agen-cies such as the Justice Department, Army Corps of Engineers, Education Department, and a number of state and local govern-ments use ADR on a routine basis. This strategy streamlines the process of resolving disputes. It avoids raising the walls created by formal grievances. Consistent with re-engineering, ADR keeps the parties focused on desired outcomes.

Partnering

As described earlier, partnering tears down barriers between agen-cies and their contractors by challenging the assumption that gov-ernment contracting must be an adversarial process. The contracts specialist no longer peers over the contractor's shoulder, and the contractor doesn't feel the need to cut corners. As seen in the Army Corps of Engineers, Arizona Department of Transportation, and other agencies, partnering lowers costs, reduces delays, raises trust and quality, and results in far fewer legal claims (Cole, 1993; Edelman, Carr, and Lancaster, 1991).

Negotiated Rule Making

Negotiated rule making, or reg neg, applies the basic partnering concept to the regulatory process. Traditionally, when an agency publishes proposed regulations, it allows a period for public com-ment. The "comment" often becomes a pitched battle in which the spokespersons for all sides duke it out, which sometimes leads to litigation, usually to delays. Negotiated rule making brings together representatives of those affected by the draft regulations *before* the regs are issued. Using a facilitator, the parties try to negotiate a consensus on the regulations. They are able to listen to each other and look for creative solutions to their differences, because the process takes place outside the glare of public scrutiny. It's less formal, more educational, and far more effective than relying solely on the public comment process, which encourages posturing and puts up nearly insurmountable walls.

In 1990, Congress passed the Negotiated Rulemaking Act, which promotes the use of regulatory negotiations. Several agencies, including the EPA and Department of Transportation, are using reg neg to break down barriers between special interests and help them develop consensus around desired outcomes.

BRAC Commission Model

The Base Realignment and Closure (BRAC) Commission is one of the federal government's best-kept secrets. The BRAC is largely unknown outside the Beltway and the communities affected by military base closures. Its story must be told, because it has handled the incredibly divisive issue of base closures in a manner few thought possible.

With the end of the Cold War we need a smaller military, and that means military bases will close. Congress could not have made reasonable decisions on which bases to close; the political pressures would have been too fierce. To its credit, Congress realized it could never make rational decisions on this process, so it established the BRAC Commission.

Members of the commission are appointed by the president. The secretary of defense establishes criteria for base closure decisions. Staff in each service branch use the criteria to recommend which bases to keep, close, or realign. The secretary presents an overall Department of Defense plan to the commission, which holds hearings in the impacted communities and with members of Congress and the armed services.

Finally, the commission votes on each recommendation, in public, and sends its list of closures and realignments to the president. The president essentially has two choices: he can approve or disapprove the BRAC plan. He cannot make individual changes. He votes it up or down in its entirety. If he approves the plan, it goes to Congress, which has the same up-or-down option. There is no horse trading; it passes or fails as presented.

The BRAC concept accepts the role of elected officials but adds an important element of nonelected expertise and judgment. Individuals with no vested interest and no need to run for reelection make decisions based on the needs of the entire country. Thus far it has worked well in dealing with the necessary but painful decisions of base closures. The BRAC concept provides an important model that government agencies at all levels can use. When the walls created by partisan bickering and special interest groups grow too high to deal with issues like budget deficits and gun control, the BRAC model can help.

Seamless Infrastructure

The new mechanisms noted in the preceding sections are necessary but not sufficient for creating seamless government service. Once the functional walls are replaced, managers need an infrastructure that supports "anytime, anyplace" seamless service. Here are elements of the emerging infrastructure.

Groupware

Groupware is a generic term for sophisticated software that enables organizations to work in a seamless fashion. It has far more power than E-mail, which works well for one-to-one and one-many communications. Groupware allows for many-to-many communications; it enables groups of people thousands of miles apart to brainstorm, plan, set priorities, and make decisions, all in real time. Groupware is radically changing the way some organizations work, abolishing the pyramidal structure by giving everyone access to information previously restricted to senior management.

With groupware, organizations can accomplish the following tasks:

- Engage hundreds of staff in simultaneous brainstorming through their PCs. Because people read faster than they speak, because everyone is working simultaneously (not sequentially, as in traditional brainstorming), and because contributions are anonymous, everyone contributes and productivity skyrockets. Some agencies report they solve problems in a day that previously took months.

- Map current organizational processes and identify bottlenecks and non-value-adding steps. Like the IDEF software used by the Defense Logistics Agency and many other organizations, this application is especially pertinent to re-engineering.

- Combine a giant database with a sophisticated message system to form an organizational on-line service, which allows staff to use internal electronic bulletin boards. Anyone with an idea can respond, and anyone tuned into the network can learn from the responses (Kirkpatrick, 1993).

Activity-Based Costing

Traditional cost accounting systems used by most organizations are not in sync with the needs of a seamless agency. Cost accounting gives managers information on the *categories* they *control*—salaries, fringe benefits, travel, supplies, equipment, and the like. Unfortunately, this information has little utility today, because it doesn't give managers accurate cost information on activities that have relevance, like the cost of responding to a fire or using a new type of technology.

Activity-based costing (ABC) shows the true costs of agency activities and processes. It allows managers to make better decisions, because it provides solid data on their current activities and the cost of alternatives.

To use ABC, employees analyze what they do each day (say, taking citizen complaints in a public works department, sending crews out, repairing broken pipes, paving sections of roadway, and so on). Next, they determine the amount of time spent on each activity and add the appropriate amount of overhead. These data show the real costs of major activities. A public works manager can compare the true cost of picking up refuse, for example, with the cost of contracting it out.

Agencies within the Department of Defense are using ABC to learn the real costs of their important business activities. Activity-based costing is helping some hospitals make better decisions (such as whether to purchase certain technology like MRI; whether to offer certain clinical services in the hospital, at outreach centers, or not at all). Activity-based costing has become the system of choice for a growing number of companies, and it will be used by government agencies that choose to organize around processes (Paré, 1993; Cooper and Kaplan, 1988, 1991).

Telecommuting

Telecommuting facilitates an "anytime, anyplace" agency by allowing staff to work away from their offices, on their own schedules. In the two most common forms of telecommuting, staff work at home or at telecommuting centers, using PCs, modems and faxes, and E-mail to stay in touch with colleagues. An estimated eight million people currently telecommute, and all levels of government are experimenting with it. California, Washington, and Hawaii have established regional telecommuting centers in the past five years, and there are four "telebusiness" centers near Los Angeles, sponsored by local governments and Pacific Bell (Master and Joice, 1993). According to a report on National Public Radio's "All Things Considered" (Jan. 27, 1994), a study of five hundred Los Angeles city employees found that their productivity rose 12 percent once they began telecommuting. California is now requiring medium-sized and large organizations to reduce the number of employee commuting days each year, in order to relieve traffic congestion and smog.

Telecommuting offers many benefits, including more employee time at home with family and community, less work-related stress, greater productivity, flatter organizational structure, greater empowerment and accountability. It also improves productivity. It benefits re-engineers in two important ways: (1) it focuses specifically on outcomes—staff are paid to accomplish certain things, not to fill time—and (2) it shatters the centuries-old assumption that work in industrialized settings occurs in a specific place at a specific time. In a global economy, government's customers and constituents often live many time zones away. It doesn't make sense to limit office hours to 8:30 to 5:00 Eastern time, if your state is trading in Asia or your drug agents are collaborating with agents in Europe. Seamless government in the global economy requires flexibility, which telecommuting provides.

Telecommuting eliminates an important non-value-adding step in every commuter's life—time on the road. It encourages staff to spend less time on the internal needs of their agency and more time focused on the needs of their customers. And telecommuting is consistent with the single point-of-contact re-engineering principle, by giving staff the systems that enable them to handle the complete job.

The Office of Personnel Management and General Services Administration studied telecommuting and found many advantages. What began as a pilot at the federal level in 1990 was formally embraced by Congress in 1992 when it appropriated

$5 million to fund four telecommuting centers in West Virginia, Virginia, and Maryland. As agencies embrace the concept of seamless service, they will challenge the assumption that all work takes place in a certain time and place. Once that assumption is rejected, widespread telecommuting will follow (Warren Master, personal communication, 1993; U.S. General Services Administration, 1993).

Flexibility for Accountability

Thus far we have looked at two requirements for seamless government service—new mechanisms to replace the old functional walls and creation of an infrastructure to support these mechanisms. A seamless government requires one other significant condition, and it's the one about which civil servants are most pessimistic: *elected officials must stop micromanaging agency staff.*

It's simply impossible to use the first re-engineering principle—organize around outcomes—if elected officials are dictating the details of agency work. Staff cannot be accountable for outcomes if elected officials (most of whom have never managed) tell staff how to do their work, just as elected officials cannot fulfill their policy-making role if staff inappropriately change those policies as they implement them.

When we learn of outrageous failure on the part of government agencies, the public's temptation is to blame lazy bureaucrats who only care about their security. A more accurate explanation is that elected officials too often micromanage the staff. In the ice rink case, for instance, New York City regulations prohibited managers from discussing the project with general contractors who might later bid on it! And a New York state law prohibited the general contractor who won the bid from selecting his own subcontractors (Wilson, 1989). When elected officials tie the staff's hands, they have little opportunity to do what they are hired to do—use their minds. They cannot organize around the outcomes; they are forced to organize around the regulations that limit their discretion.

Alas, we will never be fully rid of elected official micromanagement; the short-term political payoffs are too tempting. Moreover, people in the United States have very ambivalent feelings
about the role of bureaucracy and bureaucrats, and that ambiva-
lence goes back to our Constitutional roots.

The founding fathers did not design a system based on the values of efficiency and effectiveness. That wasn't their concern;
tyranny was. As David Marion (1985) has noted, the founders'
"deep-seated suspicion, indeed resentment, of executives and
administrators . . . cannot be overstated" (p. 20). Rather than allow
power to accumulate in any one place, the founders dispersed it,
forcing governmental agencies to please multiple masters.

The founders could not have foreseen the administrative problems that their system would create: "In the agrarian context of the
eighteenth century, they did not worry much about the capacity of
government to govern, whether the division of powers between
President and Congress would so hamper the regime that neither
branch could ever arrive at and implement the agreements needed
by an industrialized country" (Riggs, 1994, p. 65). Another com-
plication is the formal role that the Constitution grants to Congress. Many students of government believe that our system gives
Congress more power over the agencies than it gives to the president, despite the fact that most agencies are part of the executive
branch. Congress creates and destroys agencies, determines their
appropriations, defines their mission and scope, and approves high-
level presidential appointments (Woll, 1963).

Thus, Congress's intrusive role in the administration of government is built into our Constitutional roots, and the same is true
in many state governments. The council-manager form of government used in most small and medium-sized local governments does
a better job of separating policy making from administrative roles,
but there too the lines become very fuzzy.

Further, our federal system of multiple masters invites interest
groups to influence policy. In fact, James Madison welcomed the

fragmentation that our system creates; he imagined a society "broken into many parts, interests and classes of citizens" and believed that a "multiplicity of interests" would deter both the tyranny of despots and the tyranny of the majority (quoted in Wilson, 1982, p. 66). If that was the founders' strategy, it was brilliantly executed in the Constitution. Fragmentation is built in. The British have a term for it. They call it "institutionalized paranoia."

When you start with a fragmented system that forces staff to deal with multiple masters, one that gives elected officials great leverage to influence the details of administration, and add the fact that micromanagement by elected officials is rewarded politically, is there any hope for reform? I believe there is. The hope comes in the form of a new compact between elected officials and executive agencies, a compact based on the first re-engineering principle: organize around outcomes.

Oregon Benchmarks: Management by Outcomes

An excellent example of the new compact was noted in Chapter Three, the Oregon Benchmarks experience. Oregon Benchmarks is a long-term planning process that has included thousands of citizens, the state legislature, and its civil servants. The benchmarks are specific outcomes for which state agencies are accountable, in areas such as adult literacy rate, number of localities meeting pollution standards, crime rate, and so on. Every two years the agencies report on progress toward these outcomes, and their funding is tied to their accomplishments. Senior executives are responsible for high-priority benchmarks, which is critical when two or more agencies must coordinate to achieve those priorities. The state legislature has actively supported Benchmarks, through its involvement and legislation.

Oregon Benchmarks is a huge step toward organizing around outcomes. It has bipartisan support. It won't prevent elected officials from involvement in administrative details, but it will reduce that tendency. Oregon Benchmarks gives elected officials some confidence in their ability to hold the bureaucracy accountable for results that they have approved. Legislators are regularly briefed on Benchmarks progress; there are few surprises. And legislators can use the budget process to reward agencies for performance. Oregon Benchmarks is a model worth emulating. It gives agencies what they need—clear direction—and provides elected officials what they want (and are due)—accountability (Oregon Progress Board, 1992).

Government Performance and Results Act: Flexibility for Accountability

Another promising initiative is the Government Performance and Results Act (GPRA), passed by Congress in 1993. This act, like Oregon Benchmarks, focuses on agency outcomes. It requires virtually all federal agencies to develop five-year strategic plans by the start of fiscal year 1998. These plans must include specific outcome-related goals. Beginning with fiscal 1999, agencies must also submit annual performance plans that include measurable goals, a plan for meeting those goals, and the indicators that will be used to measure progress toward them. Starting in fiscal 2000, agencies must submit annual program performance reports that compare actual performance with goals.

Significantly, the GPRA allows agencies to request waivers on certain procedural requirements and controls—over staffing levels, limitations on compensation, and prohibitions on transfers among budget categories. Thus, the GPRA will give agencies the flexibility they need, in exchange for the accountability Congress wants. *Flexibility for accountability*—that's the deal. If it works as intended, it's a good deal for everyone.

To prepare for full implementation, fifty-three agencies began pilot projects during fiscal year 1994. Several pilots are being used to test the "flexibility for accountability" concept. These agencies will request waivers from certain administrative controls, as they work toward stated outcomes. Other agencies are pilots in the use of performance budgeting, a method that identifies the costs of achieving different levels of performance. Like activity-based costing, performance budgeting gives managers data about the costs of things that matter (like the number of bridges brought up to standard, percentage of babies immunized) rather than internal indicators that mean little to elected officials or citizens.

Oregon is only one state, though several states are adopting its Benchmarks principles. The GPRA is only a piece of paper; it remains to be seen if Congress and the Office of Management and Budget (which oversees the GPRA) will make good on their end of the bargain. Equally important, the agencies will have to establish meaningful outcomes and develop useful performance indicators, a task that many will find difficult. Most agencies are used to measuring inputs (such as the number of requests for service); some also measure outputs (percentage of requests responded to within a given time period). Few have learned how to measure *outcomes* (such as the percentage who were better able to meet their needs after interacting with the agency). However, the GPRA, like Oregon Benchmarks, is extraordinarily significant, because it gives agencies and elected officials principles both can affirm— focus on outcomes and flexibility for accountability. These are important starts.

Beyond the Models: A New Way of Thinking

In this chapter, we have looked at three conditions important to the implementation of seamless government service: new mechanisms to replace old functional walls, infrastructure that supports seamless service, and new relationships with elected officials that give staff flexibility in exchange for accountability.

When provided, these conditions and tools will be enormously helpful. So will the re-engineering design principles detailed in Chapter Four and models such as that described beginning in

Chapter Five. More important than any of these, however, is the foundation on which re-engineering is built: challenging fundamental assumptions. And agency staff can begin the process of unearthing and challenging their assumptions before any of these conditions and tools are fully in place.

In other words, re-engineering for seamless service requires *new ways of thinking*. As high-performing athletes often put it, "It's all a mind game." At their athletic level, there is little to distinguish number 1 from number 2 in terms of pure athletic talent or skill. The differences between those who excel and those who don't are usually based on mental preparation, not physical or technical talent.

Consider: In July 1979, Martina Navratilova won the women's tennis crown at Wimbledon for the second straight year. Minutes after the match, she was asked which victory was tougher, her first win or her second. Not even close, Navratilova replied; the second was much harder. Why? Tougher opponent? No, she said. The reason the second championship was so much harder was that the first year she was trying to win; the second year, she was *trying not to lose*.

People who toil in our public institutions frequently work hard at *not losing*. Not losing at the mundane tasks (say, filling out a travel advance form), not losing at the far more significant ones (such as choosing one's words carefully with elected officials or the media). Our system offers little forgiveness for errors, few rewards for innovation. The prudent choice is to be careful, play it safe, avoid losing. That's an assumption widely held in the civil service, and it makes all the rational sense in the world.

The problem with this rational assumption is that it creates a self-fulfilling prophecy: the less you try to change, the less likely you will be punished or disappointed. But this assumption also reduces tremendously the chances of winning. For the simple fact is, *it's extraordinarily difficult to be successful at not losing*. It diminishes human potential and energy; it lowers creativity; it drains the human spirit.

To move toward a seamless future, we will have to challenge assumptions about playing it safe and not losing. Re-engineering isn't only about sophisticated technology and process-mapping tools; like most human progress, it's about new ways of thinking and seeing the world. As John Stuart Mill wrote in his *Autobiography,* "No great improvements in the lot of mankind are possible, until a great change takes place in . . . their modes of thought."

Managers who participate in workshops on re-engineering frequently report that they have learned how to see their work world differently. When they learn how to map out current processes and challenge non-value-adding steps, start at the end and work backward, begin with a clean sheet, and set stretch objectives, they see possibilities never before imagined. They stop chuckling at the phrase "close enough for government work." They don't tolerate it; they don't believe it. They see too many new and imaginative ways to do the public's business. They are too eager to start over.

That is the promise. That is the challenge. Most civil servants enter public life eager for a challenge, believing that public service is a high calling. After years of running into bureaucratic walls and impossible roadblocks, they discover the challenge and promise are gone. Re-engineering invites us to start over, to rediscover our initial aspirations and values about work and service. If we allow ourselves to develop new ways of thinking about the world of work, those aspirations and values will be realized, seamlessly.

References

AT&T. *Re-engineering Handbook*. Indianapolis: AT&T, 1991.

Abraham, L., and others. *Reinventing Home: Six Working Women Look at Their Home Lives*. New York: Plume, 1991.

Albrecht, K., and Zemke, R. *Service America!* New York: Warner Books, 1990.

Alexander, M. "Is There a Doctor in the Network?" *Computerworld*, Dec. 9, 1991, p. 18.

Associated Press. "Creation of Border Super Agency Is Called 'Premature.'" *Washington Post*, Aug. 27, 1993, p. A16.

Barr, S. "Gore Chat with Interior Staff May Set Bobbitt Back by $38." *Washington Post*, May 18, 1993a, p. A19.

Barr, S. "Clinton Plan May Cut 140,000 Manager Jobs." *Washington Post*, Dec. 23, 1993b, p. A21.

Barr, S. "Gore Lobs Glass Ashtray at Puffed-Up Specifications." *Washington Post*, Aug. 17, 1993c, p. A19.

Barzelay, M., and Armajani, B. J. "Managing State Government Operations: Changing Visions of Staff Agencies." *Journal of Policy Analysis and Management*, 1990, 9(3), 307–338.

Behn, R. D. "Management by Groping Along." *Journal of Public Policy Analysis and Management*, 1988, 7(4), 643–663.

Bennis, W., and Nanus, B. *The Leaders*. New York: HarperCollins, 1985.

Blackburn, J. (ed.). *Time-Based Competition*. Homewood, Ill.: Business One Irwin, 1991.

Capra, F. *The Turning Point: Science, Society, and the Rising Culture*. New York: Bantam Books, 1983.

Carnevale, A. *America and the New Economy*. San Francisco: Jossey-Bass, 1991.

Carr, D. K., and others. *Breakpoint: Business Process Redesign*. Arlington, Va.: Coopers & Lybrand, 1992.

Caudle, S. "Government Business Progress Reengineering: Agency Survey Results." Washington, D.C.: National Academy of Public Administration, 1994.

CBS *Sunday Morning*, Apr. 26, 1987. Television program.

Chandler, A. D., Jr. *The Visible Hand: The Managerial Revolution in American Business*. Cambridge, Mass.: Harvard University Press, 1977.

Chase, G., and Reveal, E. C. *How to Manage in the Public Sector*. Reading, Mass.: Addison-Wesley, 1983.

Cole, E. "Partnering: A Quality Model for Contract Relations." *The Public Manager*, Summer 1993, pp. 39–42.

Cooper, R., and Kaplan, R. S. "Measure Costs Right: Make the Right Decisions." *Harvard Business Review*, Sep.–Oct. 1988, pp. 96–103.

Cooper, R., and Kaplan, R. S. "Profit Priorities from Activity-Based Costing." *Harvard Business Review*, May–Jun. 1991, pp. 130–135.

Crenson, M. A. *The Federal Machine: Beginnings of Bureaucracy in Jacksonian America*. Baltimore: Johns Hopkins University Press, 1975.

Davenport, T. H. *Process Innovation:Reengineering Work Through Information Technology*. Boston: Harvard Business School Press, 1993.

Davidow, W. H., and Malone, M. S. *The Virtual Corporation*. New York: HarperBusiness, 1992.

Davis, S. M. *Future Perfect*. Reading, Mass.: Addison-Wesley, 1987.

Defense Logistics Agency. DLA Consumable Item Management—Corporate Information Management (CIM) Business Process Improvement Project. *Final Report*. Nov. 20, 1992.

De Pree, M. *Leadership Jazz*. New York: Dell, 1992.

Dumaine, B. "Times Are Good? Create a Crisis." *Fortune*, Jun. 28, 1993, pp. 123–130.

Edelman, L., Carr, F., and Lancaster, C. L. *Partnering*. Ft. Belvoir, Va.: U.S. Army Corps of Engineers Alternative Dispute Resolution Series, Dec. 1991.

Ehrenhalt, A. "Hard Truths, Tough Choices: Excerpts from the first Report of the National Commission on the State and Local Public Service." *Governing*, Aug. 1993, pp. 47–56.

Fallows, J. *More Like Us: Making America Great Again*. Boston: Houghton Mifflin, 1989.

Feldman, D. L. "Twenty Years of Prison Expansion: A Failing National Strategy." *Public Administration Review*, 53(6), Nov./Dec. 1993, 561–566.

Galagan, P. A. "Beyond Hierarchy: The Search for High Performance." *Training and Development*, Aug. 1992, pp. 21–35.

Gardner, J. W. *On Leadership*, New York: Free Press, 1990.

Gilbert, G. R. "Employee Empowerment: Flaws and Practical Approaches." *The Public Manager*, Fall 1993, pp. 45–48.

Gleckman, H. "The Technology Payoff." *Business Week*, Jun. 14, 1993, pp. 57–68.

Gore, A. *Creating a Government That Works Better and Costs Less*. Washington, D. C.: U.S. Government Printing Office, 1993.

Hall, C. W. "Area Governments Struggle to 'Reinvent' Human Services." *Washington Post*, Oct. 4, 1993, pp. D1, D5.

Hall, G., Rosenthal, J., and Wade, J. "How to Make Reengineering Really Work." *Harvard Business Review*, Nov.–Dec. 1993, pp. 119–131.

Hammer, M. "Reengineering Work: Don't Automate, Obliterate." *Harvard Business Review*, July-Aug. 1990, pp. 104–112.

Hammer, M., and Champy, J. *Reengineering the Corporation*. New York: HarperBusiness, 1993.

Handy, C. *The Age of Unreason*. Boston: Harvard Business School Press, 1989.

Harrington, H. J. *Business Process Improvement: The Breakthrough Strategy for Total Quality, Productivity, and Competitiveness*. New York: McGraw-Hill, 1991.

The Harwood Group. *Meaningful Chaos: How People Form Relationships with Public Concerns*. Dayton, Ohio: Kettering Foundation, 1993.

Henkoff, R. "Cost Cutting: How to Do It Right." *Fortune*, Apr. 9, 1990, pp. 40–49.

Hoffman, E. B., and Wagner, J. A. "Courtbusters." *Government Executive*. Oct. 1993, pp. 29–33.

Keidel, R. W. *Game Plans: Sports Strategies for Business*. New York: Dutton, 1985.

Keller, M. *Rude Awakening*. New York: HarperCollins, 1989.

Kirkpatrick, D. "Groupware Goes Boom." *Fortune*, Dec. 27, 1993, pp. 99–106.

Kotter, J. P. "What Leaders Really Do." *Harvard Business Review*, May-June 1990, pp. 103–111.

Kouzes, J. M., and Posner, B. Z. *The Leadership Challenge: How to Get Extraordinary Things Done in Organizations*. San Francisco: Jossey-Bass, 1987.

Lathrop, J. P. "The Patient-Focused Hospital." *Healthcare Forum Journal*, July/Aug. 1991, pp. 16–20.

Lewin, K. *Field Theory in Social Science*. Chicago: University of Chicago Press, 1951.

Linden, R. M. *From Vision to Reality*. Charlottesville, Va.: LEL Enterprises, 1990.

Linden, R. M. "Meeting Which Customers' Needs?" *The Public Manager*, Winter 1992–93, pp. 49–52.

Marion, D. E. "The Federal Bureaucracy: A Bicentennial Review." Newsletter (University of Virginia), Dec. 1985, pp. 19–25.

Marshall, R., and Tucker, M. *Thinking for a Living: Education and the Wealth of Nations*. New York: Basic Books, 1992.

Marsters, M. E., and Williams, H. S. "Prototyping: When Planning Becomes Designing." *Innovating*, Winter 1993, pp. 33–48.

Martin, J. "Re-engineering Government." *Governing*, Mar. 1993, pp. 27–30.

Master, W., and Joice, W. "Reinventing the Workplace: Interagency Telecommuting Centers." *The Public Manager*, Fall 1993, pp. 11–13.

Mechling, J. "Reengineering: Part of Your Game Plan?" *Governing*, Feb. 1994, pp. 42–52.

Mill, J. S. *Autobiography*. New York: H. Holt, 1873.

Mintzberg, H. *Mintzberg on Management*. New York: Free Press, 1989.

Monden, Y. *Toyota Production System*. Norcross, Ga.: Industrial Engineering and Management Press, 1983.

NBC News (Producer). *Dateline*. Dec. 14, 1993. Television program.

Naisbitt, J., and Aburdene, P. *Reinventing the Corporation*. New York: Warner Books, 1985.

National Commission on the Public Service. *Leadership for America: Rebuilding the Public Service*. Washington, D.C.: GPO, 1989.

National Performance Review. *Transforming Organizational Structures*. Draft, Red Cover Version, Accompanying Report. Washington, D.C.: n.p., 1993.

Ohno, T. *Toyota Production System: Beyond Large-Scale Production*. Cambridge, Mass.: Productivity Press, 1988.

Oregon Progress Board. *Standards for Measuring Statewide Progress and Government Performance*. *Report to the 1993 Legislature*. Portland: Oregon Progress Board, 1992.

Osborne, D., and Gaebler, T. *Reinventing Government*. Reading, Mass.: Addison-Wesley, 1992.

Paré, T. P. "A New Tool for Managing Costs." *Fortune*, June 14, 1993, pp. 124–129

Pascale, R. T., and Athos, A. G. *The Art of Japanese Management: Applications for American Executives*. New York: Warner Books, 1981.

"People, Processes, and Partnerships: A Report on the Customs Service of the 21st Century." U.S. Customs Service, 1994.

Peters, T. J. "Leadership: Sad Facts and Silver Linings." *Harvard Business Review*, Nov.–Dec. 1979, pp. 164–172.

Peters, T. J. *Liberation Management*. New York: Knopf, 1992.

Peters, T. J., and Waterman, R. H., Jr. *In Search of Excellence: Lessons from America's Best Run Companies*. New York: HarperCollins, 1982.

Porter, E. A. "What Government Can Learn from Business About Quality." *Governing*, Aug. 1993, pp. 10–11.

Riggs, F. W. "Bureaucracy and the Constitution." *Public Administration Review*, Jan.–Feb. 1994, pp. 65–72.

Savage, C. M. *Fifth Generation Management: Integrating Enterprises Through Human Networking*. Maynard, Mass.: Digital Equipment Corporation, 1990.

Schaffer, R. H., and Thomson, H. A. "Successful Change Programs Begin with Results." *Harvard Business Review*, 1992, pp. 81–89.

Schwartz, E. I. "The Power of Software." *Business Week*, June 14, 1993, p. 76.

Senge, P. *The Fifth Discipline: The Art and Practice of the Learning Organization*. New York: Doubleday/Currency, 1990.

Stalk, G., Jr., and Hout, T. M. *Competing Against Time*. New York: Free Press, 1990.

Starr, P. *The Social Transformation of American Medicine*. New York: Basic Books, 1982.

Stewart, T. A. "Reengineering: The Hot New Managing Tool." *Fortune*, Aug. 23, 1993, pp. 41–48.

Stewart, T. A. "The Search for the Organization of Tomorrow." *Fortune*, May 18, 1992, pp. 92–98.

Swiss, J. E. "Adapting Total Quality Management (TQM) to Government." *Public Administration Review*, July-Aug. 1992, 52(4), 356–361.

Takeuchi, H., and Nonaka, I. "The New, New Product Development Game." *Harvard Business Review*, Jan.–Feb. 1986, pp. 137–146.

Toffler, A. *The Third Wave*. New York: Bantam Books, 1980.

Trojanowicz, R., and Bucqueroux, B. *Community Policing: A Contemporary Perspective*. Cincinnati: Anderson, 1990.

U.S. Department of Agriculture. *What If We Could Just Start Over?* Washington, D.C.: U.S. Department of Agriculture, 1987.

U.S. Department of Defense, Office of the Assistant Secretary of Defense for Command, Control, Communications, and Intelligence. *The DoD Enterprise Model, Vol. II*. Washington, D.C.: Jan. 1994.

U.S. Department of Labor. *Workforce Investment Strategy—A Comprehensive Worker Adjustment Proposal with One-Stop Career Centers*. Washington, D.C.: n.p., 1993.

U.S. Department of the Treasury. *A Plan for Reinventing the IRS*. Washington, D.C.: U.S. Department of the Treasury, 1993.

U.S. Forest Service. *Chartering a Management Philosophy for the Forest Service*. Washington, D.C.: U.S. Forest Service, 1989.

U.S. General Services Administration. *Reclaiming Your Rush Hour: Guidelines for Telecommuting*. Washington, D.C.: U.S. General Services Administration, 1993.

Verity, J. W., and McWilliams, G. "Is It Time to Junk the Way You Use Computers?" *Business Week*, July 22, 1991, pp. 66–69.

Waterman, R. H., Jr. *The Renewal Factor: How the Best Get and Keep the Competitive Edge*. New York: Bantam Books, 1987.

Waterman, R. H., Jr., Peters, T. J., and Phillips, J. R. "Structure Is Not Organization." *Business Horizons*, June 1980, pp. 17–26.

Watson, P., and others. "Operational Restructuring: A Patient-Focused Approach." *Nursing Administration Quarterly*, Fall 1991, 16(1), 45–52.

Weber, D. O. "Six Models of Patient-Focused Care." *Healthcare Forum Journal*, July/Aug. 1991, pp. 23–31.

Webster, D. *The DoD Initiative in Concurrent Engineering*. Washington, D. C.: U.S. Department of Defense, 1992.

Welch, J. *Work in America*. Paper presented at the Seventh Annual Awards Dinner of the Work in America Institute, New York, Nov. 13, 1990. Scotia, N.Y.: General Electric, 1990.

White, L. D. *The Jacksonians: A Study in Administrative History, 1829–1861*. New York: Macmillan, 1963.

Wilson, J. Q. *Bureaucracy: What Government Agencies Do and Why They Do It*. New York: Basic Books, 1989.

Wilson, J. Q. "The Rise of the Bureaucratic State." In F. S. Lane (ed.), *Current Issues in Public Administration*. (2nd ed.) New York: St. Martin's Press, 1982.

Woll, P. *American Democracy*. New York: Norton, 1963.

Womack, J. P., Jones, D. T., and Roos, D. *The Machine That Changed the World: The Story of Lean Production*. New York: HarperCollins, 1990.

Index